MW01618491

112 illustrations, 105 in color

Robert Hughes

Lucian Freud
paintings

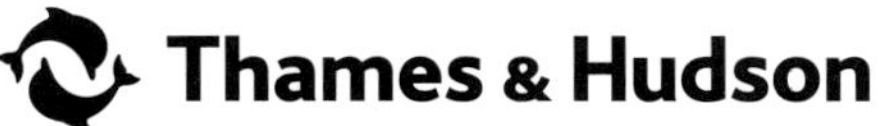

First published in the United States of America in 1987 by
Thames & Hudson Inc., 500 Fifth Avenue,
New York, New York 10110

thamesandhudsonusa.com

First paperback edition (revised) 1989
Reprinted 2001

Library of Congress Catalog Card Number 89-51234
ISBN 0-500-27535-1

Designed by Derek Birdsall RDI

Printed and bound in Singapore by C.S. Graphics

Contents

Robert Hughes On Lucian Freud

All quotations from Lucian Freud come from private conversations with the author

The first painting by a living British artist that I can remember seeing – not just noticing – was a Lucian Freud, hanging in the Tate Gallery more than twenty-five years ago. It was his 1952 portrait of Francis Bacon. A small picture, about the size of a shorthand note-pad, and one whose extreme compression makes it even more compact in memory; one remembers it as a miniature. The thought of 'miniature', with its Gothic overtones, was affirmed by the surface: tight, exact, meticulous and (most eccentrically, when seen in the late fifties, a time of urgent gestures on burlap) painted on a sheet of copper. There seemed to be something Flemish about the even light, the pallor of the flesh, and the uniform cast of the artist's attention. But there, on the edge of familiarity, its likeness to the modes of older portraiture stopped. What a strange, ophidian modernity this small image had, and still retains! One did not need to know it was the head of a living artist to sense that Freud had caught a kind of visual truth, at once sharply focused and evasively inward, that rarely showed itself in painting before the twentieth century.

In 'normal' portraiture, a tacit agreement between painter and subject allows the sitter to mask himself and project this mask – of success, of dignity, of beauty, of role – upon the world. But here the face with its lowered, almond-shaped eyes and eyelids precisely contoured as a beetle's wing-cases is caught in a moment between reflection and self-projection. It is as naked as a hand.

The point is not that the artist has 'penetrated the character' of his sitter, that commonplace requirement of portraiture which is, in fact, only a little more sophisticated than the pleasure people express when the eyes of a subject 'follow them around the room'. Rather, it is that he has seen everything with such evenness, while conveying the utter disjuncture between the artist's gaze and the sitter's lack of response. Everything is there, down to the shadow cast on the forehead by an escaped curl of hair whose strands you can count; but every particular, like the long horizontal S made by the curl of the eyebrow and a shading on the crease between the eyes, seems to obey the strictest impulses of artifice. Here, the fluent continuity of Ingres's form-world seems to have been refracted through the detailed spikiness of northern Renaissance art, but in no antiquarian way: Bacon's pear-shaped face has the silent intensity of a grenade in the millisecond before it goes off.

In the thirty-five years since he painted this, Lucian Freud has become the greatest living realist painter. To grasp what he has done one needs to set aside one or two shibboleths of contemporary culture, ideas meant to distinguish a 'post-modernist' state of mind from others allegedly less up-to-date. The main one is the idea that painting can still enrich itself by incessantly quoting other visual media – film and print, still photography and particularly television, in whose amniotic glare every foetal mind in Europe and America for the last two generations has been left to float. The history of painting's relationship to visual mass media is almost (and in the case of photography, literally) as old as the media themselves, but one does not need to know very much about the history of painting to sense that the expressive powers of the older art have changed, not necessarily for the better, as a result. The difference between, say, Pierre Bonnard using a Kodak snapshot of Marthe Boursin on the terrace at Le Cannet as one of the *données* of a composition, and Andy Warhol repeating the photographed face of Marilyn or Liz 100 times on a single canvas forty years later, is absolute, not relative; one of kind, not of degree. The former takes it for granted that, whatever machines and memory-aids it may use, whatever visual madeleines trigger recollection, painting and its direct conversion of sight into mark are still on top. The latter takes it equally for granted that the 'Big Media' are the primary and given field of an artist's demotic posture. It simply assumes that culture and nature have reversed themselves, that the image on the television screen or the tabloid page is the one that counts in our visual understanding of the world; that it makes no practical difference whether a painter objects to that or, like Warhol, greets it with hierophantic rapture: there is nothing he can actually do about it, since the small audience of art is powerless against the vaster solicitations and generalizations of mass media.

These media, we learn, are reality, and all culture had better get on board. Or else, the artist can set himself up as a 'diagnostician' of mass culture, reserving the right not to be in it (mingled with a little envy at its star-making power) while devising glosses on it. For this, a carefully primped irony, that cuirasse of art in the early 1980s, is necessary – a distance so affected as to constitute a hopeless impediment to feeling. Nothing is fresh. Or, nothing can be seen to be fresh without exposing author and audience to the charge of naivety, of not understanding one's 'true' and inescapably media-bound cultural circumstances. Mass visual media are the dog; painting, the tail; there is no question which wags which. The intellectually 'respectable' way for painting to confront mass media while retaining some shreds of its old avant-garde credentials is to acknowledge this and then give in to it. 'Only by embracing the intensity of empty value at the core of mass-media representation and the fierce recycling of styles used to twist and pervert every intention,' claimed one recent apologist for this state of affairs, 'only then can the perennial challenge be met of finding and constructing significant meaning in the midst of declining values for images and words.' (Lisa Phillips, *David Salle* catalogue, Whitney Museum, 1987) That use of 'only' is fairly breathtaking but that is what the argument in essence comes down to: and it is on this philistine counsel of despair that a number of big contemporary reputations, from late Warhol to David Salle in America, from Richard Hamilton to Gilbert and George in England, find their footing.

Perhaps we are stuck with the notion that the mass visual media exercise such a broad mandate over human imagination in the late twentieth century that they have their own kind of *Tausendjahrige Reich*. Perhaps the fate of the visual arts, as a consequence, can only be to oscillate between this sort of entropic aetherialization and the lumpy, hot rhetoric of expressionism – suffering, either way, from a mannerist denial of the specific, the keenly somatic and the authentically felt.

But then, perhaps not. Painting is a sublime instrument of dissatisfaction, of dissent from any kind of visual orthodoxy and received idea, not excluding those of late modernist mannerism. No work of art can ever be experienced at first hand by as many people as a network news broadcast or the commercials that grout it. That does not matter. It never has. What does count is the energy and persistence with which painting can embrace not 'empty value' but lived experience of the world; give that experience stable form, measure and structure; and so release it, transformed, into one mind at a time, viewer by viewer, so that it can work as (among other things) a critique of the more 'ideological' and generalized claims of mass media. There is no great work of art, abstract or figurative (and especially none figurative) without an empirical core, a sense that the mind is working on raw material that exists in the world at large, in some degree beyond mere invention. Painting is, one might say, exactly what mass visual media are not: a way of specific engagement, not of general seduction. That is its continuing relevance to us. Everywhere, and at all times, there is a world to be re-formed by the darting subtlety and persistent slowness of the painter's eye. We are never loose from our bodies and the re-embodiment of our experience of that world – its delivery from the merely conceptual, the unfelt, the second-hand or the rhetorically transcendent – is what painting offers. Hence the present interest (belated enough but better late than never) in the work of Lucian Freud, a man of 64 whose first American retrospective exhibition this is.

Lucian Freud was born in Berlin, in December 1922. His father, Ernst Freud, the youngest son of Sigmund, was an architect who had painted as a student (but entertained no ideas of being a professional artist). His mother, Lucie Brasch, was the daughter of a well-off grain merchant. Lucian was the second of their three sons. He grew up in an elegant quarter of Berlin near the Tiergarten; the family spent part of each summer on the Baltic, and as a child Lucian was taken to his maternal grandfather's country estate near Kotbus, where his lifelong love of horses was set: one of his earliest memories is of a fire in the stables, the panic, the animals plunging and whinnying. But life in Berlin was protected, cosseted, close, and rendered all the more so by the anxieties of an Austrian Jewish family under the lengthening shadow of Nazism and the street eruptions of Brownshirt gangs. Freud remembers being watched all the time by parents and governesses, escorted each day to the Französisches Gymnasium (by a route that sedulously avoided the sight of the burnt carcass of the Reichstag) – a childhood that prepared him, as no other could, for an adult obsession with solitude and unpredictable movement. To know exactly where one is, and for no one else to know it; to control one's social distances and apportion one's availability to others; to see without being seen, and to slip at will between the layers – these are unnegotiable conditions of Freud's life. 'All the real pleasures were solitary. I hate being watched at work. I can't even read when others are about.'

The family flat had art in it, as one would expect any house belonging to cultivated Jews in the late 1920s to do, but Freud's father was no collector. Freud remembers Hokusai prints, reproductions of Brueghel's *Seasons* and in particular some plates of Dürer watercolours – one depicting a tangle of grass stems, 'dense but not congested', and the other (from the Albertina) of Dürer's famous crouching hare. They seemed very big to him but he can no longer tell whether this was due to their real size or their strong visual impact; however, when he was eight, he combined their motifs in a drawing of a man lying down in tall grass. He also remembers nursery toys that piqued him visually, whose structure made him curious, particularly a jointed wooden horse whose screws and bolts gave him 'a sense of the mechanical attachment of ligaments to bone'. Like all children, Freud started scrawling early; unlike most, he continued with it until, by the time he was twelve, drawing was his constant passion. But its skills he had to learn by himself.

In 1933 Hitler became Chancellor and there was little doubt what the fate of Jews in Berlin would be. Lucian Freud's father came to England to find a suitable school for the children and soon after the family moved to London. (Grandfather Sigmund more obstinately remained in Vienna, until just after the *Anschluss* in 1938, before seeking refuge in England – like the Rabbi Yochanan ben Sakkai, as he later put it, departing for Jabneh to open a school of Torah studies after Titus' destruction of the temple. Though harried by the Gestapo and tormented by cancer of the mouth, he was able to ship his collections, books and papers to London, where he settled in Hampstead. The painter remembers his illustrious grandfather by his jokes, and by the gifts of money.)

School in the new country did not always go smoothly. Lucian Freud was not quite eleven when he arrived in England – he became a naturalized British subject in 1939 – and his parents seem to have assumed (as he did well before his sixteenth birthday) that he would grow up to be an artist. Theoretically, the school he went to should have made this easier. Dartington Hall, near Totnes in Devon, had been set up by Leonard Elmhirst and his wife, an American heiress of strongly liberal views, as an experiment in training the young to social responsibility by giving them freedom of choice; in the mid-1930s this self-contained community, with its farm and forestry departments, its own stables, textile studio and construction workshops, was as far from the cloistered, philistine, flogging-and-fagging stereotype of an English boarding school as a school could get. Its freedom seemed anarchic and Freud exploited it. Disliking his art teacher, he skipped art classes, spent his whole time riding the school horses, objected to anyone else handling them, and even had fancies about being a jockey. His only known sculpture is a sandstone carving of a horse, done when he was fourteen.

Three-legged horse, 1937
sculpture, sandstone, *c.* 56 cm
Private collection

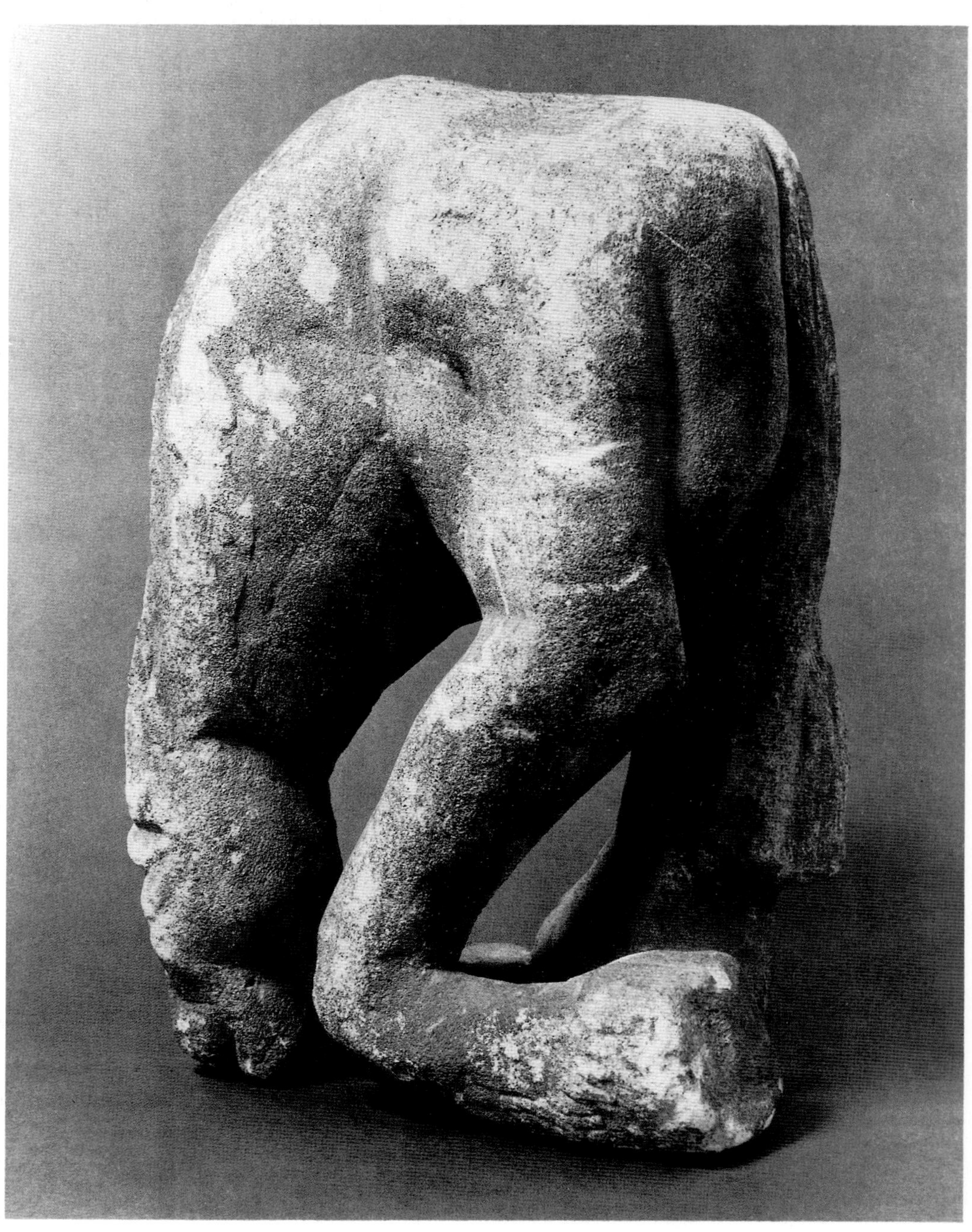

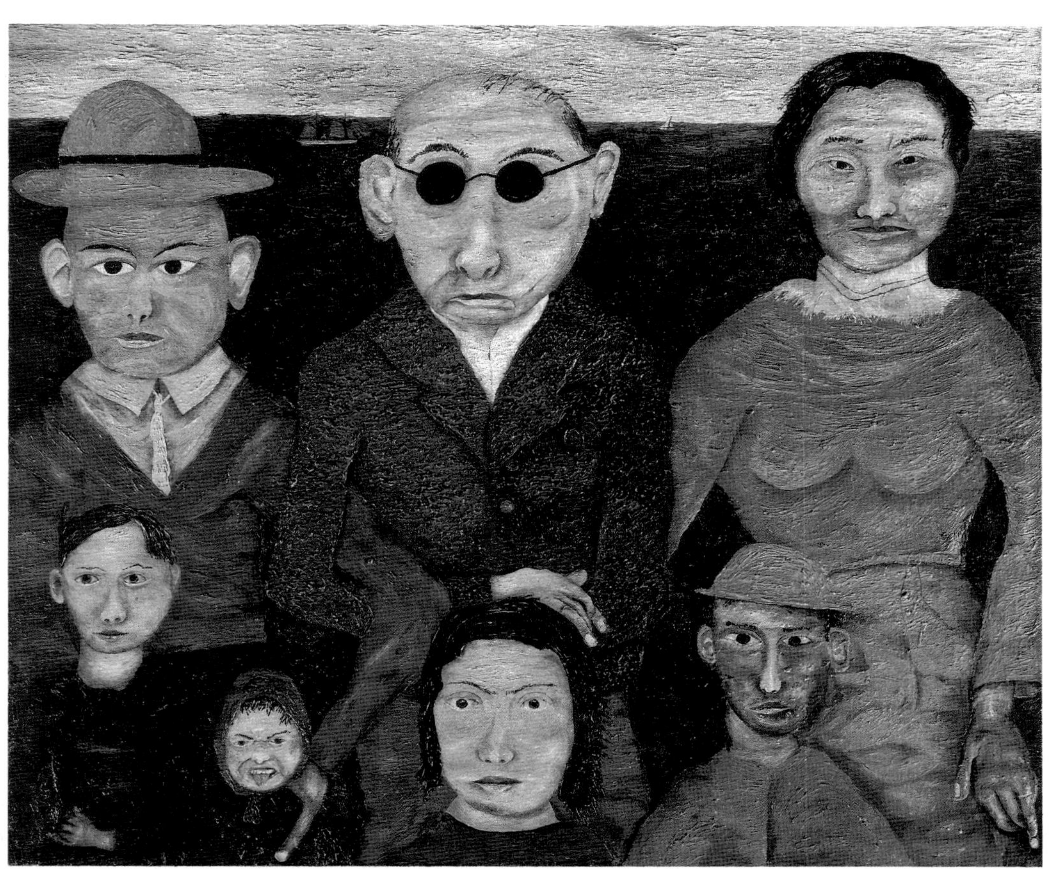

The refugees, 1941
oil on panel, 50.8 × 61 cm
Private collection

Plucked out of Dartington, he finished his schooling at Bryanston, a more sober but still 'progressive' public school in Dorset. In 1938 the stone horse gained him admission to the Central School of Arts and Crafts, from which in 1939 he moved to a smaller and more atelier-like institution, the East Anglian School of Drawing and Painting, run at Dedham by the painter Cedric Morris. Morris was a self-taught painter and inventive gardener whose original style affected the way Freud worked. One night he accidentally burned the place down, and in 1942 he ran away to sea on a Merchant Navy vessel but was invalided out of service a few months later. Convalescing from his illness, he returned to Morris's tutelage, drawing incessantly.

The affinities of Freud's early paintings and drawings seem German in their linearity, their spikiness, their sense of the alienated single figure and the isolated single detail. As a boy Freud had not looked at much German expressionism, and in England between 1939 and 1945 there was, in any case, none to see. But there is a distinct likeness, accidental or not, between some of Freud's early work and *Neue Sachlichkeit* painting. Freud as a child had seen and liked certain drawings by George Grosz – mask-like faces, indifferent or sly, glimpsed in the street or on the bus – and to these, as an influence on his fledgling essays like *The refugees*, 1941 (not in this exhibition), one should certainly add the work of Otto Dix. Today Freud is apt to dismiss the more ostentatiously neurotic, cocaine-nervy aspects of *Neue Sachlichkeit* – Christian Schad's portraits of freaks and café socialites, for instance – as predictable illustrations. But there is no doubt that part of his reputation as a boy prodigy in London art circles in the war years rested on his single-minded commitment to linear description rather than painterly evocation, and

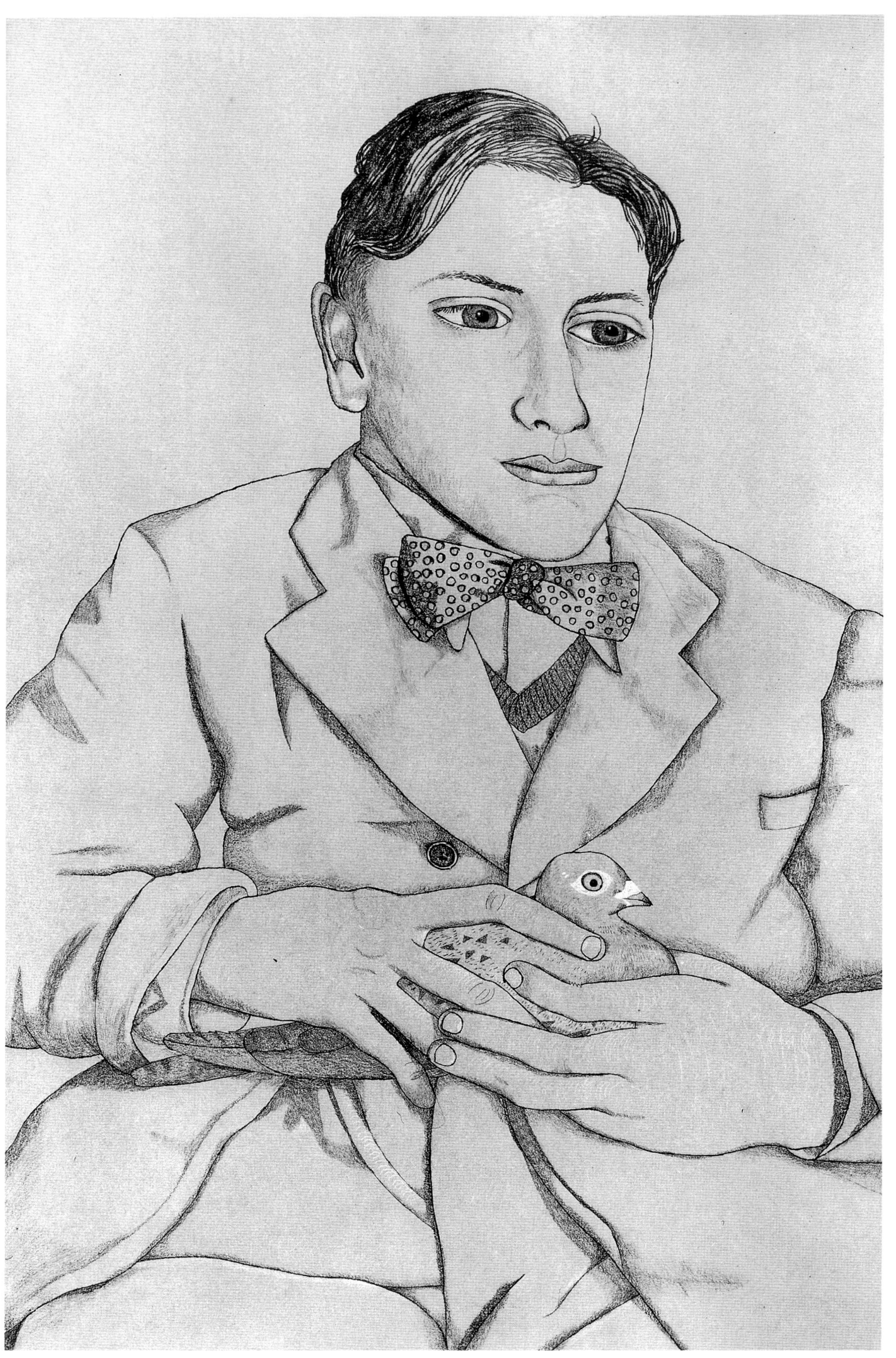

Boy with a pigeon, 1944
conté and pencil heightened with white, 50 × 33 cm
Private collection

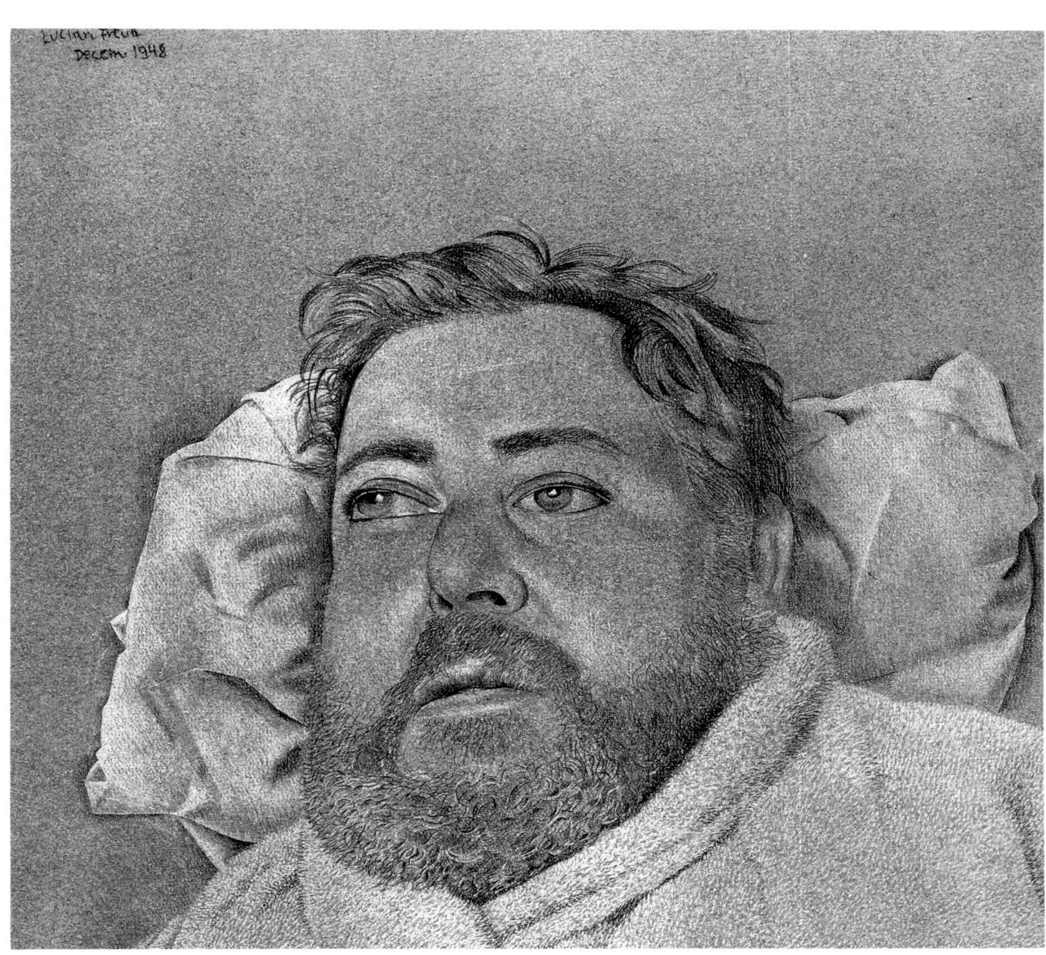

Christian Bérard, 1948
black and white conté, 41 × 44 cm
Private collection

his refusal to let intense personal interests dominate a painting or a drawing. The precocity of the early work, some of which, like *Boy with a pigeon*, 1944, reveals a degree of control extraordinary in an artist of 21, lies in the fierce independence of its delineation. By 1948, his study of Christian Bérard is already among the best European drawing of its time. The habit of young, neo-romantic painters in England in the early 1940s was to generalize and go after painterly effects, in which an evocative nostalgia for place was mingled with a tardy School-of-Paris cuisine; whereas one senses rebellion in the mannered, spiky forms of Freud's drawing. Everything is equally there, and must be equally described. This objectivity, this evenness of attention mingled with a barely veiled anxiety about the otherness of all objects – rooms, faces, plants, furniture – lies at the core of Freud's early work. It gave rise to the impression, among some critics, that Freud had connected himself to Surrealism. A tenuous link, no more than a whisper of feeling, was there; these days, Freud is inclined to discount it altogether:

As a young man I was not obsessed with working in a specific way, even though I felt very little freedom. The rigidity of Surrealism, its rigid dogma of irrationality, seemed unduly limiting. I could never put anything into a picture that wasn't actually there in front of me. That would be a pointless *lie, a mere bit of artfulness.*

But the touch of Surrealism cannot quite be dismissed; one would be mildly surprised if it were, given Freud's quickness of response and the cultural milieu of wartime London. He had

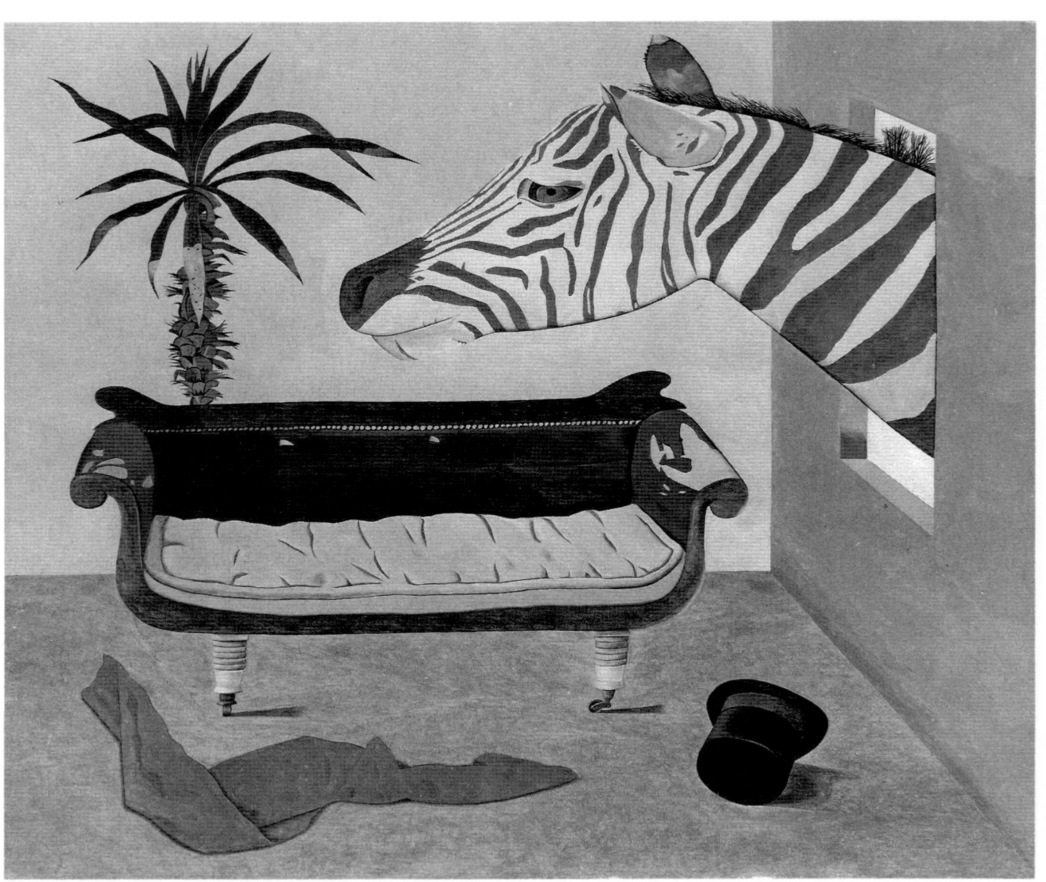

The painter's room, 1943
oil on canvas, 62.2 × 76.2 cm
Private collection

seen and admired work by Miró and de Chirico. Freud's image of a giant zebra's head poking disconcertingly through the window in *The painter's room*, 1943, or straining towards the still-life in *Quince on a blue table*, is a classic de Chirican trope, the encounter of incompatibles, a homage to Lautréamont's passage about the sewing-machine, the ironing-board and the umbrella. It happened that Freud did have a stuffed zebra's head, that it sat in his studio, and that in the 1940s there was no shortage of English rooms with stuffed trophies on their walls, so that the effigy might have looked less weird then than it seems now. Doubtless this was as close as Freud could come to having a horse in a rented London room. But the head still looms, sad and incongruous, gazing at the scraggy, embrowned indoor palm behind the burst sofa, as though remembering Africa.

Juvenile Freud looks excruciatingly conscious of style: very literal and, at the same time, mannered. It is also tinged with death, since Freud had a yen for organic things that were past movement: dead chickens (autopsy subjects from a local veterinarian, which had perished from 'not too horrific' causes) and dead monkeys supplied by a louche pet-shop owner who also sold snakes, like liquorice, by the foot. The mannerisms, Freud now thinks, came out of his lack of flexibility:

I always felt that my work hadn't much to do with art; my admirations for other art had very little room to show themselves in my work because I hoped that if I concentrated enough the intensity of scrutiny alone would force life into the pictures. I ignored the fact that art, after all, derives from art. Now I realize that this is the case.

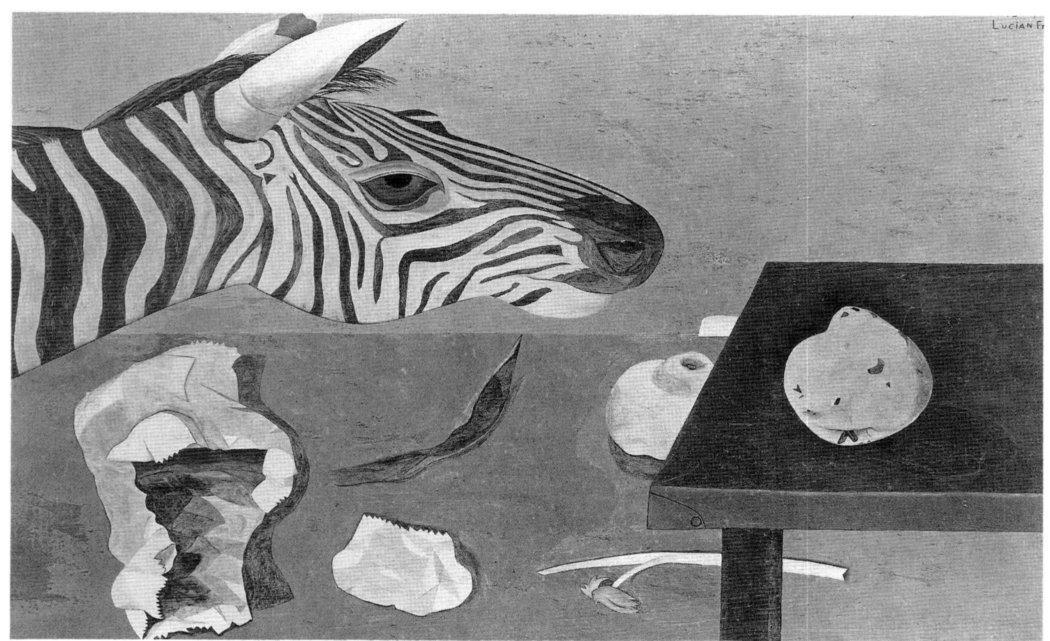

Quince on a blue table, 1943/44
oil on canvas, 36.8 × 58.4 cm
Private collection

All the same, the image has some quality of surprise, of confrontation. In conversation, Freud cites a casual-seeming reference from T. S. Eliot's play *The Family Reunion* (Part II, Scene III, Faber and Faber Ltd and Harcourt Brace Jovanovich Inc., 1939):

CHARLES
.... I felt safe enough;
And now I don't feel safe. As if the earth should open
Right to the centre, as I was about to cross Pall Mall.
I thought that life could bring no further surprises;
But I remember now, that I am always surprised
By the bull-dog in the Burlington Arcade.

The dog in the Burlington Arcade was a stuffed bulldog straining at a leash, which a canine outfitter had placed outside his door to draw customers. Freud remembers seeing it: 'It frightened everyone for about a second. I was really affected by the thought of this.'

That sense of slippage, of the moment in which the world declares its disconcerting alienness, permeates Freud's work and is the warp of its intensity. (The weft, as we shall see, is his privacy about his models as 'people in my life'.) One does not know the name of the young man in *Interior in Paddington*, 1951, but he looks familiar from middle-European painting of the 1920s, this shabby, pale, tight-wound fellow with an unlit cigarette, who wears his raincoat indoors. What rivets one's attention in the painting as *theatre* is the way Freud has distributed the unease, between the curious gesture of the man's right hand – the fingers clasped, hiding or about to lob something, but what? – and the slicing, whipping, minutely observed leaves of the indoor palm, as much a protagonist as the man. This treatment could approach melodrama were it not for its containment by cool pictorial devices: the strict formality of the folds of trouser-leg and gaberdine, the internal rhymes (such as those between the lower folds of the raincoat and the discreet curve of the iron window-railings, the man in the room and the distant boy in the street, the topknot of the palm and the street-lamp outside); and, above all, the light, which is quiet, clear, enveloping and frontal. It throws no deep shadows. It favours flat shapes and linear, rather than tonally modelled, roundings. It is, in fact, the light emitted by the saint of Freud's imagination and of modernist classicism generally: Ingres.

Ingres had been on Freud's mind ever since he began seriously to paint. To study this perfection in drawing, he recalls, is 'like gazing across a barrier at something unreachable.' What seemed to constitute the 'modernity' of Ingres – the ground from which an artist so long dead could speak to the present – was his detachment, read by Freud as amounting almost to solitude within Ingres's idea of history: his sense of 'the grandeur *and remoteness* of the classical past to which he was appealing.'

Ingres's history painting has the humour of madness. He couldn't draw without inventing. His drawing is evocative in a way that forces us to believe in it. A line, any single line, of his drawings is worth looking at.

Freud does not think of himself as an 'expressive' colourist, and he cites with approval a reply Ingres is supposed to have made when a student asked him what he considered to be most beautiful in art: 'A colour adjacent to another which most closely resembles it.' All Freud wanted to do was draw and go somewhere from there. 'My colour has no symbolic function whatever', he declared some forty years later:

I don't want any colour to be noticeable. I want the colour to be the colour of life, so that you would *notice it as being irregular if it changed. I don't want it to operate in the modernist sense as colour, something independent; I don't want people to say, 'Oh, what was that red or that blue picture of yours, I've forgotten what it was.' Full, saturated colours have an emotional significance that I want to avoid.*

There was no question where Freud stood in the unending squabble between *Rubéniste* and *Poussiniste*; he felt the same kind of conviction that lay behind Blake's objurgations against Reynolds: 'The Man who asserts that there is no Such Thing as Softness in Art, & that every thing in Art is Definite & Determinate, has not been told this by Practise, but by Inspiration & Vision, because Vision is Determinate & Perfect.'

Ingres surfaced especially in Freud's portraits, such as the exquisite sequence on his first wife Kitty Garman, daughter of the sculptor Jacob Epstein, of which the best-known is *Girl with roses*, 1947–8. It is masterly in the smoothness of its transitions, from the detail of hair (in which every strand seems to be in place, with its own stated kink and highlight, nothing skimped) to the finely modulated flatness of the flesh, mapped by a drawing so rigorous and discreet (the lines of eyelashes, the curl of the mouth with its hint of looseness) that detail and stylization cannot be separated. Everything is equally scrutinized, the broken caning of the chair and the exact bloom of light on the dark skirt no less than the rose-petals and the minuscule structure of reflections in those huge, tawny, apprehensive eyes. What other modernist portrait, one asks oneself, has deployed such a consideration of detail amassed and refined to so haunting an erotic tenderness? Surely, none: *Girl with roses*, painted under the spell of Ingres and the Flemish *quattrocento*, but conveying a sense of dislocation – 'It seems impossible that she should not have been trembling', wrote Lawrence Gowing (*Lucian Freud*, 1982, p. 84) – is one of those rare effigies in which nothing seems elided yet everything is pictorially operative. It is the work of a young artist to whom style is breath but who has learned to abolish mannerism in the interests of feeling. Along with *Girl in bed*, 1952, and the portrait of Francis Bacon painted in the same year, it is the masterpiece of Lucian Freud's twenties. If one were to look for a counterpart in English poetry of the time to the sense of erotic life in Freud's paintings between 1947 and 1952 – tender, edgy, hotel-bound, absorbed, delirious in escape and vulnerable to intrusion – it could be George Barker (*Collected Poems 1930–1955*, Faber and Faber Ltd, 1957):

Turn on your side and bear the day to me
Beloved, sceptre-struck, immured
In the glass wall of sleep. Slowly
Uncloud the borealis of your eye
And show your iceberg secrets, your midnight prizes
To the green-eyed world and to me. Sin
Coils upward into thin air when you awaken
And again morning announces amnesty over
The serpent-kingdomed bed . . .

'The Ingres of Existentialism', as Herbert Read dubbed Freud, had in fact been spending a lot of time in Paris once the war released Europe from its iron grip. Freud has never been much of an aesthetic tourist; he visited Greece after the war, and with Francis Bacon went to the Ingres exhibition in Paris in 1967; he made small pilgrimages to Colmar for Grünewald's Isenheim Altarpiece and to Haarlem for Frans Hals; but it was in Paris that the European could get back to Europe, and he went there as soon as he could after the war, in 1946. World War II had brought the small and peripheral-feeling artworld of London to a halt, but (despite the schematic picture we are given these days of the sudden shift of the 'centre' to New York) Paris, after the war, had a cultural density and reality no other city could match, especially for a young painter. Living in a room in the Hotel D'isly, frequenting the cafés and the studios, Freud was exhilarated to find that the French 'took the idea of being an artist seriously; they accepted the fact that one was an artist and found nothing odd about it. *La peinture, elle marche bien?* Nobody in London would pose such a question.'

Ingres would stay with him forever, but his style did mutate, as styles must. It began to move towards chiaroscuro; one sees this first in *Girl with a white dog*, 1951–2, where Freud's abiding sense of complicity between the human and the animal (which would later take such offensive form in *Naked man with rat*, 1977–8) is expressed in the likeness of form between the girl's pale, exposed breast and the white, bullet head of the dog, and the rhyme between nipple and muzzle.

By the mid-1950s Freud's armoury of illusion was fully assembled and he had begun to experience the discontents of Pygmalion, if one is to take literally what he wrote in the July 1954 issue of *Encounter*:

A moment of complete happiness never occurs in the creation of a work of art. The promise of it is felt in the act of creation but disappears towards the completion of the work. For it is then that the painter realizes that it is only a picture he is painting. Until then he had almost dared to hope that the picture might spring to life. Were it not for this, the perfect painting might be painted, on the completion of which the painter could retire. It is this great insufficiency that drives him on. Thus the process of creation becomes necessary to the painter perhaps more than it is in the picture. The process in fact is habit-forming.

The turning point in Freud's work with the human clay, when he moved decisively away from the *Ingriste* modulation of flatness by contour, came in 1958 and 1959 with *Woman smiling.* It was attended by a change of instrument, the paint (in Gowing's words) being 'driven across the surface with the springy bristles of a hog-hair brush quite unlike the touch of the pliant sable, which had followed the forms with obedient literalness.' (*Lucian Freud*, 1982, p. 118) The marks are brusquer; they find their equivalents for stringy hair and blotched complexion with improvised force, and their light from the white ground shows through. Now the small forms beneath the skin, the small bunches of muscle and little tossing wedges and crescents, claim Freud's attention. In their folding, puckering and slippage there is more protuberance and pressure, linked to greater agility and freedom of drawing. The shadow under the left cheekbone, prolonged in a line to the raised corner of the mouth and joined by the serpentine shadow of the buccal muscles, is disturbing, almost like a scar: it perverts the wholeness of the face, while giving it a pleated solidity.

At a certain point after *Woman smiling*, around 1960, Freud started pushing hard against the envelope of form given by the face. There had long been traces, in his work, of a sense of detachment of skin from structure; the corner of a mouth (as in *Girl with roses*, or more vividly in the tiny *Boy's head*, 1952) came a little loose, showing the slackness and elasticity of pulled skin. He began to translate into a faster and coarser tempo this sense of the flesh as a membrane that could be manipulated, in a sequence of portraits – some of a long-jawed woman with bouffant hair, some of himself – that were a startling departure from the flat forms of his earlier work. There was no loss of concision but a gain in impetus. The hog-hair brush sweeps and loops, drawing *in* the paint, pushing the muscular structures around. It may be that Freud had gained something from the smearing and displacement of facial wholeness in the work of his close friend Francis Bacon. These portraits record his fascination with Frans Hals, an artist 'fated always to look modern, to the point of coarseness – when people are shocked by Hals, I think they have a real sensibility.'

Thinking about Hals attuned Freud's tonic sense of protuberance and flattening, the elastic vigour of form, and what it could gain from direct strokes with stiff bristles. This reaches one extreme in *Man's head (self portrait)*, 1963, with its diagonal thrust of the painter's forearm and hand against his cheek, pulling it away from the nose and mouth; and a further one in the weird amplitude of the big *Sleeping head*, 1962, by which the unseen forms of the rest of the body – thigh, buttock, breast – seem to have been translocated into the swellings of that single cheek and puffy jaw, seen from below.

Freud's aim was less effigy than presence. 'In a culture of photography we have lost the tension that the sitter's power of censorship sets up in the painted portrait.' To be photographed, Freud says, makes him feel that something disagreeable is being done to him. The main difference between a painted and a photographed portrait is simply 'the degree to which feelings can enter into the transaction from both sides. Photography can do this to a tiny extent, painting to an unlimited degree.'

There was no formal system in this integration of discovered shapes, no sphere-cone-cylinder devices for making a reliable little pictorial engine out of that most unreliable, mutable and fierce of pictorial objects, the human head. The work is full of radical elisions but these are not so much the result of a liking for certain kinds of distortion as 'the result of forced necessity from moment to moment': 'I feel it is immoral to put anything in that isn't there. But it is not necessarily immoral to leave out something that is there.'

The *Sleeping head* was another hinge-point in his work. 'I was going to do a nude,' Gowing quotes Freud as saying of it, 'then I realized that I could do it from the head.' (*Lucian Freud*, 1982, p. 151) The task was to expand the plasticity Freud had learned to discover in the head through to the body as a whole. Hence the nudes of the 1960s and 70s.

It is unlikely that any painter since Picasso has made his figuring of the naked human body such an intense and unsettling experience for the viewer as Lucian Freud. Certainly no realist artist, working within the boundaries of likeness (and one may note that 'Naked portrait' is a recurrent phrase in Freud's titles) has done so. As John Russell remarked, 'Freud carries the experience so far that we sometimes wonder if we have any right to be there.' (*New York Times*, 13 January 1983) But that experience, for all its dislocating intensity, is one with historical roots. Freud is one of those painters whose work flatly contradicts the *idées reçues* about the Englishness of English art, its mildness, anecdotalism, pastoral leanings and eccentricity. It is at one with the great tradition of European painting, but it addresses a crisis in that tradition: the crisis of the Ideal Nude, which happened around 1890 in the work of Degas and Rodin. Much that can be said about the explicitness of Freud's nudes was said, a hundred years ago, by writers like Huysmans and Félix Fénéon about those of Degas. These images were not 'spiritual', not even 'psychological'. 'I show them deprived of their airs and graces, reduced to the level of animals cleaning themselves,' Degas remarked to George Moore ('Degas, the Painter of Modern Life', *Magazine of Art*, September 1890). What Huysmans called the 'icy fever' of Degas's probing draftsmanship could shock the bourgeois precisely because it did not idealize. The anguish of decorum they caused in the viewer, whose eye the artist jams against a keyhole, who is forced against his most earnest cultural convictions to feel like a voyeur, was described by Félix Fénéon in a passage that is virtually a proleptic description of Freud ('Les impressionistes en 1886', republished in *Au-delà de l'impressionisme*, Hermann, 1966):

A bony spine sticks out; upper arms shoot past juicy pear-shaped breasts and plunge straight down between the legs. . . . There's a collapse of hair on shoulders, bosoms on hips, stomach on thighs, limbs on their joints, and viewed from above as she lies on the bed, with her hands plastered against her buttocks, the slut looks like a series of bulging jointed cylinders. . . . And it is in obscure furnished rooms, in the humblest circumstances, that these richly patinated bodies that bear the bruises of marriages, childbirth and illness divest themselves and spread their limbs.

It was in part this friction of carnality against cultural expectation that gave the late pastels of Degas their hypnotic leverage on the mind. Freud is after the same quarry:

The task of the artist is to make the human being uncomfortable, and yet we are drawn to a great work by involuntary chemistry, like a hound getting a scent; the dog isn't free, it can't do otherwise, it gets the scent and instinct does the rest.

Degas's violence to conventional representation of the nude lingered in France, healed by Matisse for his Apollonian purposes but exacerbated by Picasso for his Dionysiac ones.

Across the channel, it became one of the motifs of English extremism. It was imported by Degas's friend Walter Sickert, and it locked into native traditions of empiricism and 'natural vision' to produce such outbursts of candour as Stanley Spencer's so-called 'Leg-o'-Mutton Nude', the 1936 *Self-Portrait with Patricia Preece*. Freud's nudes take up this stand. We are shown what is there, exposed, with an utter lack of sentimentality (but in this case without Spencer's Protestant anxiety too): the fine-drawn ligatures and muscular rhythms of the blonde in *Naked girl*, 1966, and the assonances between the parts of her body, the eyelids, the parted lips, the twin pink leaves of her sex, all painted with an inquisitorial and even-handed completeness, a will to see, to engage, but not to peep, that is the mark of Freud's temperament. No modern nudes are more densely packed with bodily life. One experiences the obdurate, sullenly comatose physical power of *Naked portrait*, 1980–1, Freud's painting of a pregnant woman near her term, with a fascination and reluctance: there has been no pubic patch like this in painting since Courbet's *Origin of the World*; but in the end it is the way the flesh is seen and rendered that sticks in the memory, the figured sense of its distended sheen, blue discoloured veins, blotchy nipples and, overall, the terse and perfect relation between the movements of the brush and the tactile sense of the body. This ability to re-form the naked body in terms of clear, energetic shape while seeming not to lose a pore, not a hair, of its tensely scrutinized nocturnal presence – as in *Naked portrait with reflection*, 1980, with its extraordinary drawing of the girl's breasts and thorax – seems to define Freud's idea of pictorial truth. The body is new every time. 'When I look at a body I know it gives me choices of what to put in a painting; what will suit me and what won't. There is a distinction between fact and truth. Truth has an element of revelation about it. If something is true, it does more than strike one as merely *being so*.' Because of its unfamiliarity, because he wanted the body to carry the expressive force that the face would otherwise pre-empt, 'I used to leave the face until last. I wanted the expression to be in the body. The head must be just another limb. So I had to play down expression in the nudes.' Hence the inward, reflective, ineloquent quality of the Freud face, a faithful reflection of studio fatigue: expression turned inward upon itself, eyes that do not evade but simply do not meet the viewer's gaze.

To scrutinize the body in this way, stiff or spreadeagled in the cone of light for 30, 50, 100 sessions, you must have the trust of the sitter. All Freud's models are people in his life. Rather than speak of painting 'from the nude' – implying distance and even a certain subtraction – Freud is careful to say 'with', implying collaboration, a conspiracy towards the image mutually arrived at. The body on the burst couch in the upstairs studio represents itself in posture and gesture and is not just a thing that sets a formal problem for the painter. 'One of the ways in which I could get them to sit was by involving them,' Freud declares.

The painting is always done very much with their co-operation. The problem with painting a nude, of course, is that it deepens the transaction. You can scrap a painting of someone's face and it imperils the sitter's self-esteem less than scrapping a painting of the whole naked body. We know our faces, after all. We see them every day, out there at large in the mirror or the photo. But we don't scrutinize our bodies to the same degree, unless we are professional models, whom I don't use, or extreme narcissists, whom I can't use.

He has never dictated a pose, because 'I am only interested in painting the actual person; in doing a painting *of* them, not in *using* them to some ulterior end of art. For me, to use someone doing something not native to them would be wrong.'

The model is not an instrument of the painter's fantasies and he is not free to paint her or him any way but head-on. The idea of 'expressive freedom' evokes a sardonic whinny from Freud. 'There is no free will and the only real work you can do is on yourself. I paint the sort of paintings I can, not the ones I necessarily want.' The realist's work means summoning up imaginative reserves to get to the visual truth at angles, to outwit but not evade the resistant surface. Freud cites Eliot's advice to himself in *Portrait of a Lady* on how to get in the right mood for creating art (*Collected Poems 1909–1962*, Faber and Faber Ltd and Harcourt Brace Jovanovich Inc., 1963):

And I must borrow every changing shape
To find expression – dance, dance,
Like a dancing bear,
Cry like a parrot, chatter like an ape.

The strangeness of Freud's paintings comes in large part from the circumstances of their making: they bypass decorum while fiercely preserving respect. As Lawrence Gowing emphasized, they do not come out of domesticity, as Bonnard's, Picasso's or even Giacometti's did, but neither are they grounded in formal atelier poses. They narrate fragments of a psychic life we cannot reassemble for ourselves. It is hard, sometimes impossible, to figure out what kind of a life Freud is painting slices of. Who is the muscular, red-haired youth splayed *à la crapaudine* on the couch in *Naked man with rat*, 1977–8, his face reflecting an anxious vacuity, his hand raised as though to ward off the painter's eye? And why is the rodent's tail draped over his thigh, so amiably close to his thick cock? Who are the women, one pregnant and the other not, in *Annie and Alice*, 1975, and what is the intimacy expressed between them under the painter's gaze? It is the sense of a secret life – the inherent strangeness of unexplained friendships and liaisons that bears on visual truth – which links Freud's work to Bacon's, and causes Freud to quote jokingly, apropos of Bacon's situations, a couplet from a skit on *These Foolish Things*: 'And when you came to visit / The neighbours said, "My god, what is it?"' But not all in Freud is disjuncture and some is healing. His reputation for edginess should not occlude the fact that he has painted some of the most intensely registered tributes to others in the history of portraiture: his head of the painter Frank Auerbach in the act of concentration, for instance, its forehead articulated with a difficult, bulging sculptural plasticity; and above all the portraits of his mother Lucie (a series which began in 1972 when she began to recover from depression, following her husband's death in 1970) which involved more than a thousand sittings and reached an apogee of grave and measured devotion with *The painter's mother*, 1982–4.

Freud's cave of making is on the top floor of a large house in Paddington, still seedy-looking despite the primping and upgrading of the neighbourhood around it. The little entrance-hall is blocked by a massive dark guardian, which turns out to be the medium-size bronze of Rodin's *Balzac*, naked and straddling; one realizes, on seeing it, that the relation between Rodin's violent plasticity and the kneading of tissue in such Freuds as the portrait of Frank Auerbach, 1975–6, is closer than one had supposed. The studio is to the right, a nondescript room of medium size; its walls are faded, mottled and in places peeling. Through a window there is a panoramic view of rooftops; one recognizes the background of certain portraits, and, looking down into the yards behind, some of the litter of cardboard, burst mattresses and trash that constitutes the subject of that *tour de force* of inspection, *Wasteground with houses, Paddington*, 1970–2. One recognizes the furniture, the bed of scrutiny, the burst upholstery of the analytic couch. On the wall to the left of the door four words are written in emphatic capitals: URGENT SUBTLE CONCISE ROBUST. The wall to the right of the door is covered, to a height of some three feet, with a sandbag-like wadding of white rags stuck to the plaster by long-dried paint; this is the odd configuration that runs across the background of *Red-haired man on a chair*, 1962–3. Hanging from the ceiling near the easel is a single light, an interrogator's 500-watt incandescent bulb in a conical shade, burning powerfully down on the couch: clinical exposure. This set-up is for Freud's 'night' paintings, done by artificial light; they have a character easily distinguished from the 'day' paintings, because their pools and clefts of shadow on the flesh are darker, larger, and done with Prussian blue, a pigment of vehement dyeing power, instead of the daytime ultramarine and Payne's grey.

Freud draws direct on the canvas, 'without doing lots of little studies for a hand, a neck, a shoulder', or even a layout for the whole figure: 'I'd rather it ran off the edges of the canvas than have to cramp the forms.'

His basic pigment for flesh is Cremnitz white, an inordinately heavy pigment which contains twice as much lead oxide as flake white and much less oil medium than other whites. It granulates and 'I think of the granules as atoms'. A general fattiness of paint developed out of Freud's nudes, but the peculiar graininess of Cremnitz white enabled him to give skin some of the peculiar quality one sees in Bacon, where the swiping brush leaves a mark on the canvas akin to a deposit of raw tissue. 'I wouldn't use Cremnitz on anything that wasn't alive; I use it for flesh, or even on the hairs of a dog, but never, for instance, on a woman's dress. It is simply a code.'

Direct quotations from other paintings are fairly sparse. Now and again the model will assume a pose reminiscent of Michelangelo (or Bronzino's quotation of him in the London National Gallery's *Venus and Cupid*); one also picks up echoes of Correggio and Rembrandt. But there is only one painting conceived by Freud as a deliberate paraphrase from an old master, and that is perhaps his own masterpiece, at least in terms of size and pictorial ambition: *Large interior, W.11 (after Watteau)*, 1981–3.

The Watteau on which *Large interior* is based is an early one, *Pierrot Content* (in the Thyssen-Bornemisza Collection in Lugano): it shows a group of characters from the *commedia dell'arte*. Later, Watteau gave such groups a more complex, irregular structure, but this early painting has an almost naive and schematic stiffness: five figures symmetrically disposed, man, woman, Pierrot, woman, man, the first four on a garden bench, the fifth sitting on the ground. The theme is jealousy. Pierrot is happy because two women are competing for him. He sits like Buridan's ass between two equally desirable objects, looking sly and silly, hands symmetrically on his thighs. The girl on the left serenades Pierrot with her guitar, while the man in pink costume to her left fixes her with an attentive ogle. The one on the right recoils and looks jealous, while the youth seated on her right leans inwards, his arm across her lap.

One can see why Freud, whose sexual history is long and labyrinthine, might have been amused by this charade of jealousy. What he made of it, however, is quite another matter. In 1981 a group of paintings from the Thyssen-Bornemisza Collection went on show at the Royal Academy in London, including *Pierrot Content*, one of Baron Thyssen's favourite objects. Near that time, Freud painted a portrait of Thyssen and although Freud had never seen the original, included a detail from it in the background of the portrait – the two left-hand

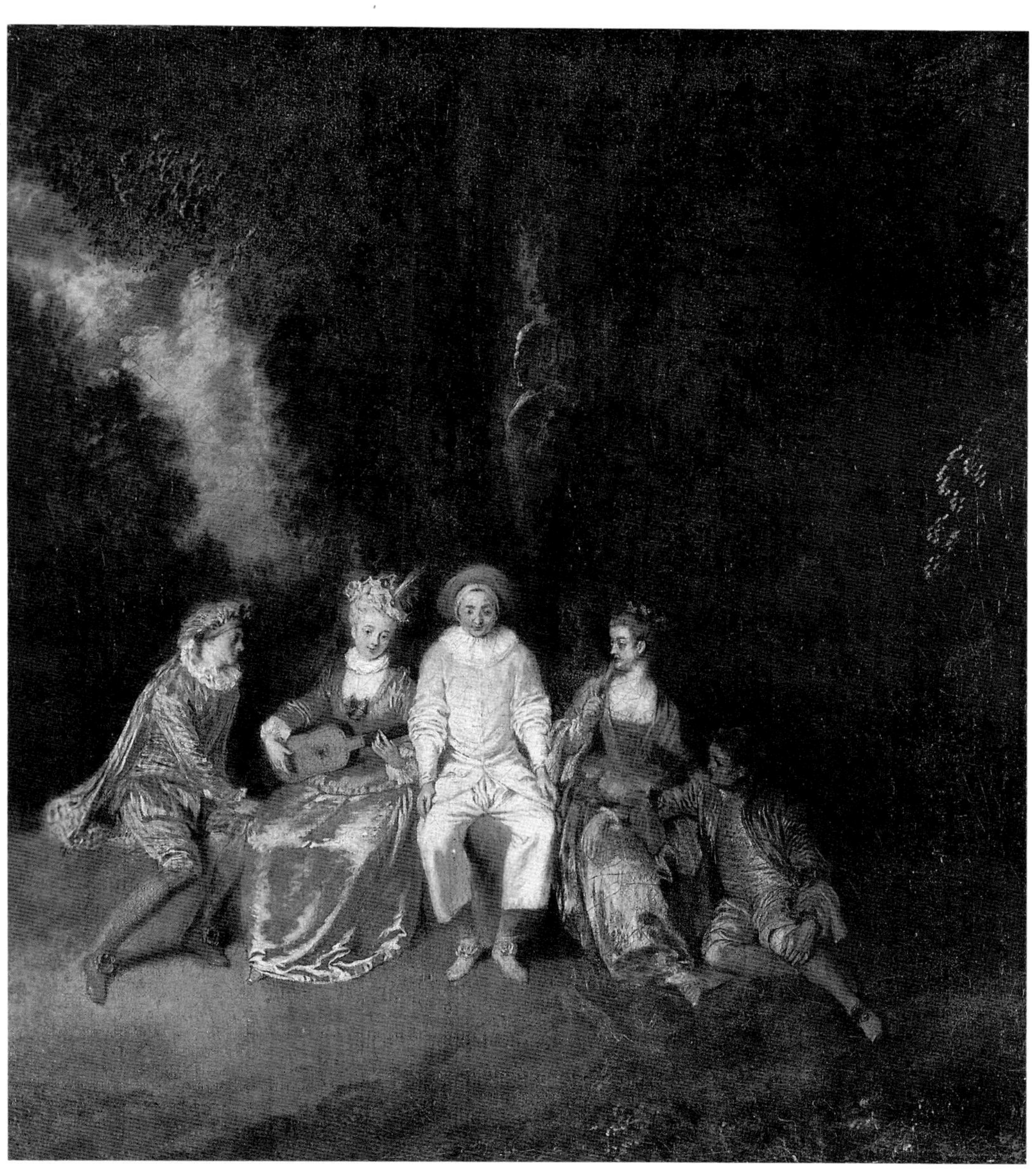

Antoine Watteau, *Pierrot Content*, *c.* 1712
oil on canvas, 35 × 31 cm
Thyssen-Bornemisza Collection,
Lugano, Switzerland

figures of the attentive man and the serenading woman, slyly putting the Baron, by implication, in the place of Pierrot. In the meantime he had begun work on a complete recapitulation of the painting, much larger than its original (the Watteau is only just over a foot either way; *Large interior*, more than six feet by six, by far the biggest canvas Freud had ever attempted). The result, painted between 1981 and 1983, is a strenuous and fascinating enterprise of absorption, homage and reversal: what Balthus precociously did with Courbet in *La Montagne*, and with Piero della Francesca in *The Street*, is done by the mature Freud to the immature Watteau in *Large interior*.

Nature and culture are here reversed. Watteau's feathery and artificial park – 'nature' in quotes, as theatre – becomes the more credible and dingy interior of an upstairs room in Paddington, his studio as usual. Watteau's trees are telescoped down into one indoor plant, an exuberantly writhing pelargonium, and it may be that a trace of Watteau's herm, a faun in profile rising amid the shrubbery, is preserved in the vertical duct for pipes set in the wall, a raw slot of bricks. Whereas Watteau's figures expand across the painting and have plenty of air between them, Freud's are close and the air around them seems congealed in the grey light of afternoon, compressing them all the more. Everything seems static except the water running from a tap on the sink, which is certainly there in Freud's studio but also naggingly recalls a detail from Ingres's *Bain Turc*, or the Valpinçon nude, (both in the Louvre), the thin flow of water issuing from its pipe into the pool below.

Watteau's figures are secured in their static grace by the conventions, postures and gestures of the theatre. Freud's are not; they are jostled together like a family in an amateur photograph who have been told to cram into the shot (this is emphasized by the spare room at both ends of the meagre bed) and they do not quite know what to do with their arms and hands, though Freud does. It is as though Freud had chosen to rework a painting of the utmost theatricality in order to assert his own mistrust of theatre. This huddling looks defensive, especially against the 'waste' space of the rest of the room and the rushing brown vista of the floorboards; it has its own pathos. But the ache of space is resisted by the bodies – solid, pasty flesh, in all its presentness and granularity, Freud's physical exuberance working at full pressure.

There are five figures, as in the Watteau, but they are all (except for 'Pierrot') girls.

For the first time in my life the individuals were secondary to the plan of the painting. I got them to look at the Watteau; and told them the idea of reworking it; and said I wanted a similar composition. I didn't want period costume, but I wanted variety in the clothes, and that they could dress up a little bit. The child on the ground has nothing to do with the Watteau. I needed her there to break the Watteau composition. I borrowed her. She was one of a pair of twin sisters. Why choose this twin and not the other? The choice was obvious. I felt she had an inner life and therefore hoped that posing would be less arduous for her.

All the rest are members of Freud's clan, by birth or affinity: the girl with the guitar is his daughter Bella, the part of Gilles is played by his son Kai. They are so present to us, so heavy with materiality, that the effect of Watteau's painting is reversed: one sees them, not as skilled actors in a little drama whose artifice the painter celebrates, but as rather awkward players of a charade whose meaning has dwindled and left only the facts of body and cloth behind. Freud preserves nothing of Gilles's silly contentment, none of the jealousy of the girl on the right or the coquettishness of the one on the left. Instead, a realist to the root, he paints once again the condition of posing for an artist over a long period of time, which is one of fatigue, boredom and a doffed loyalty to the painter: all five faces have the resigned, inward-turned look of other passengers seen across the carriage of an underground train, and the big hands and feet (their structure of tendon and bone so admirably defined in clear strokes of the brush) slump into positions where they get the most rest. One is made poignantly aware of Freud's desire to show how the strictest formal expressiveness of the body comes from the body's own forms and not from the narratives it can be made to enact. And because one does expect narrative of some kind from any composition involving a number of figures, one is tempted to attribute to *Large interior* a pathos that Freud did not put into it. It is, in fact, a painting of the most steely concision, a veritable manifesto of Freud's deeper intentions: to assert, with the utmost plastic force, the advantages of scrutiny over theatre, without for a moment falling into the formalist trap of regarding the body as a mere inventory of potentially abstract forms, or the idealist one of mistaking it for a cultural construct without pores or orifices, without the sag and sheen of flesh – without, in sum, the humanity that Freud's art so alertly hunts from the body's cover.

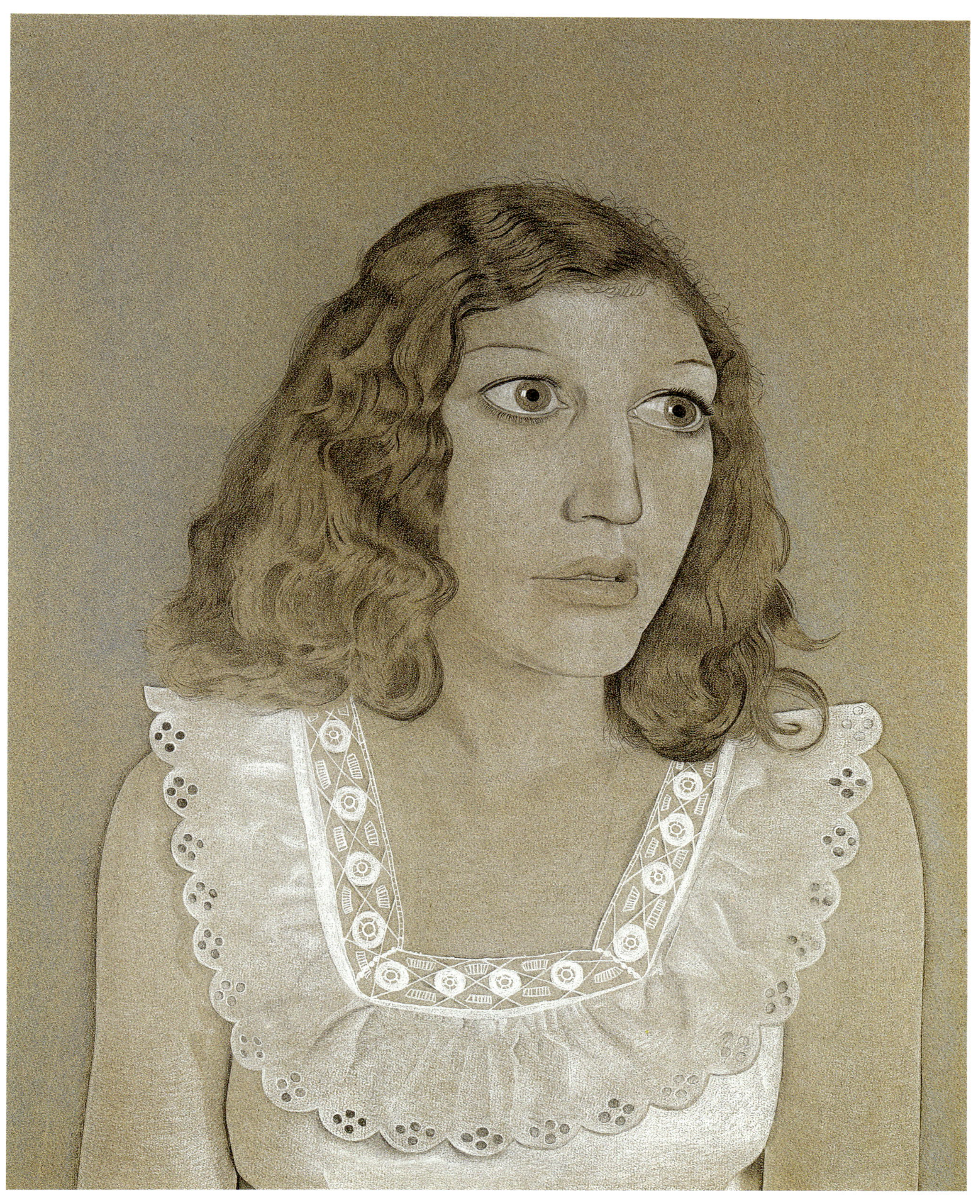

I

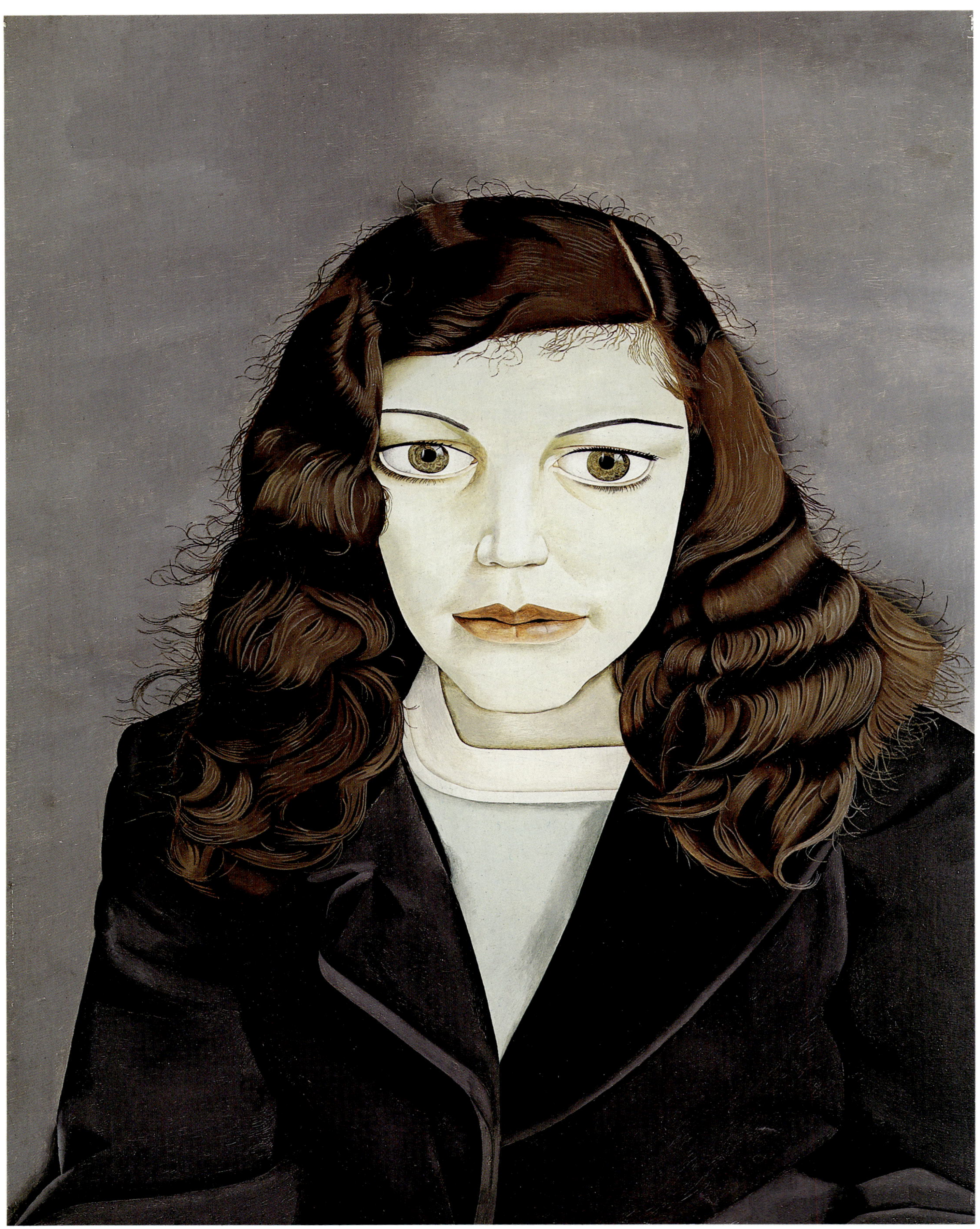

2

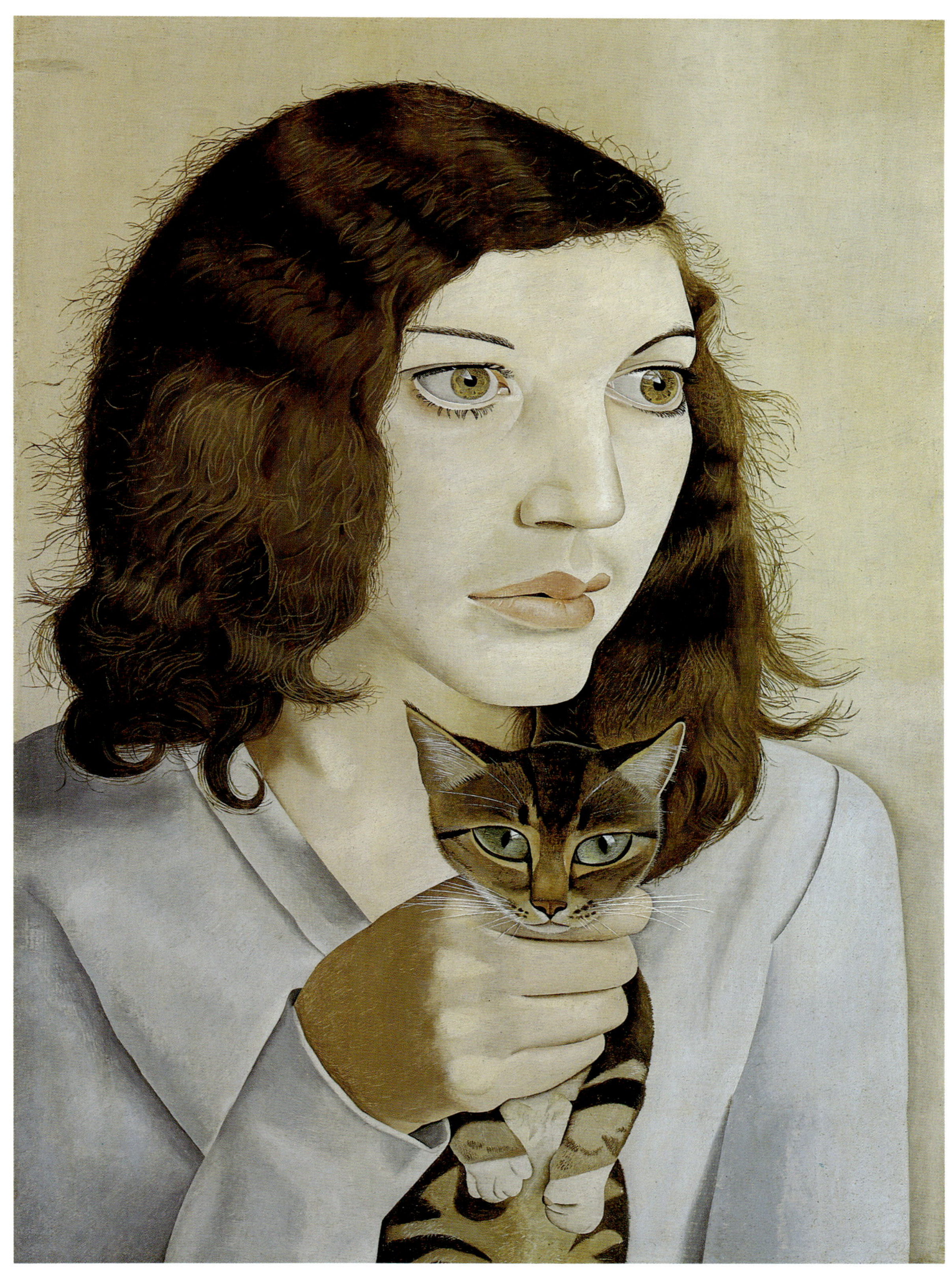

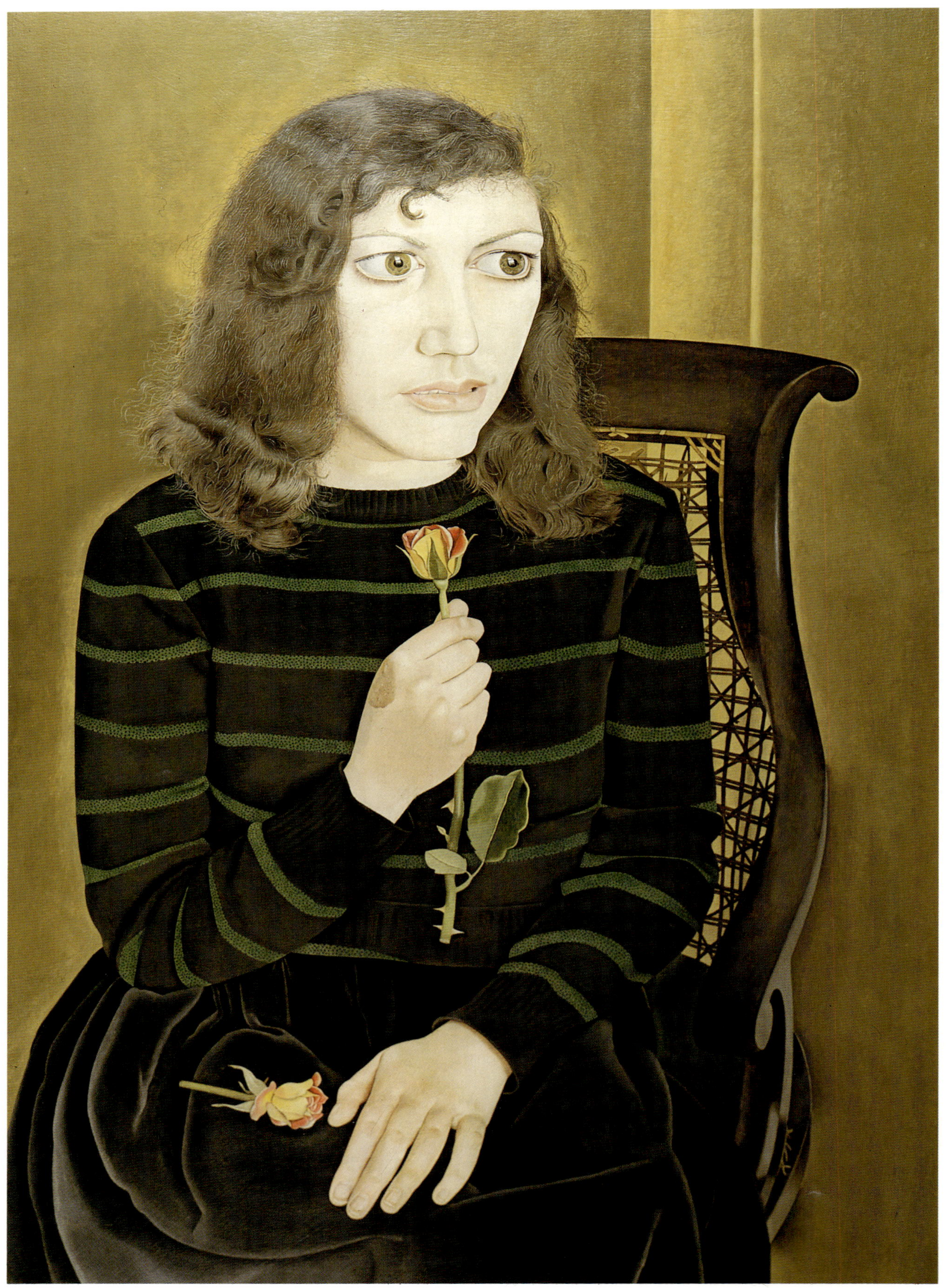

4

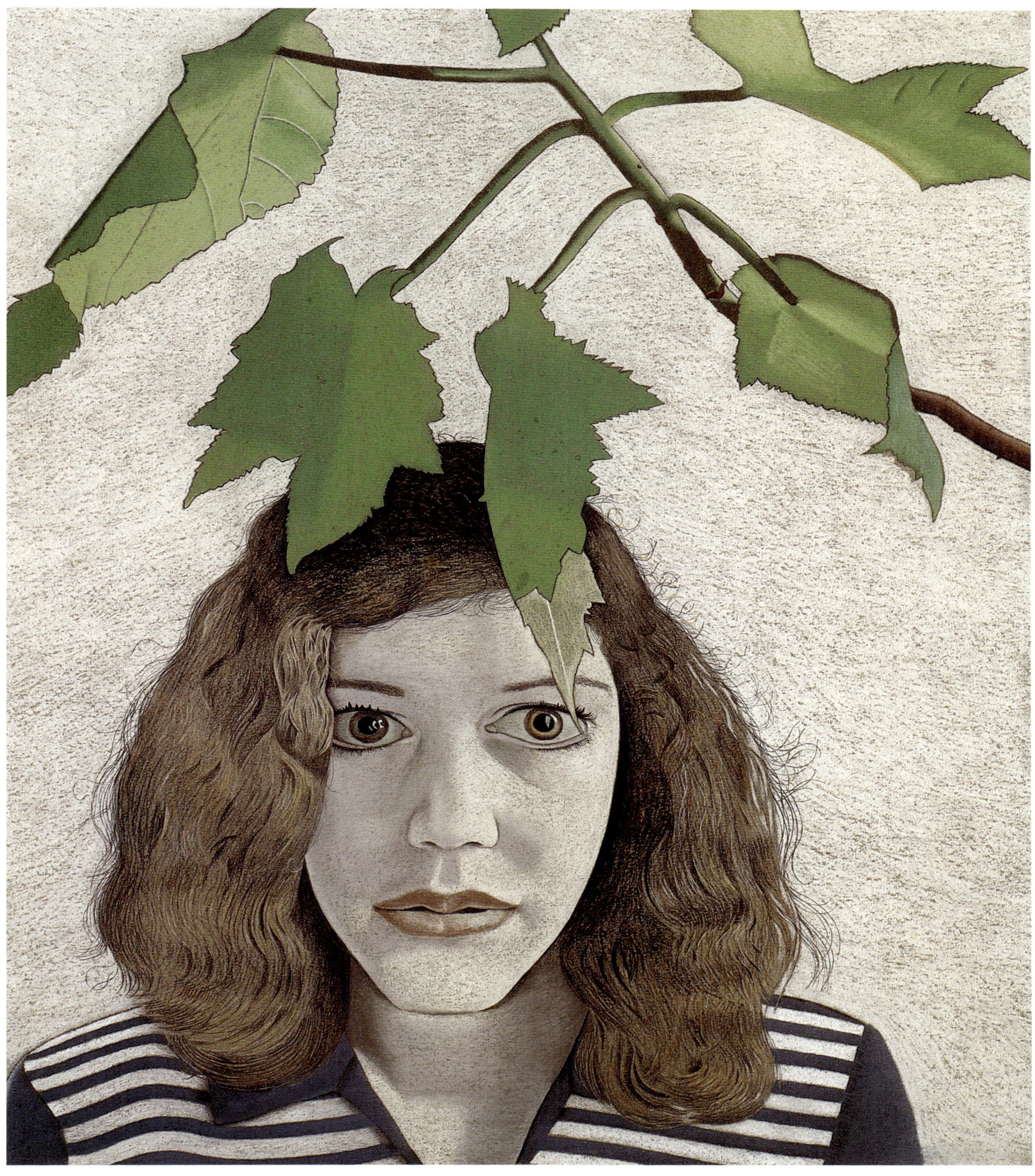

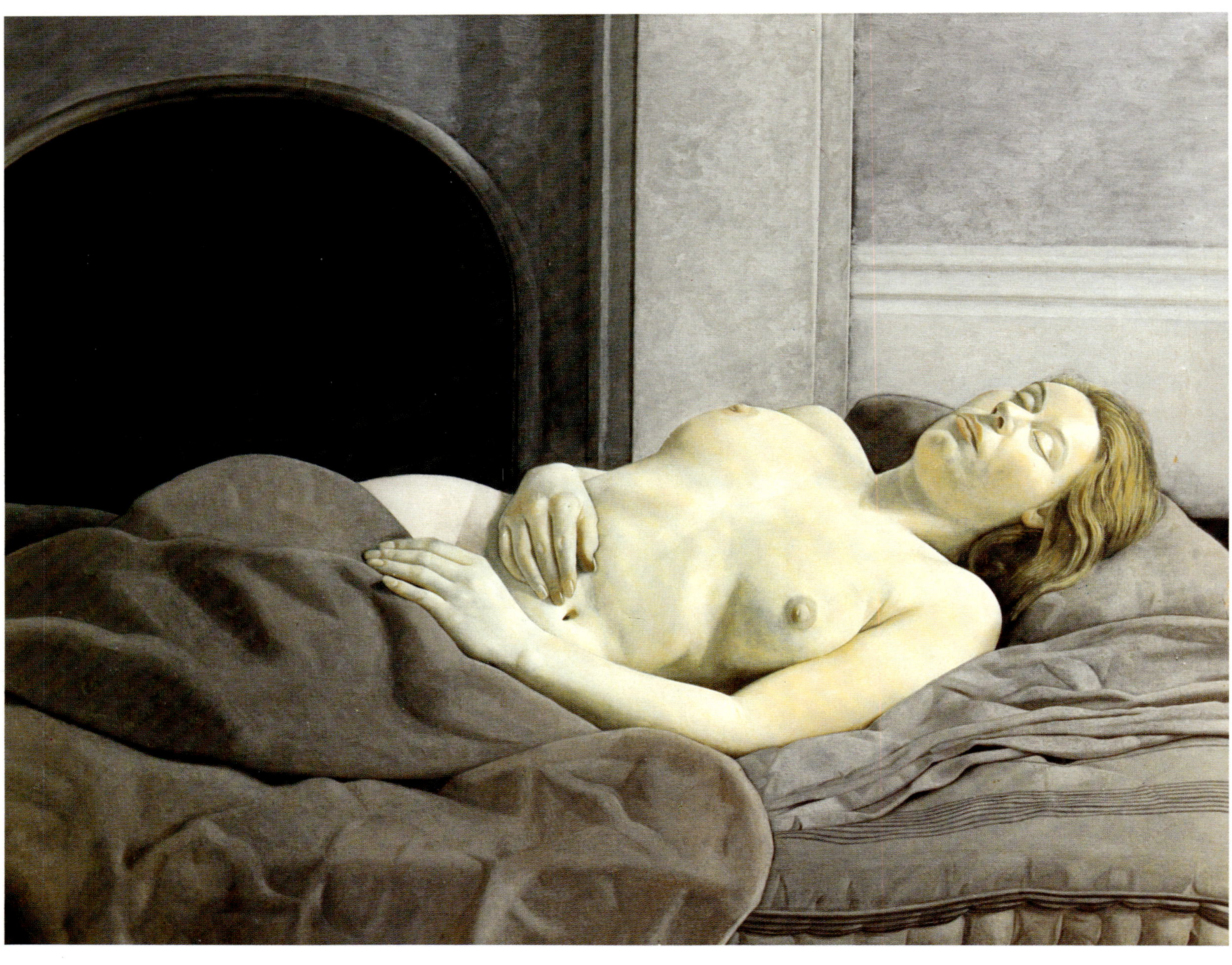

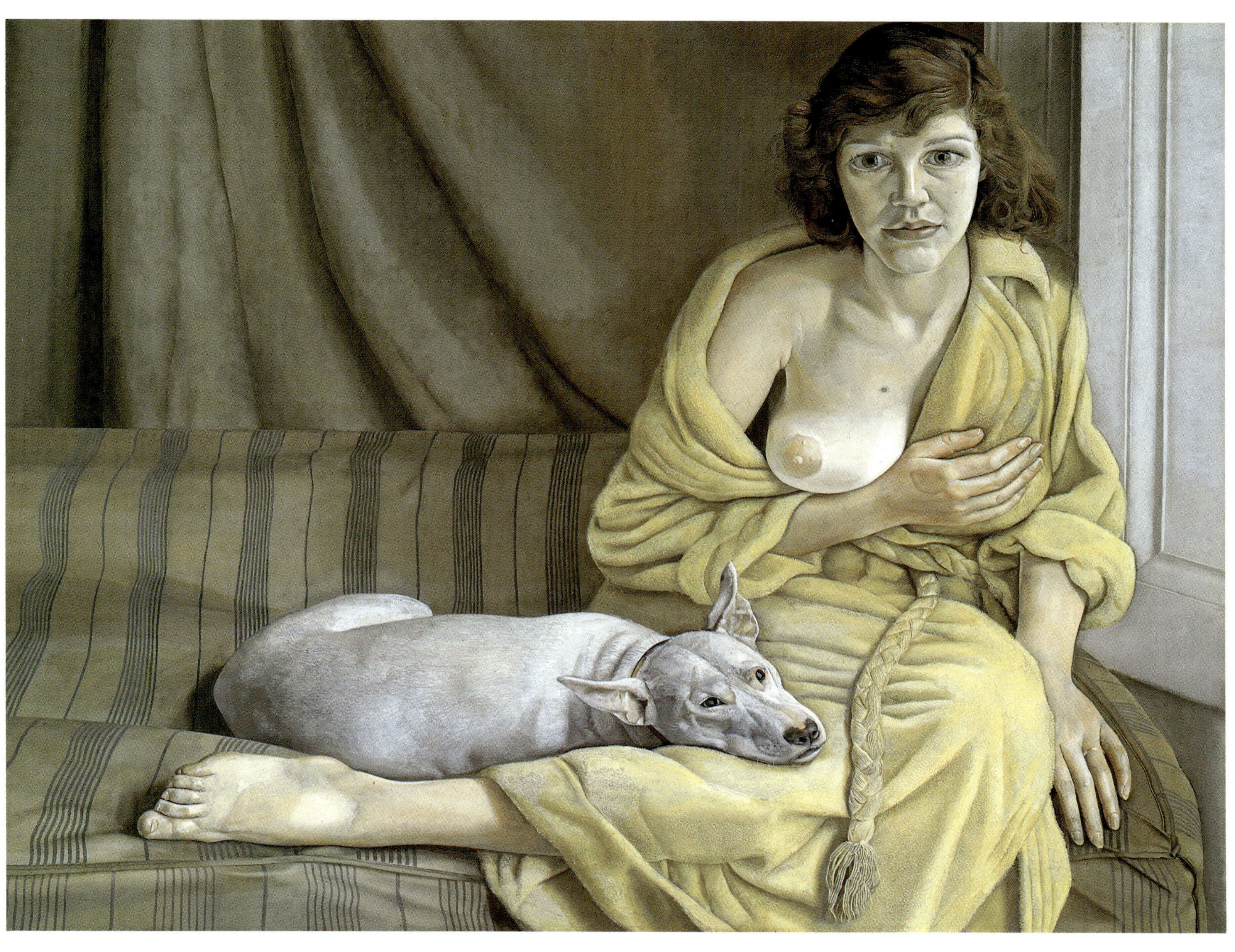

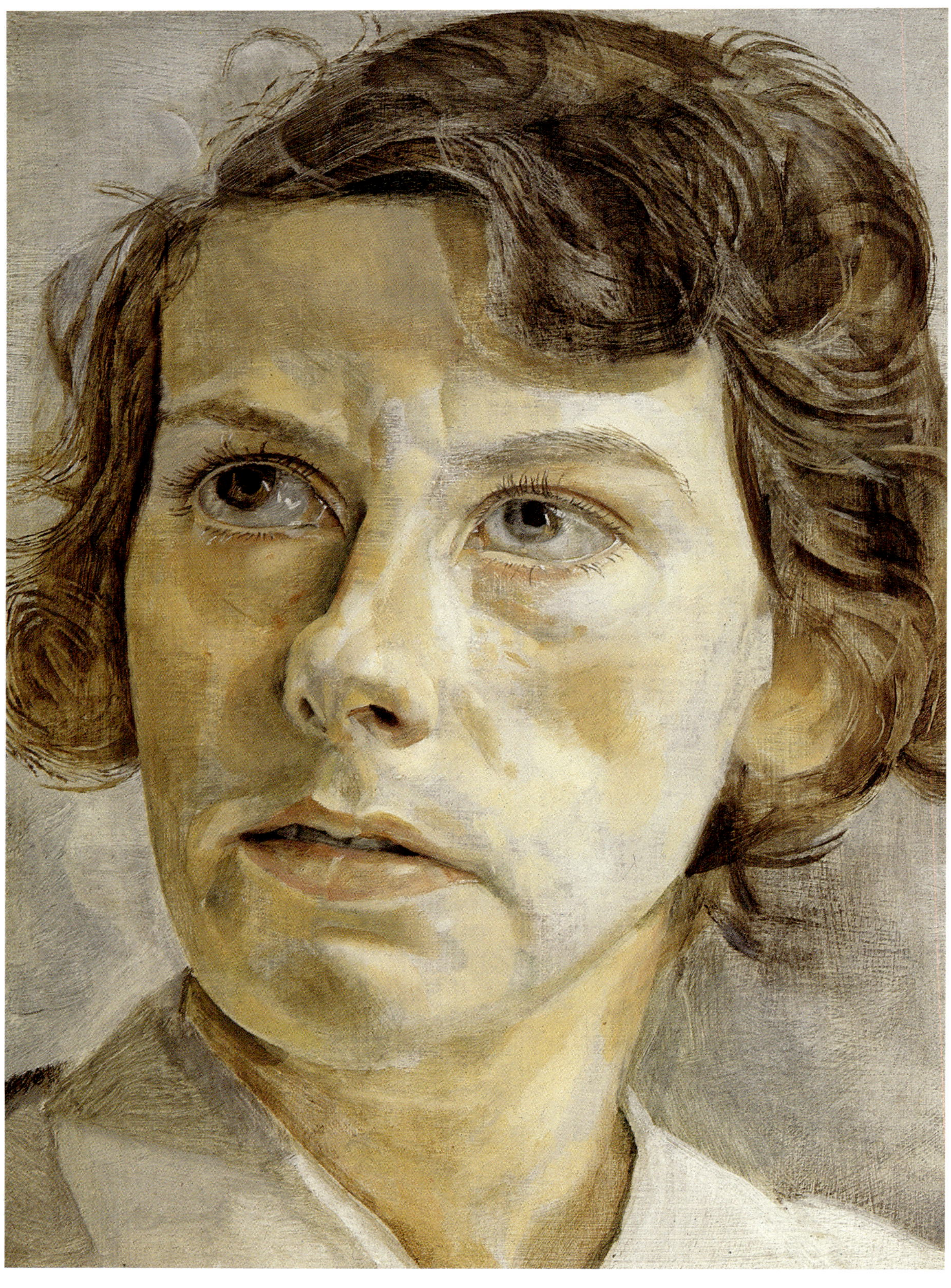

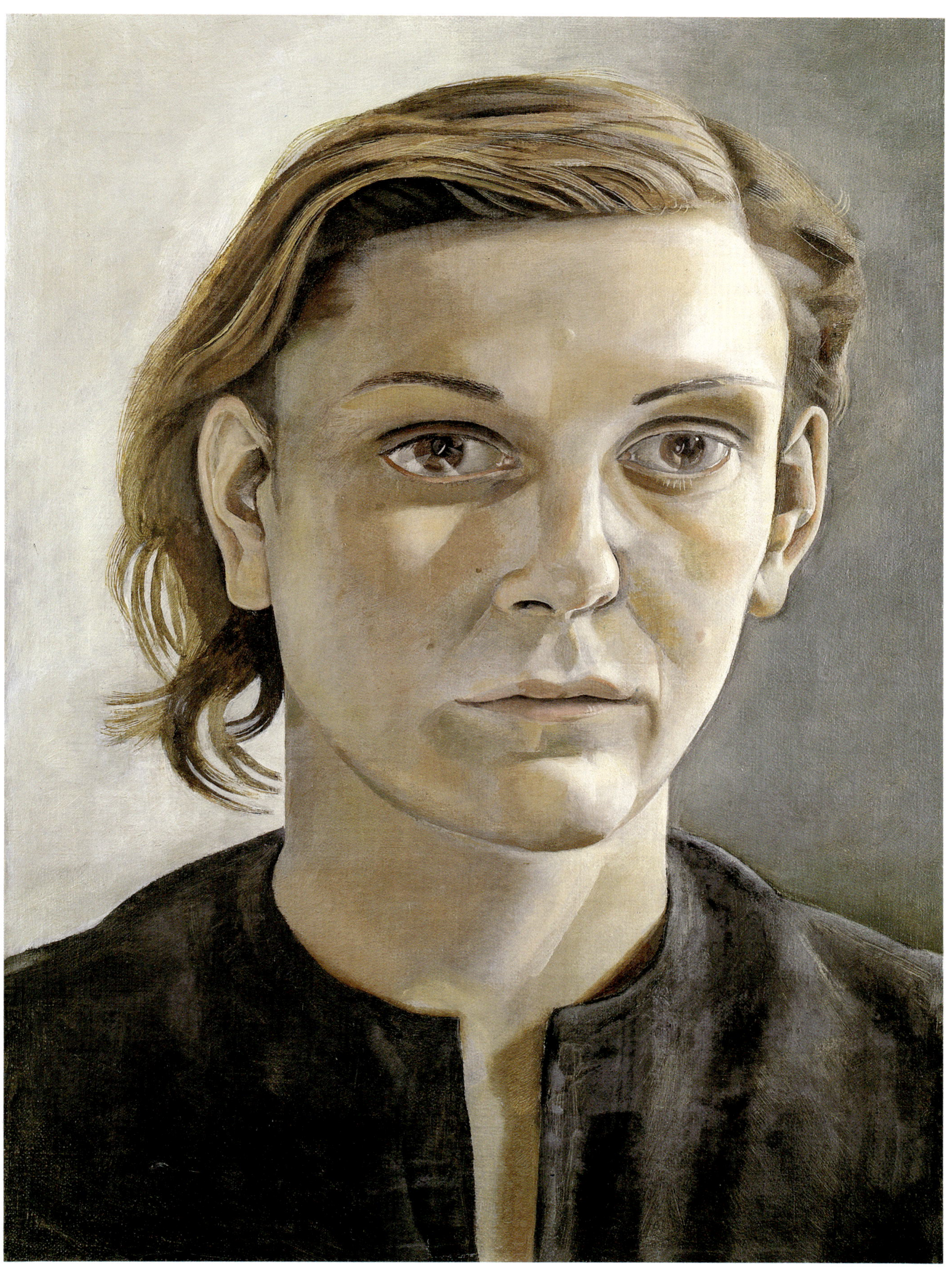

9

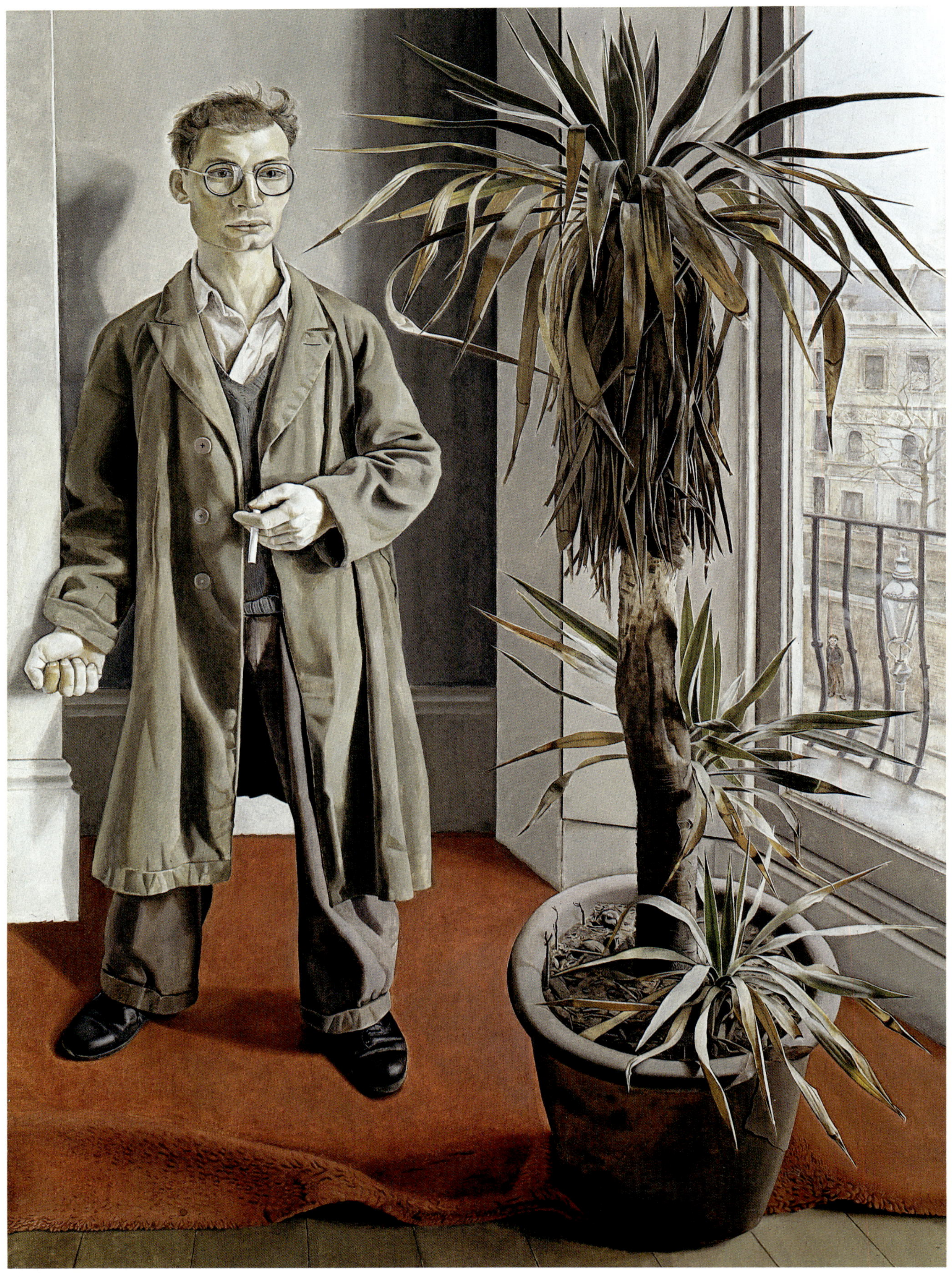

10

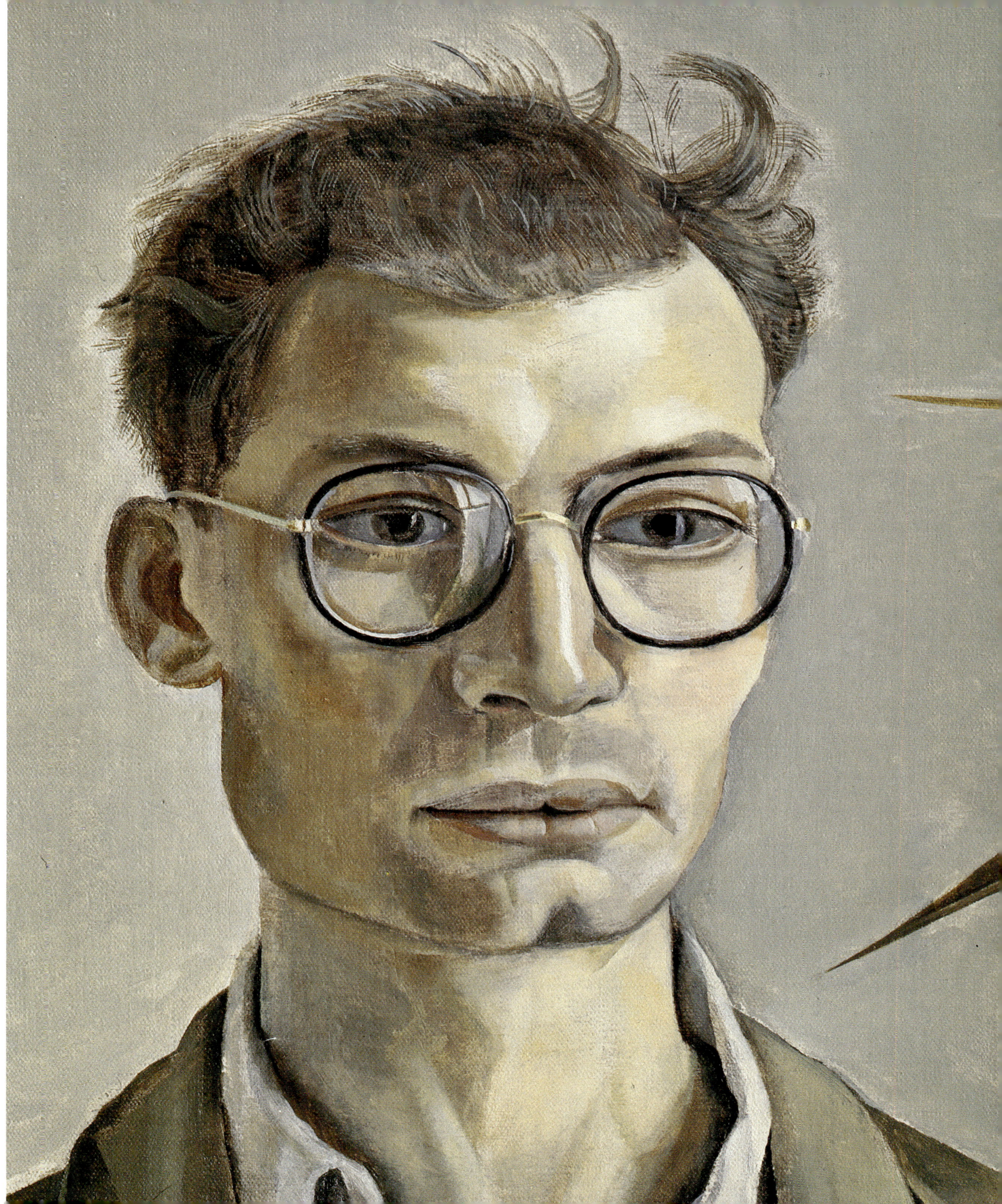

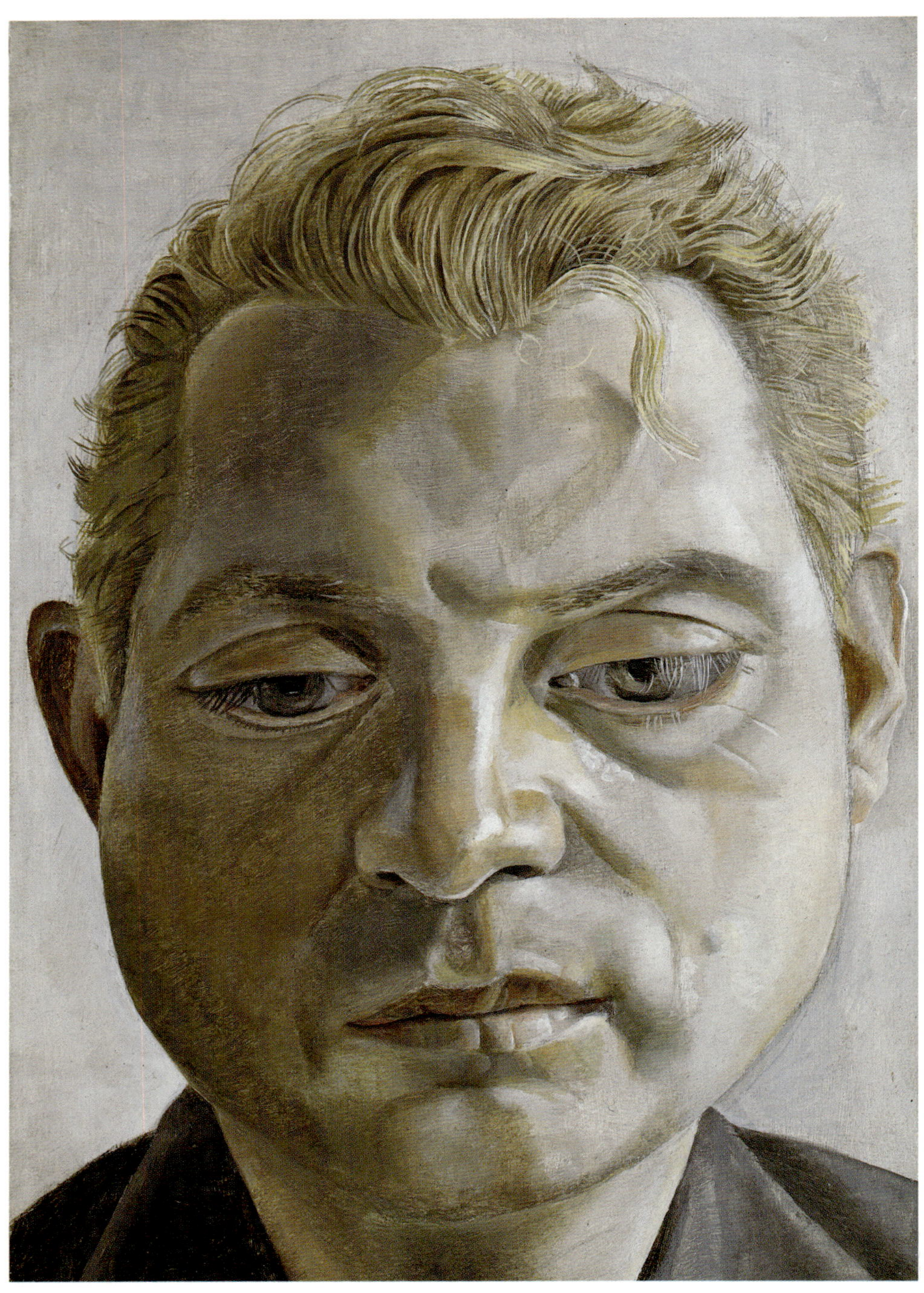

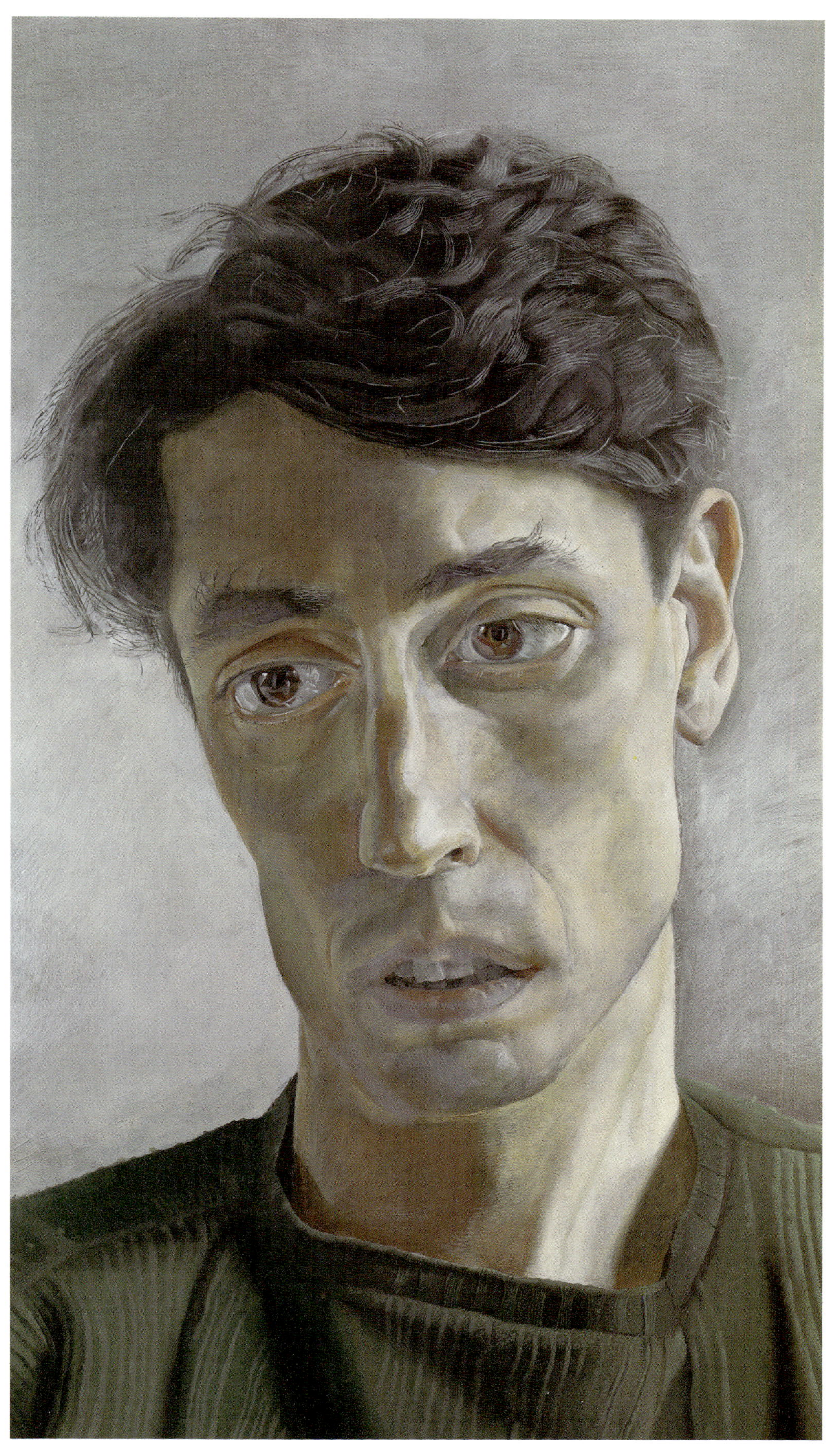

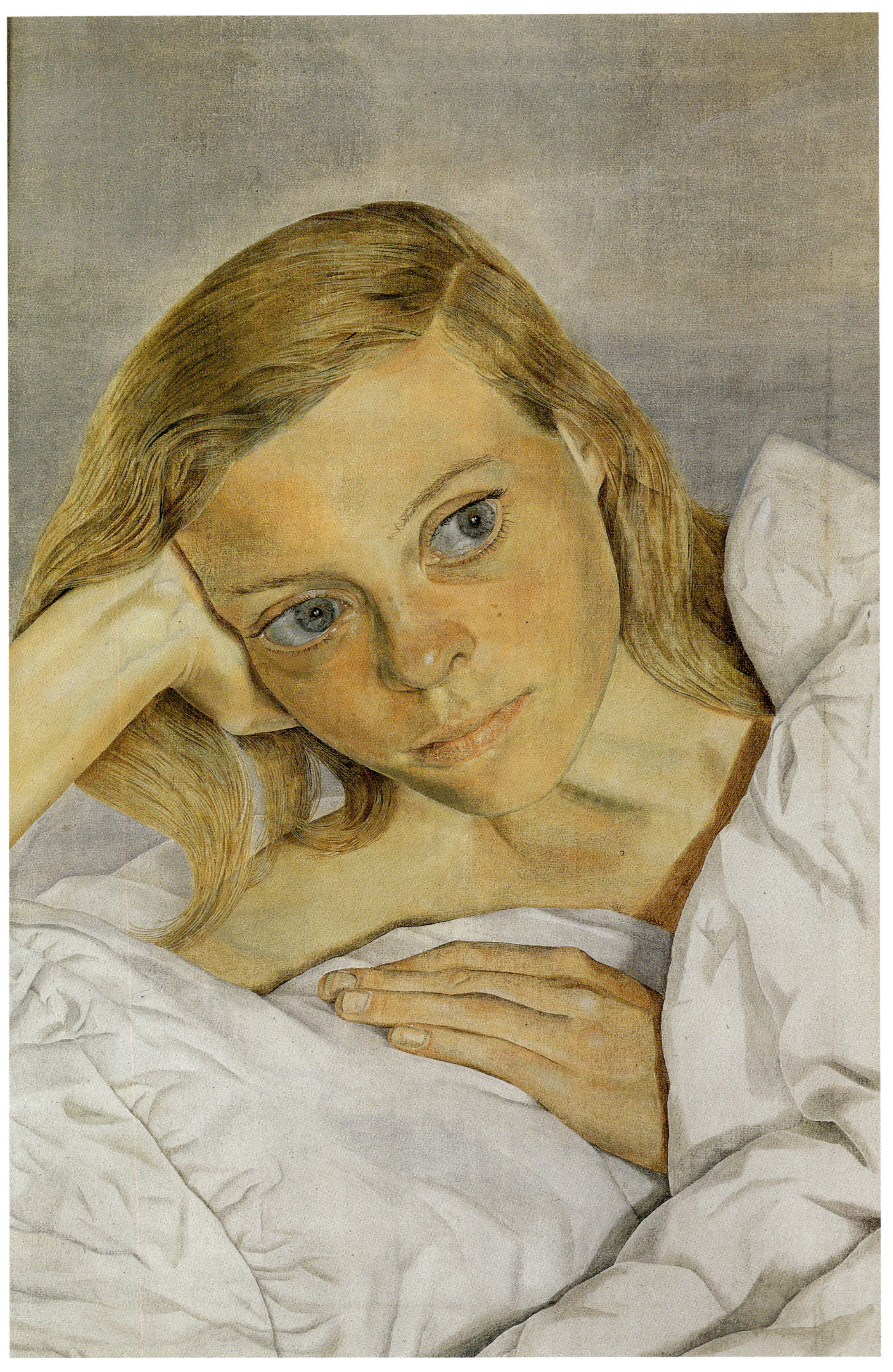

13

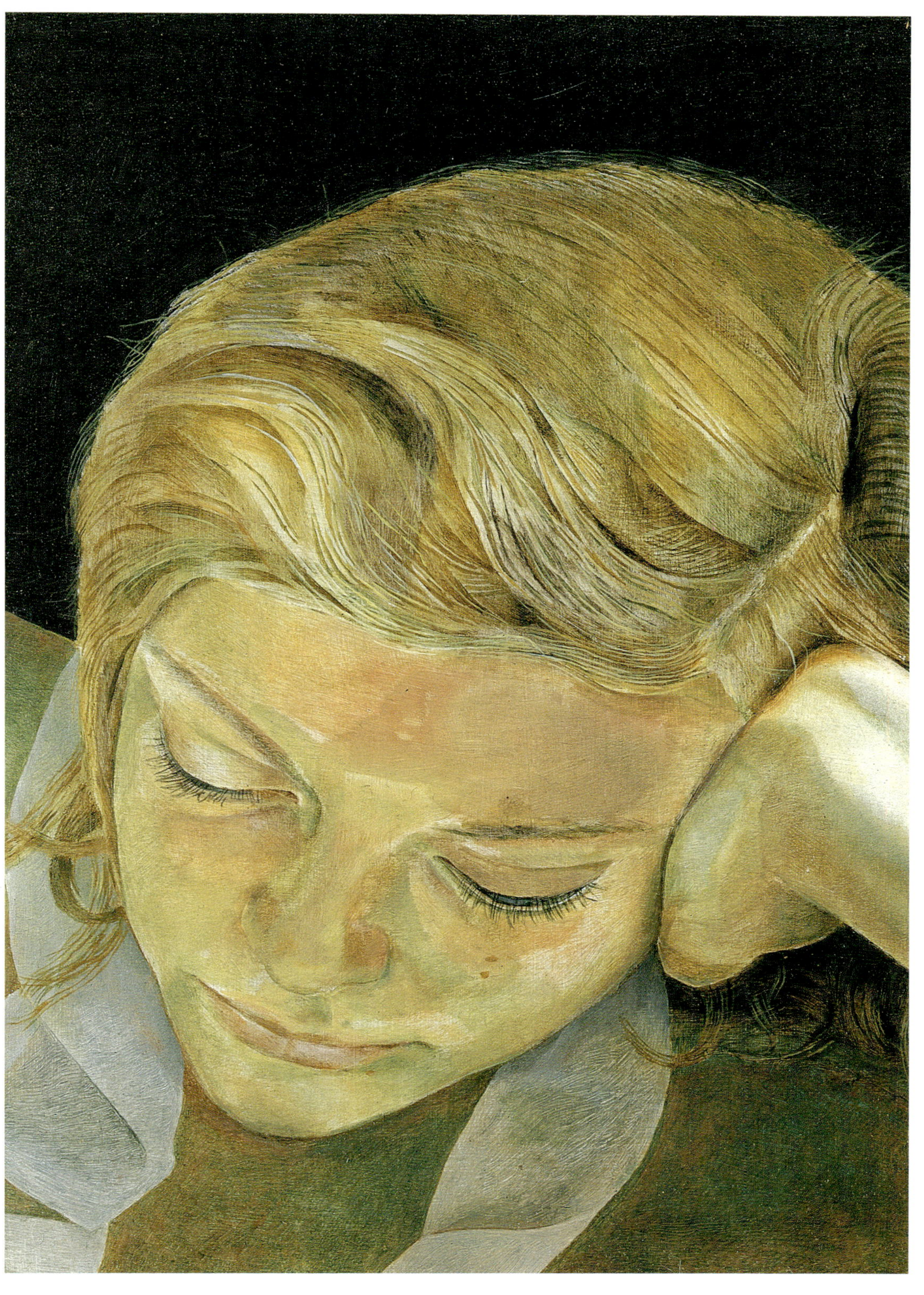

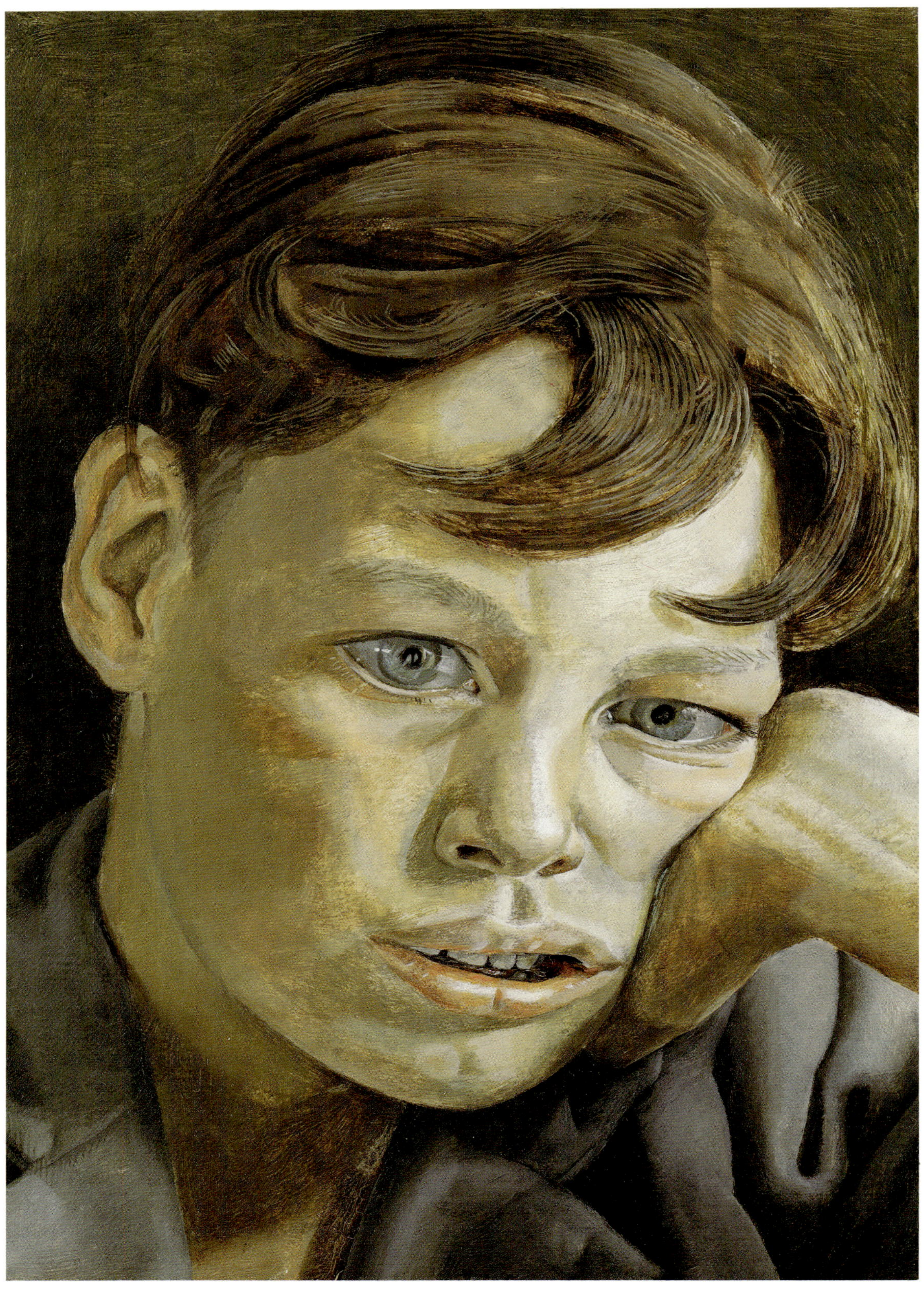

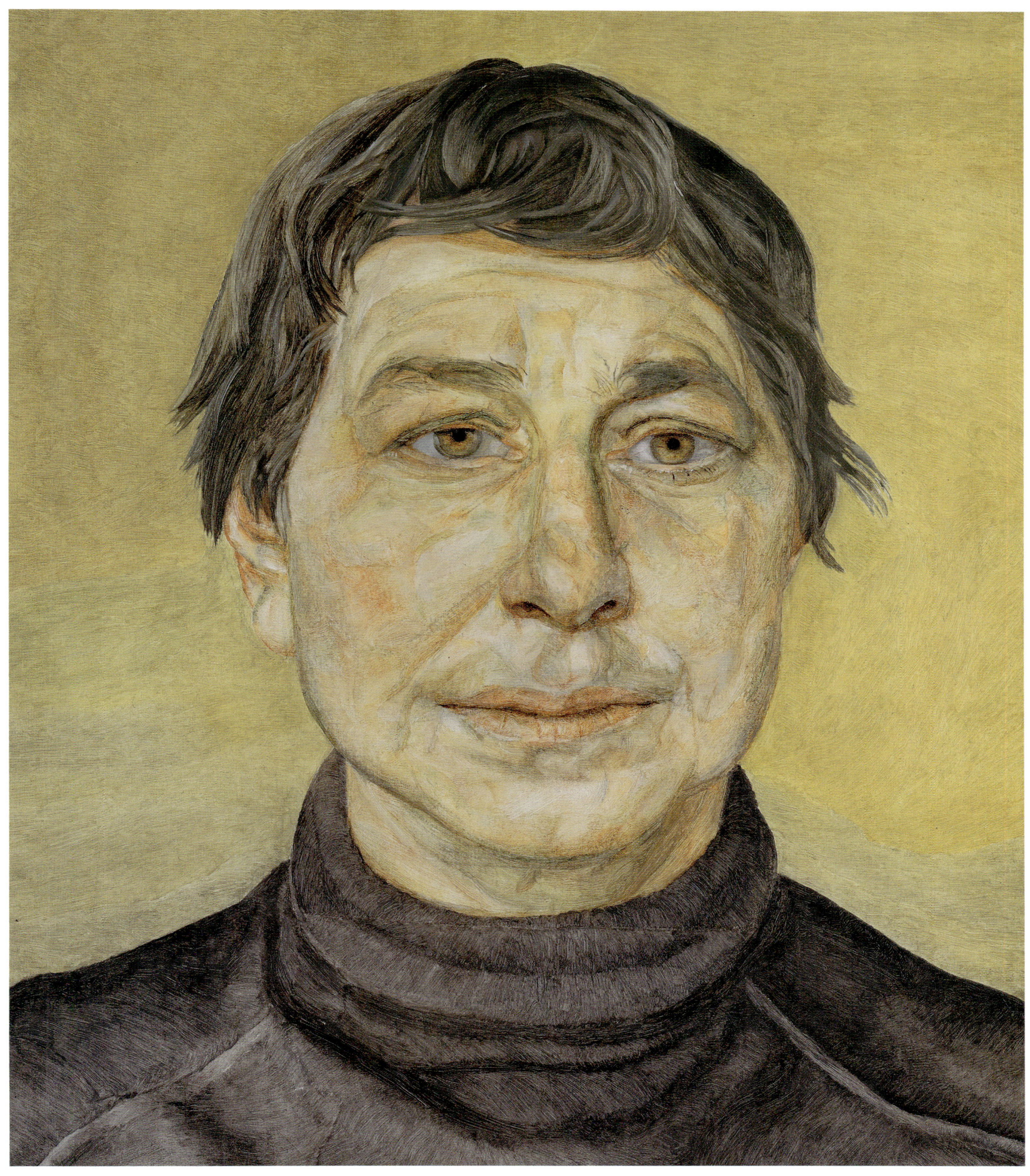

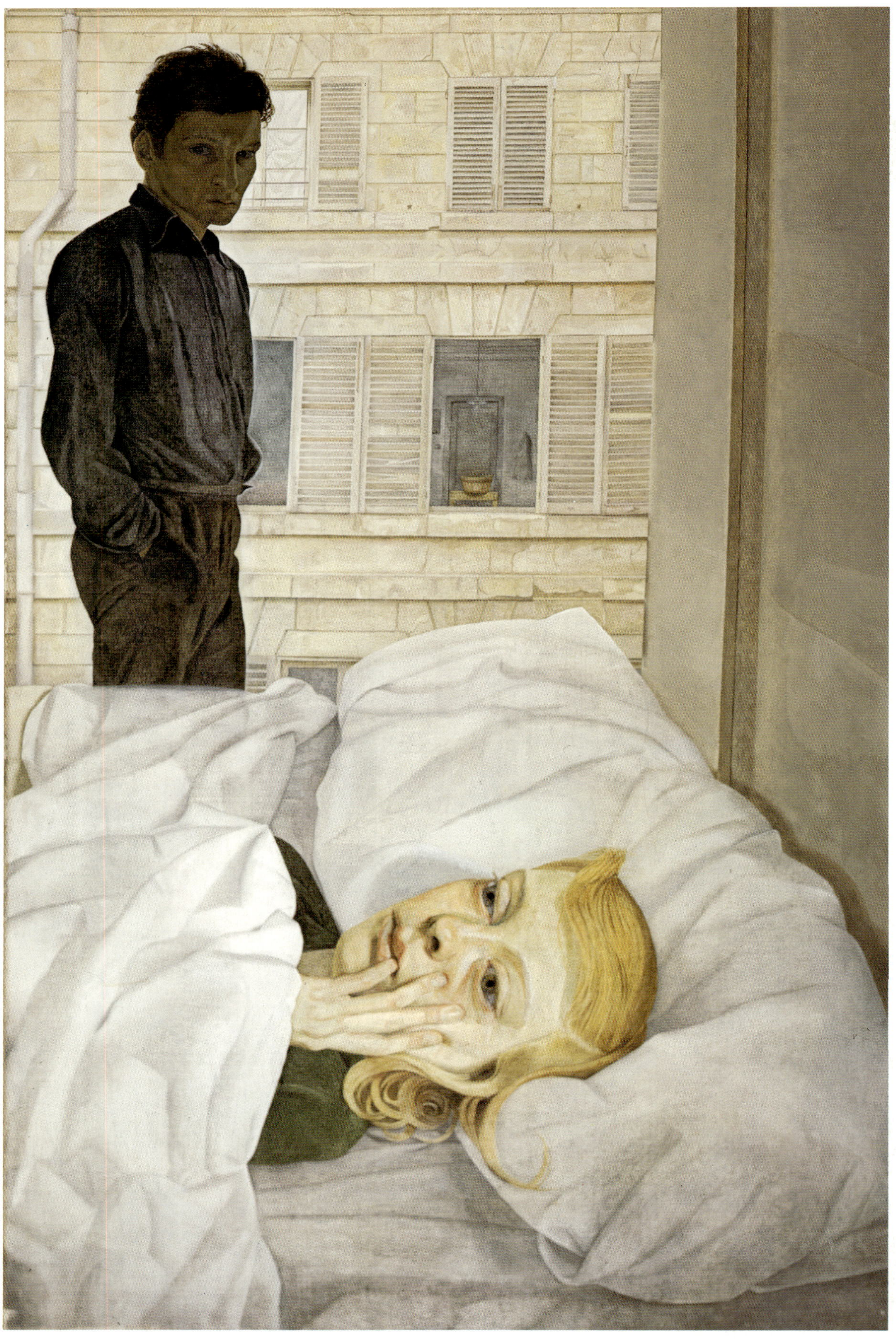

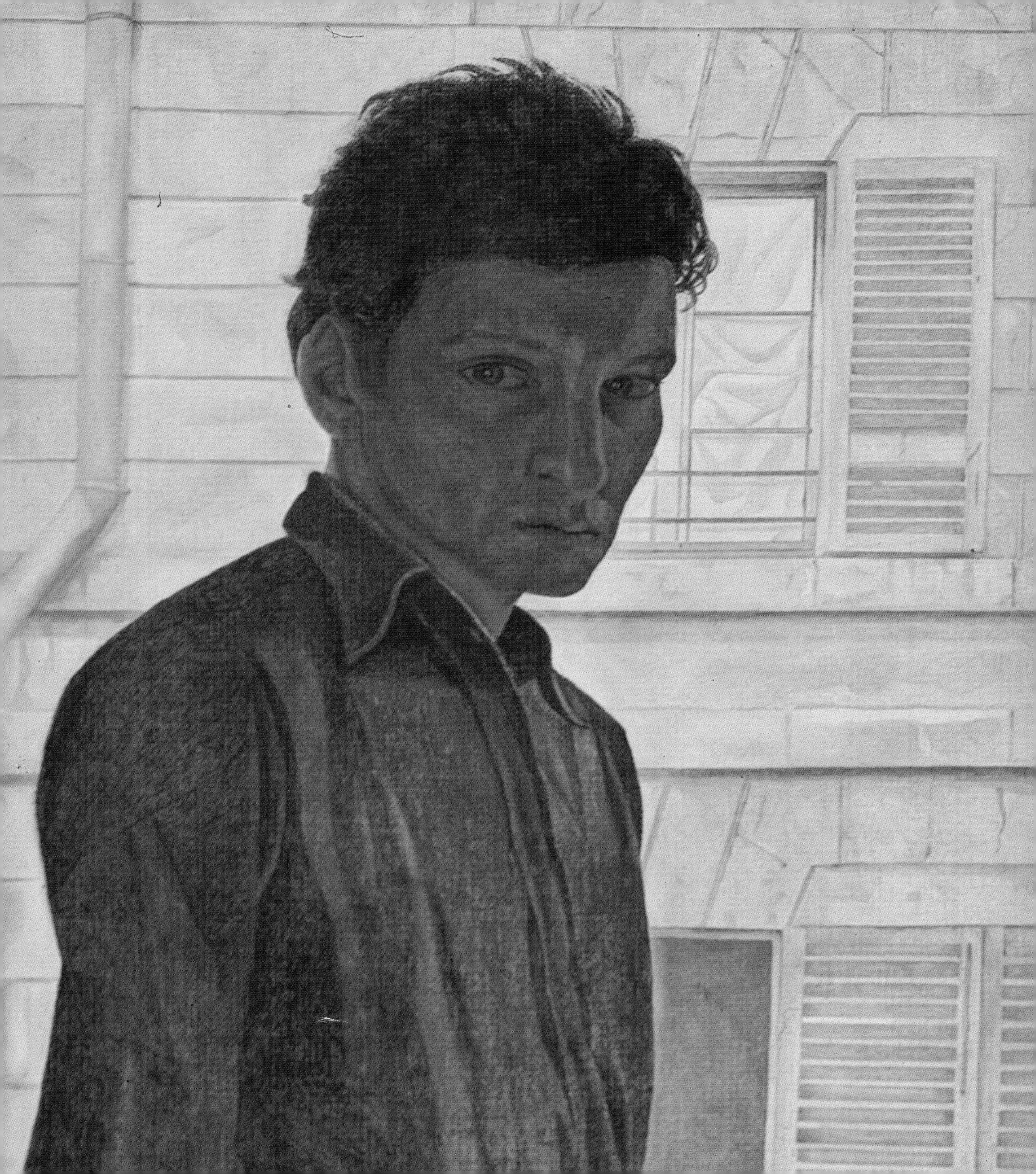

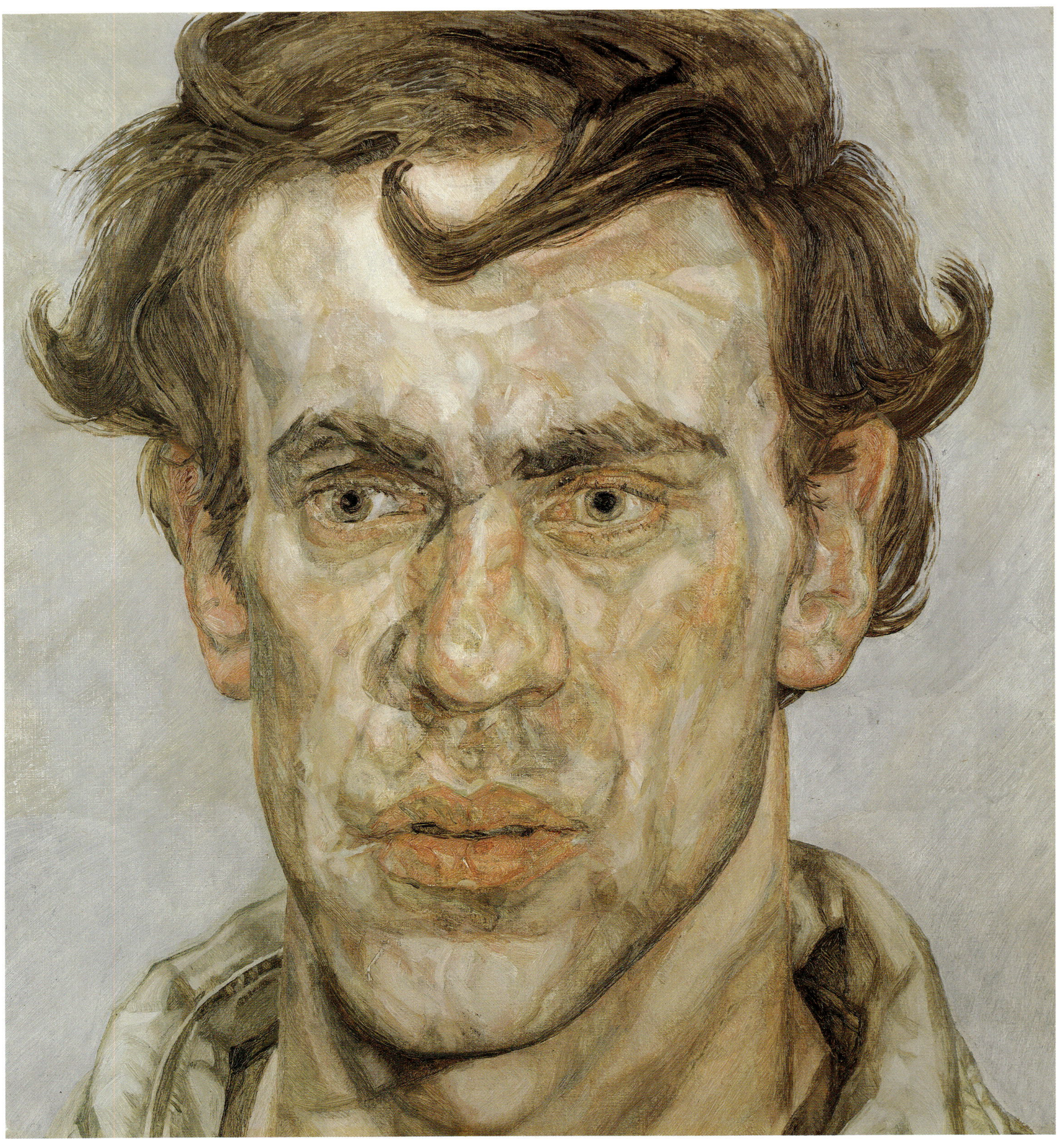

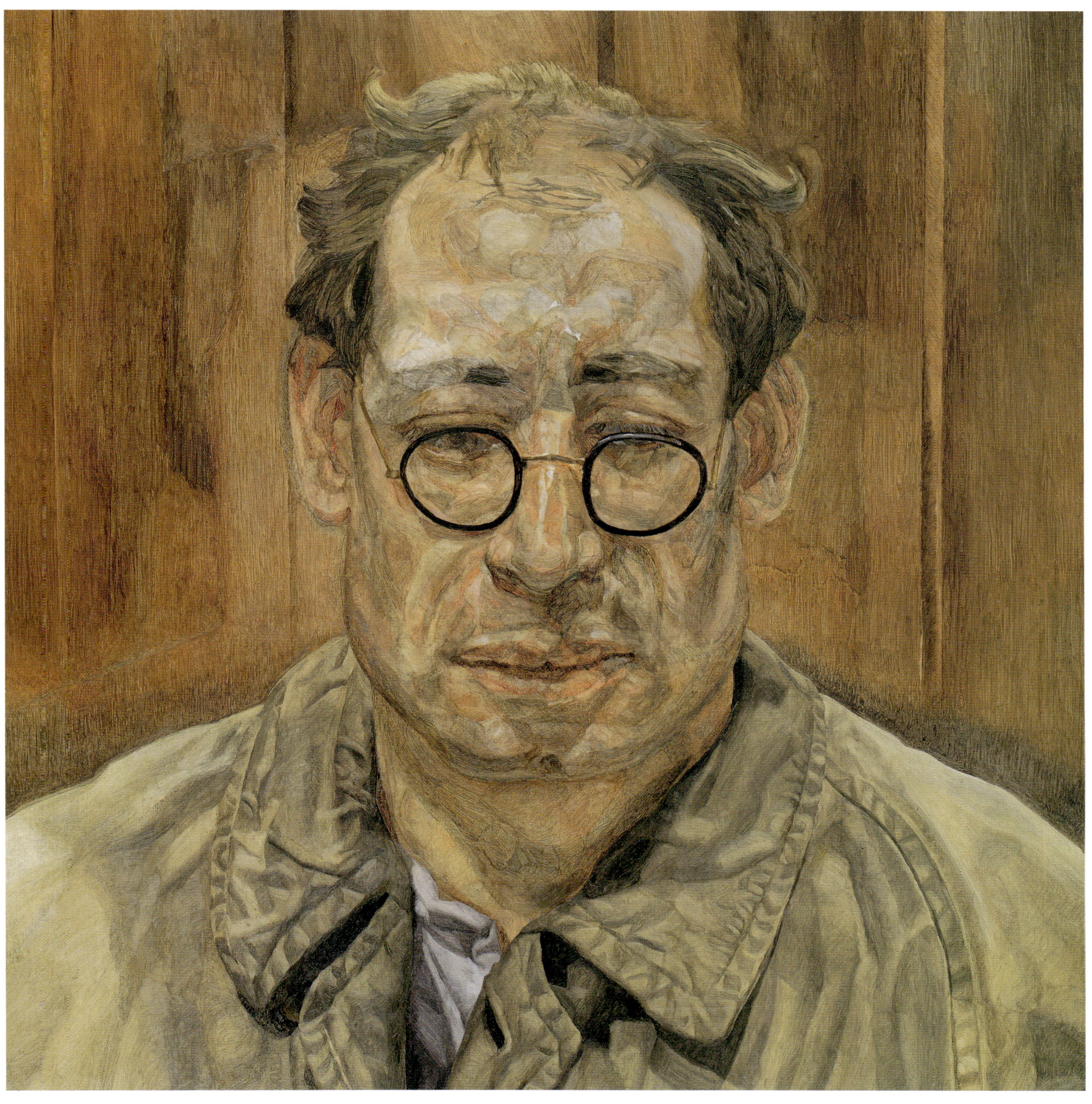

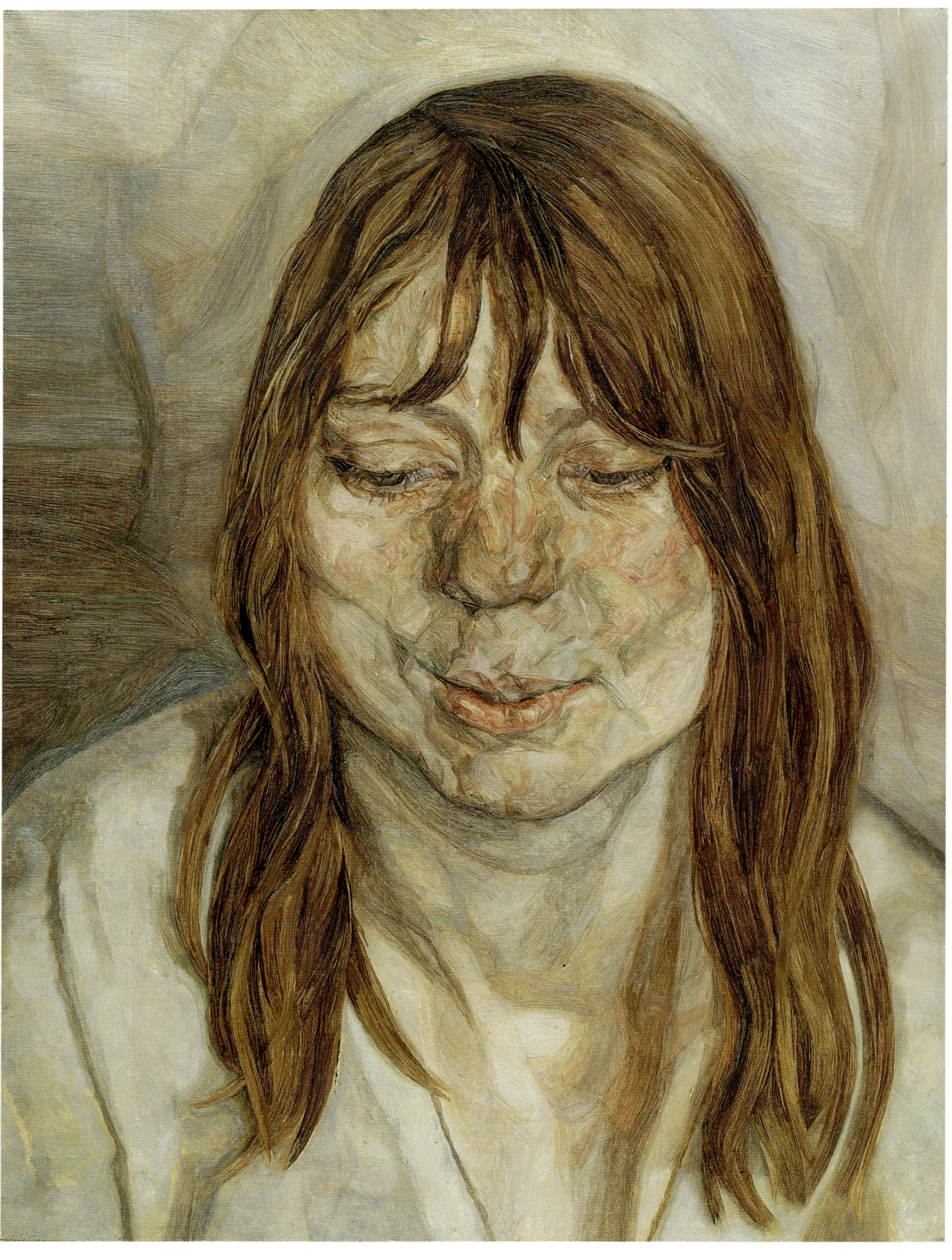

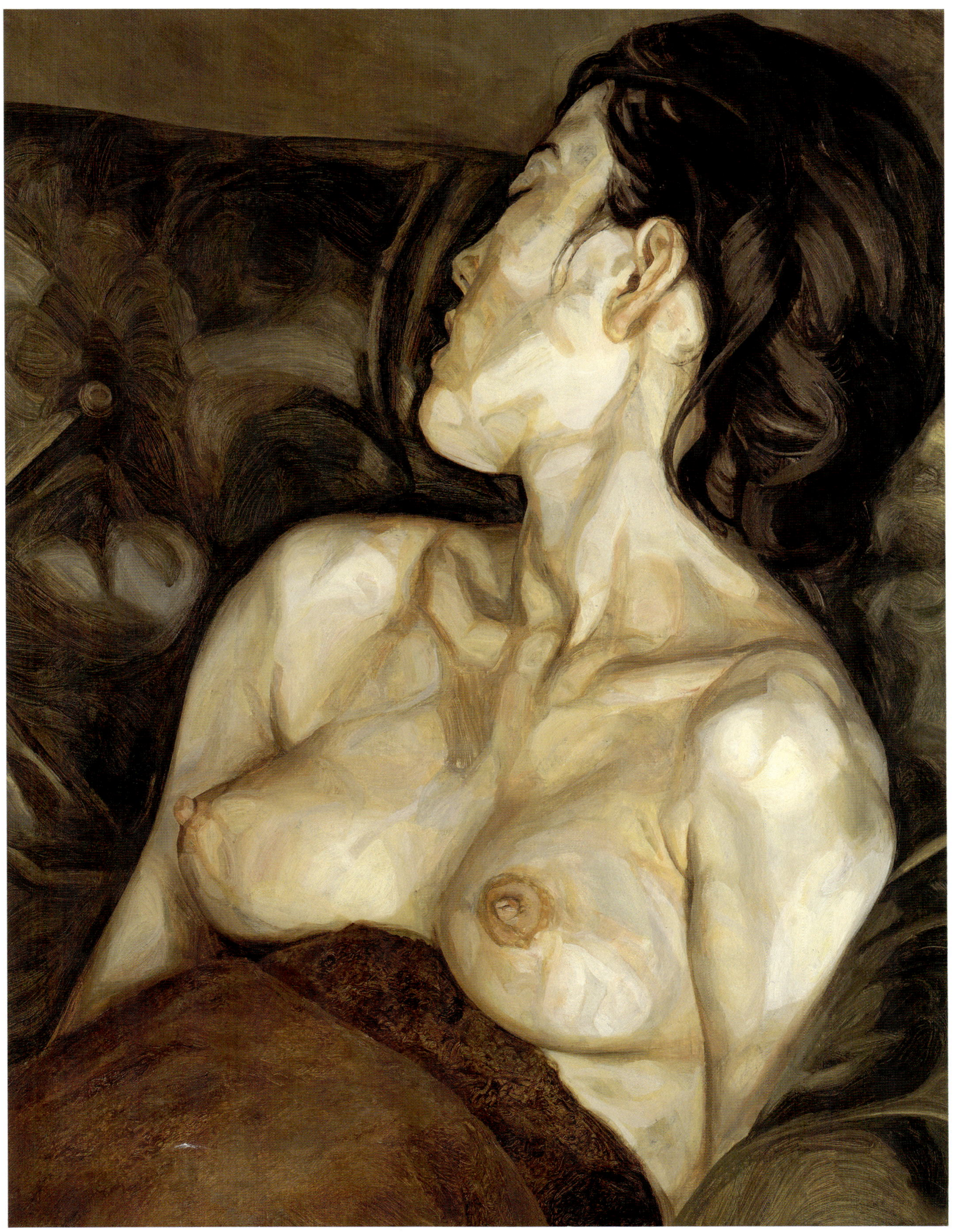

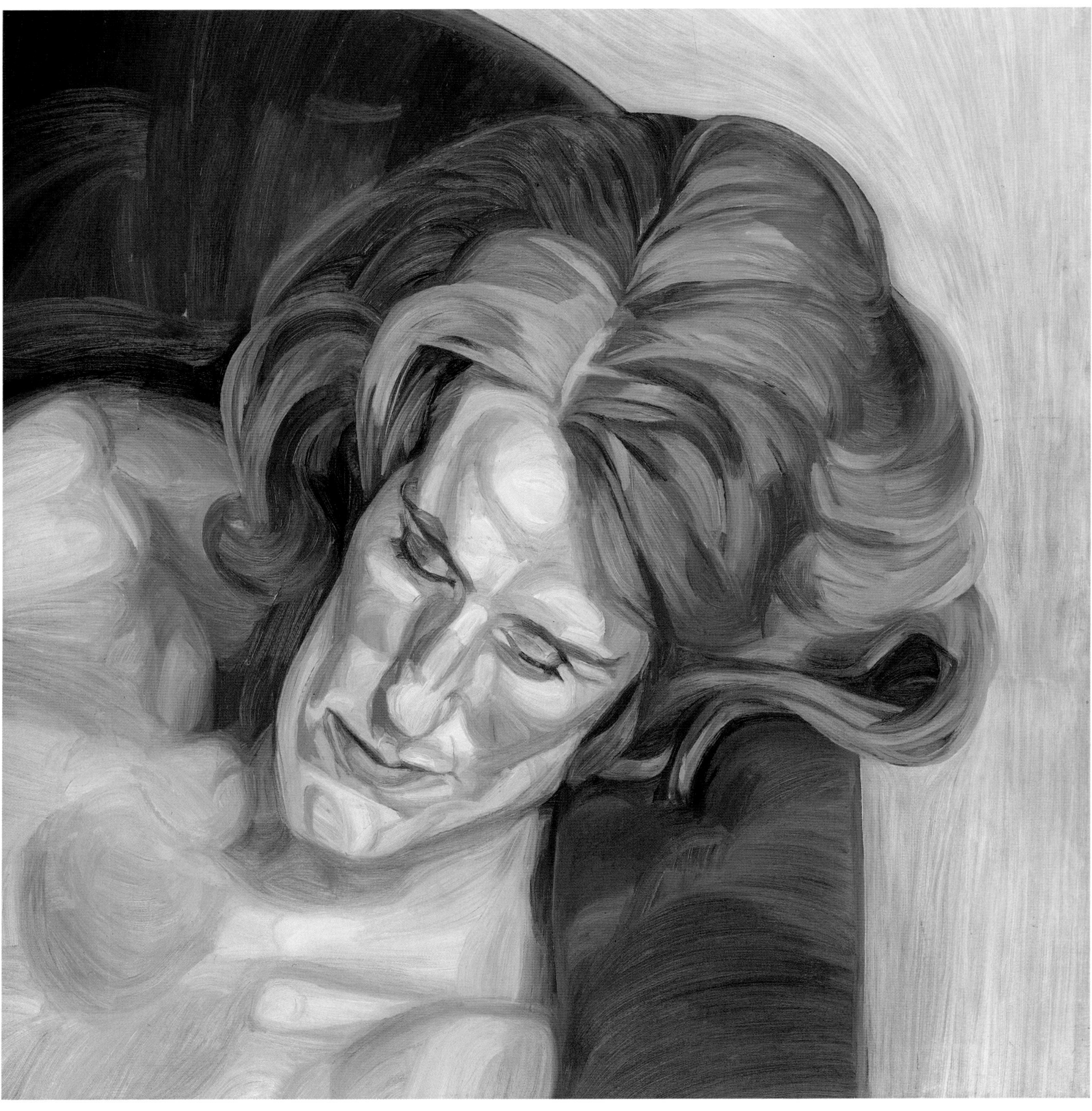

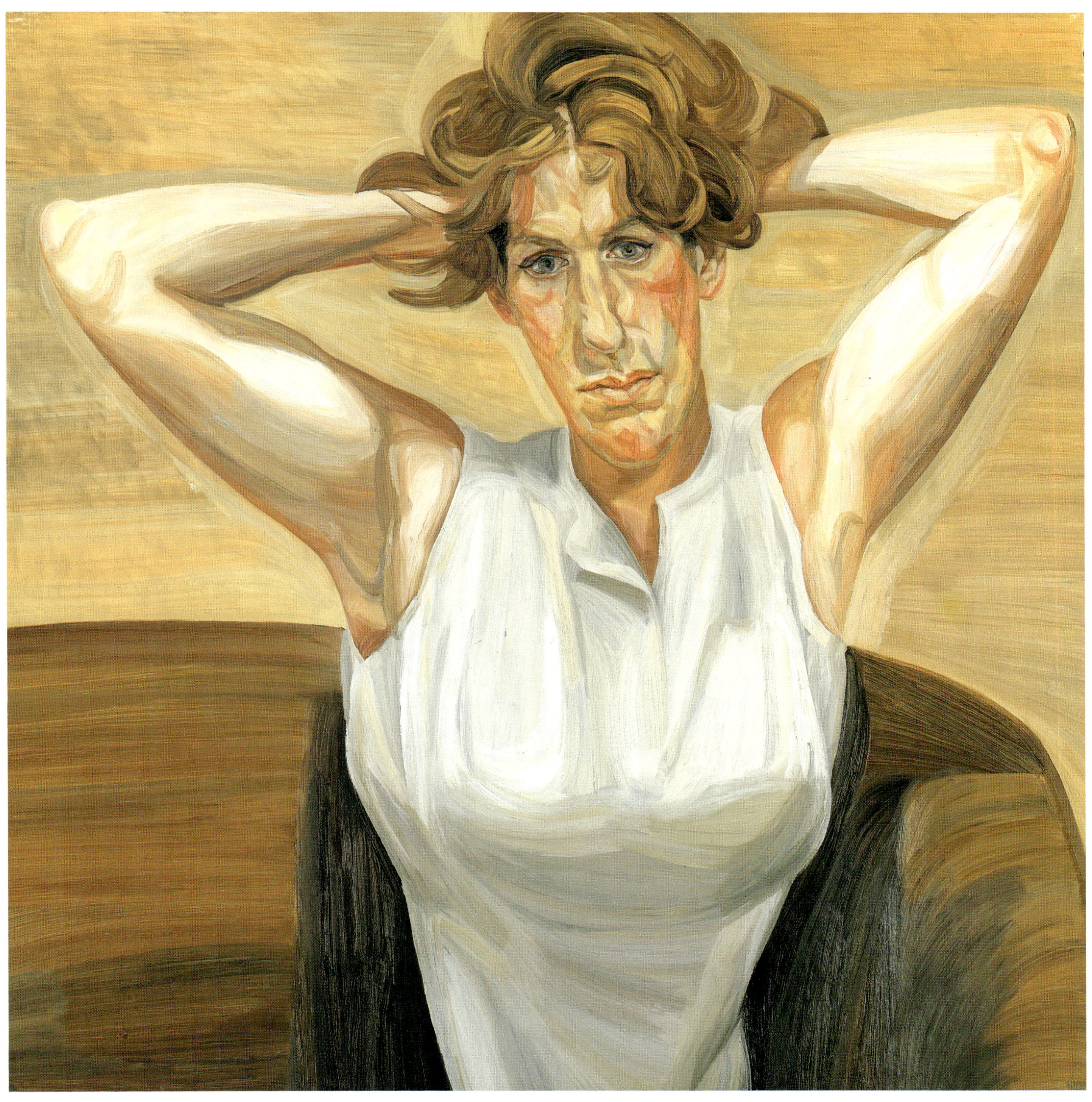

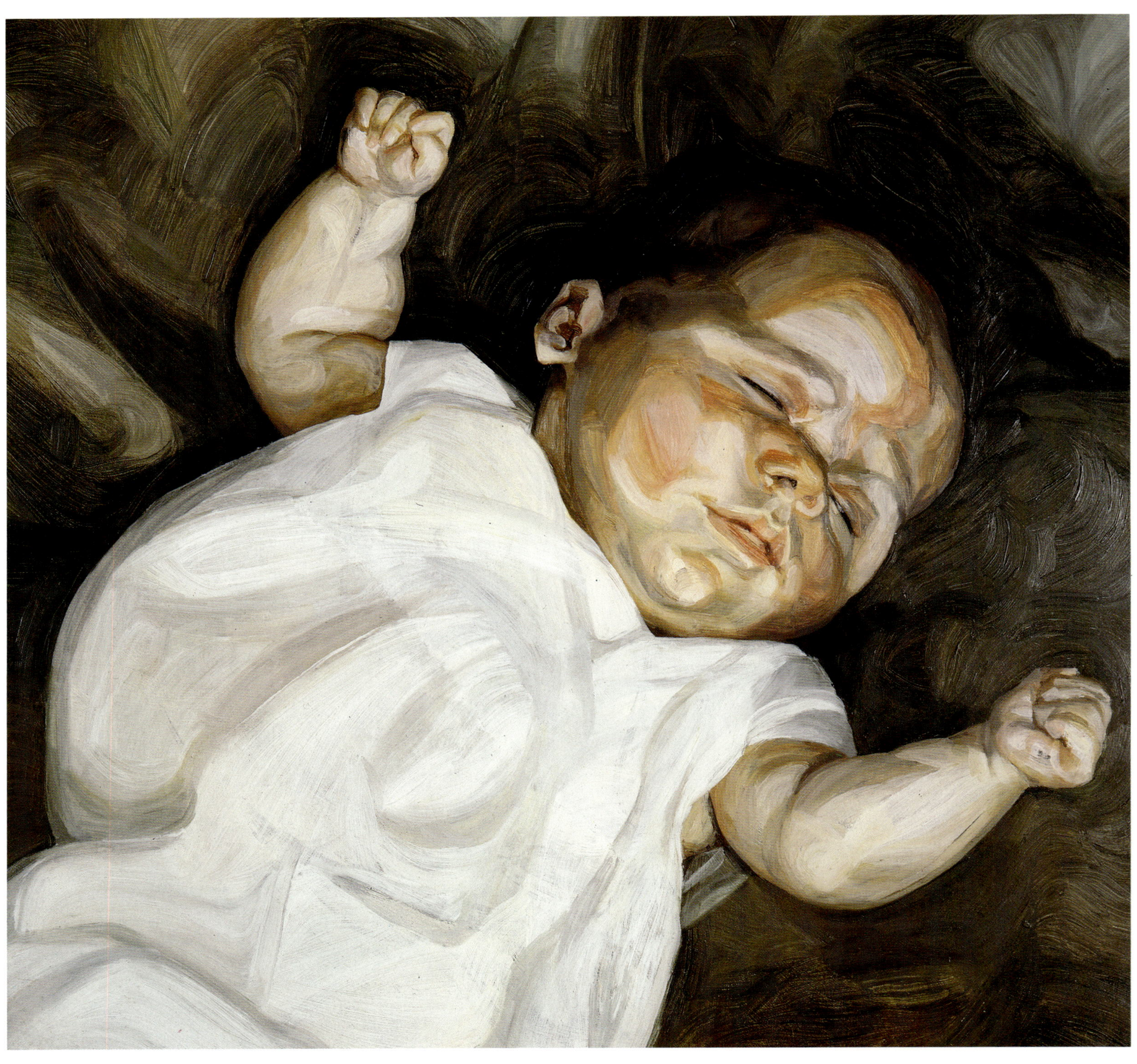

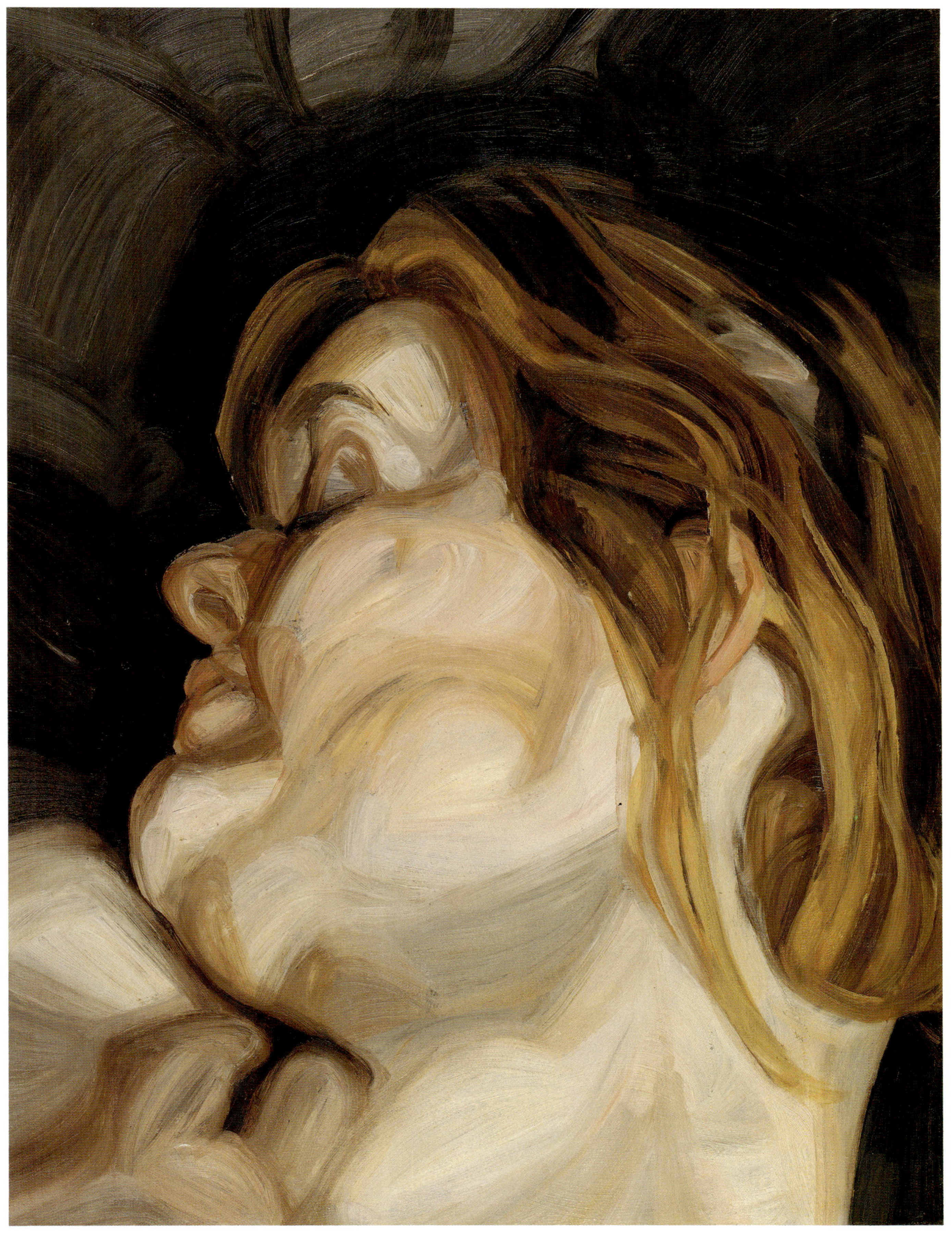

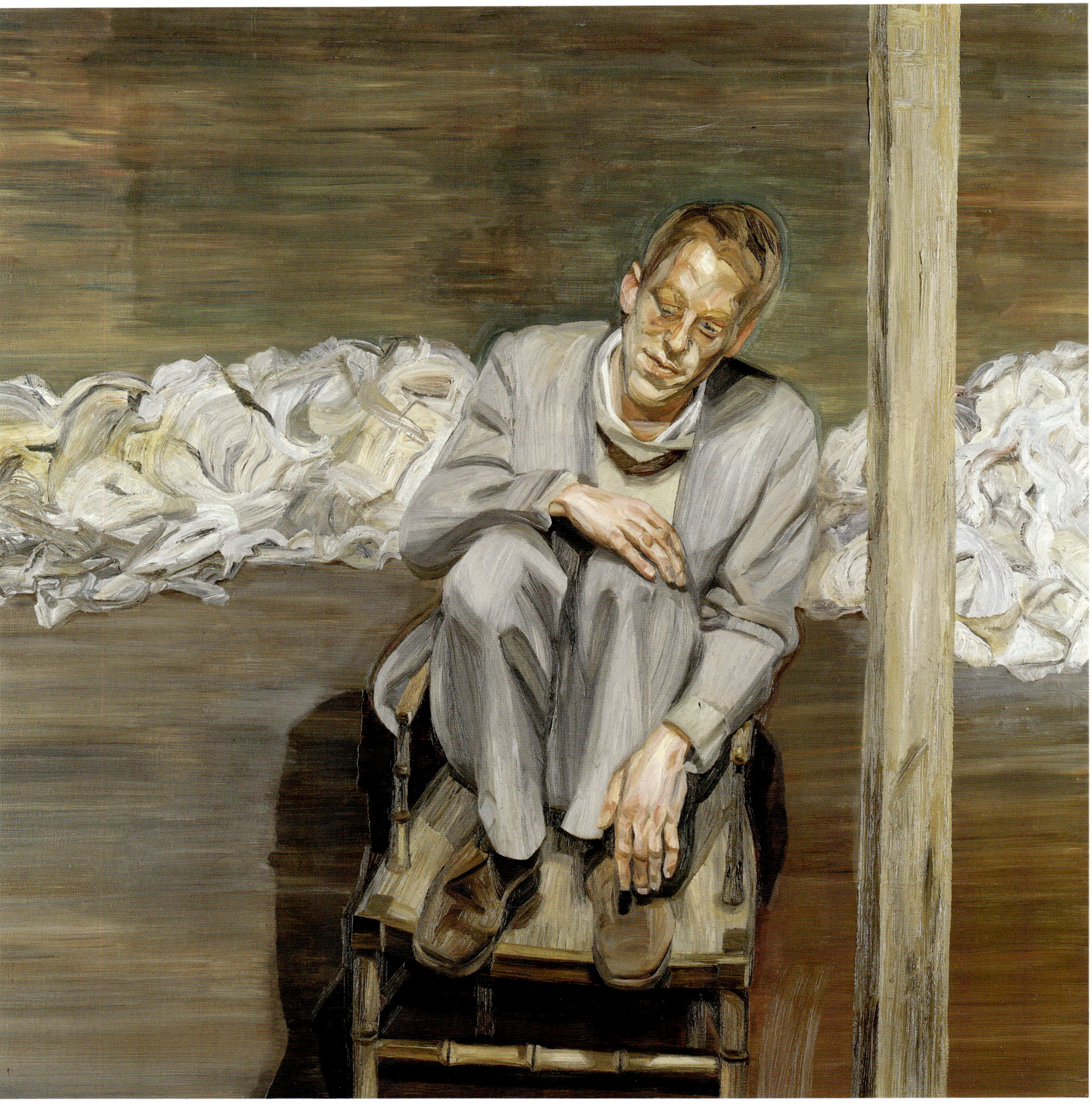

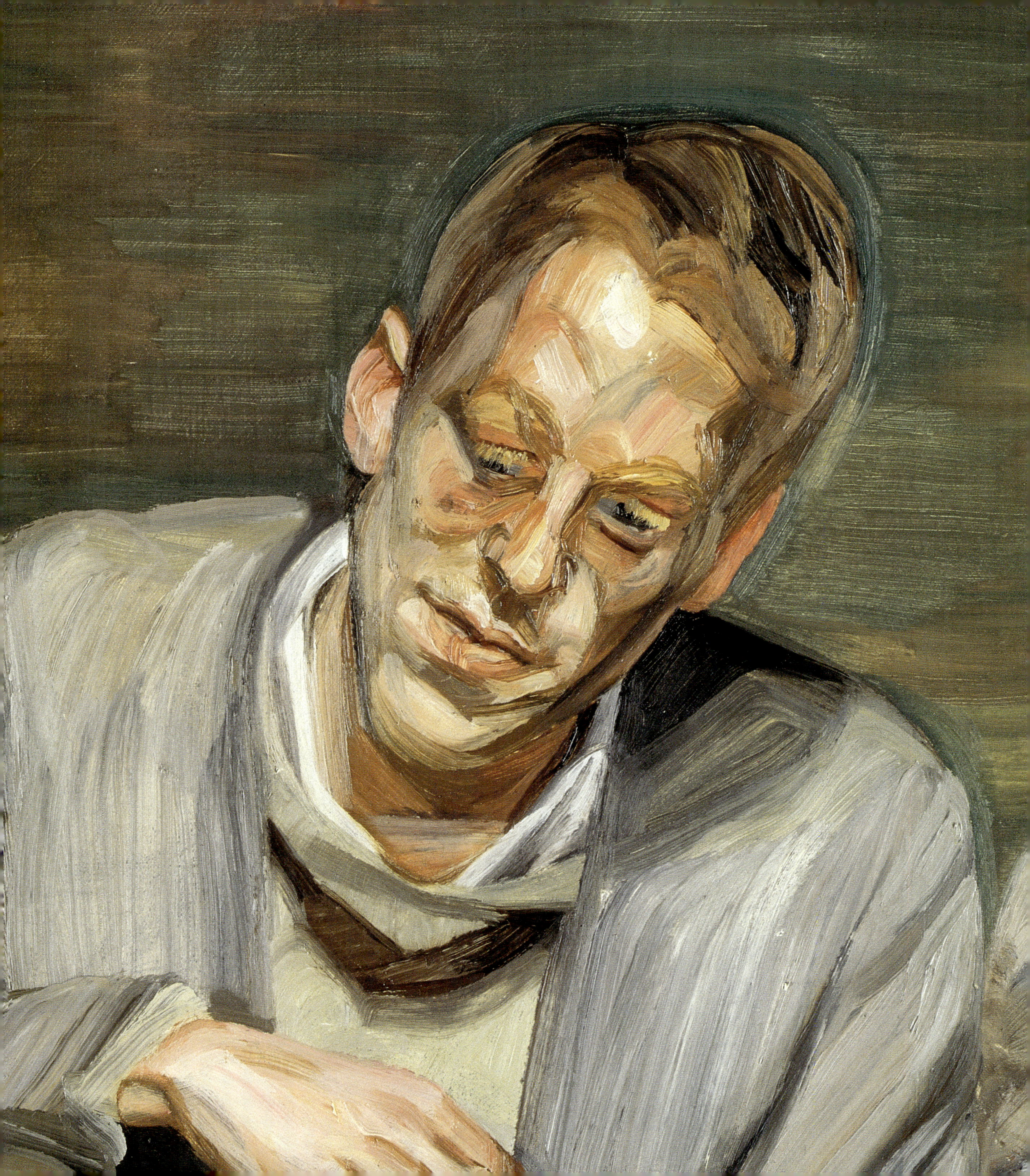

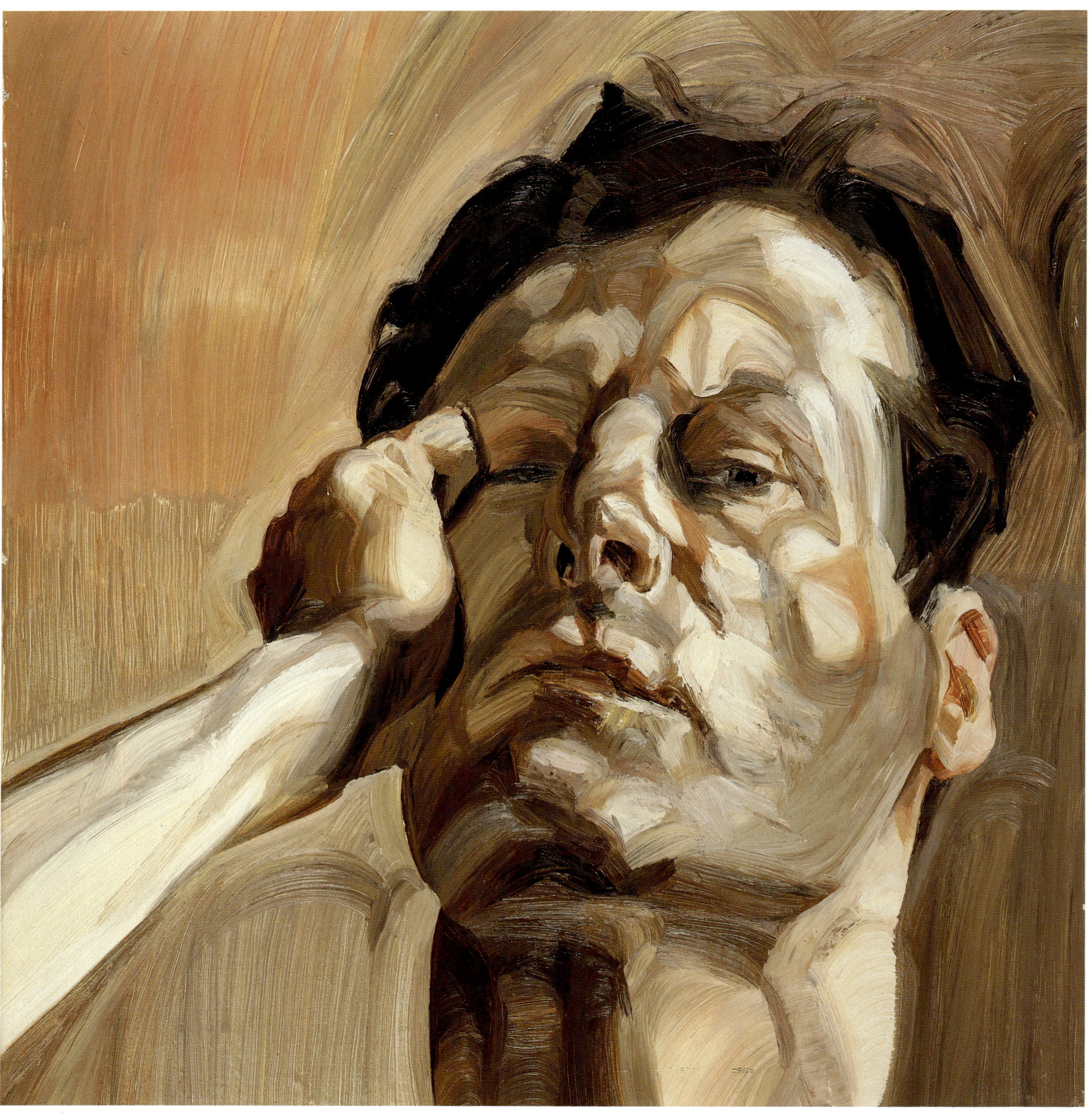

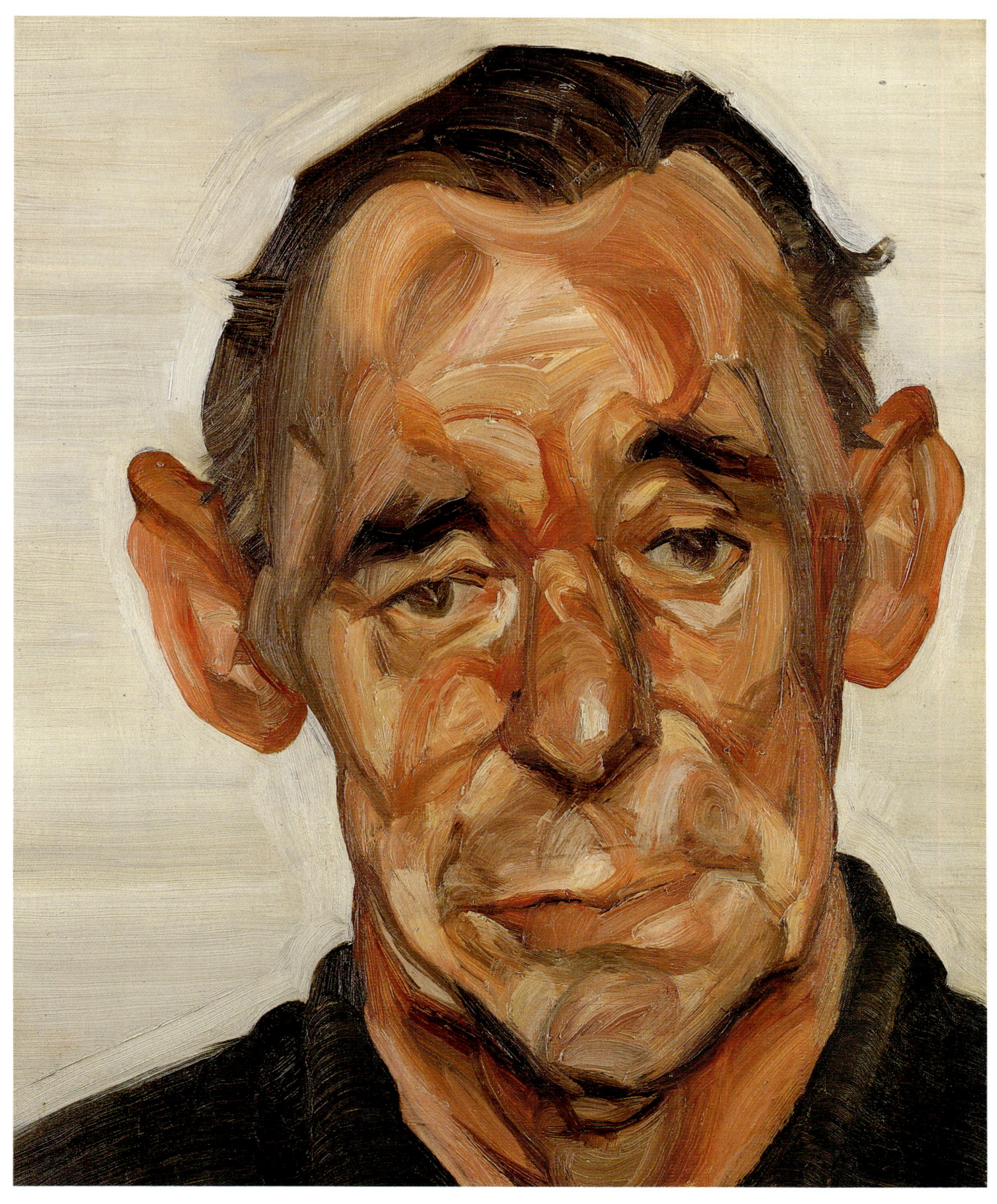

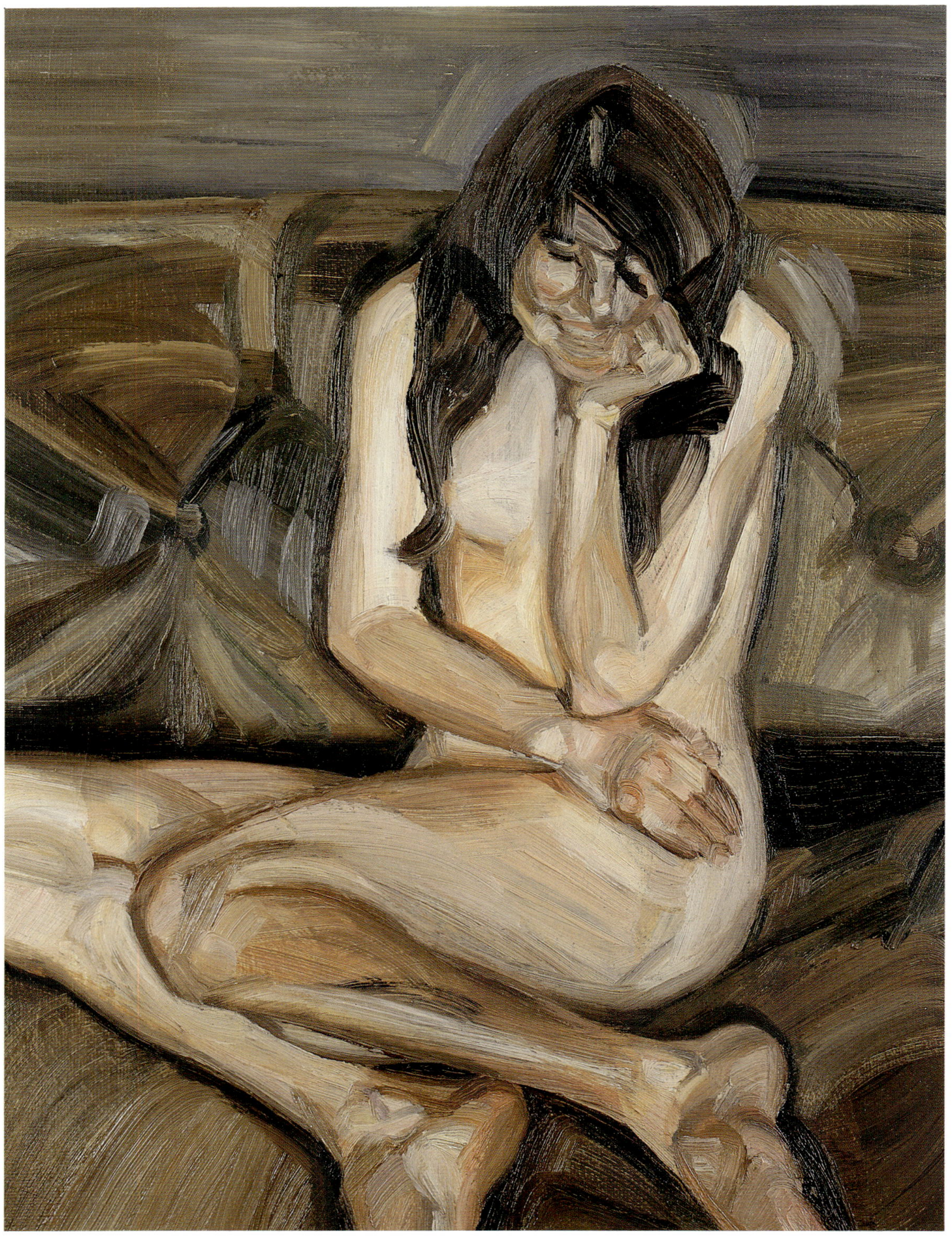

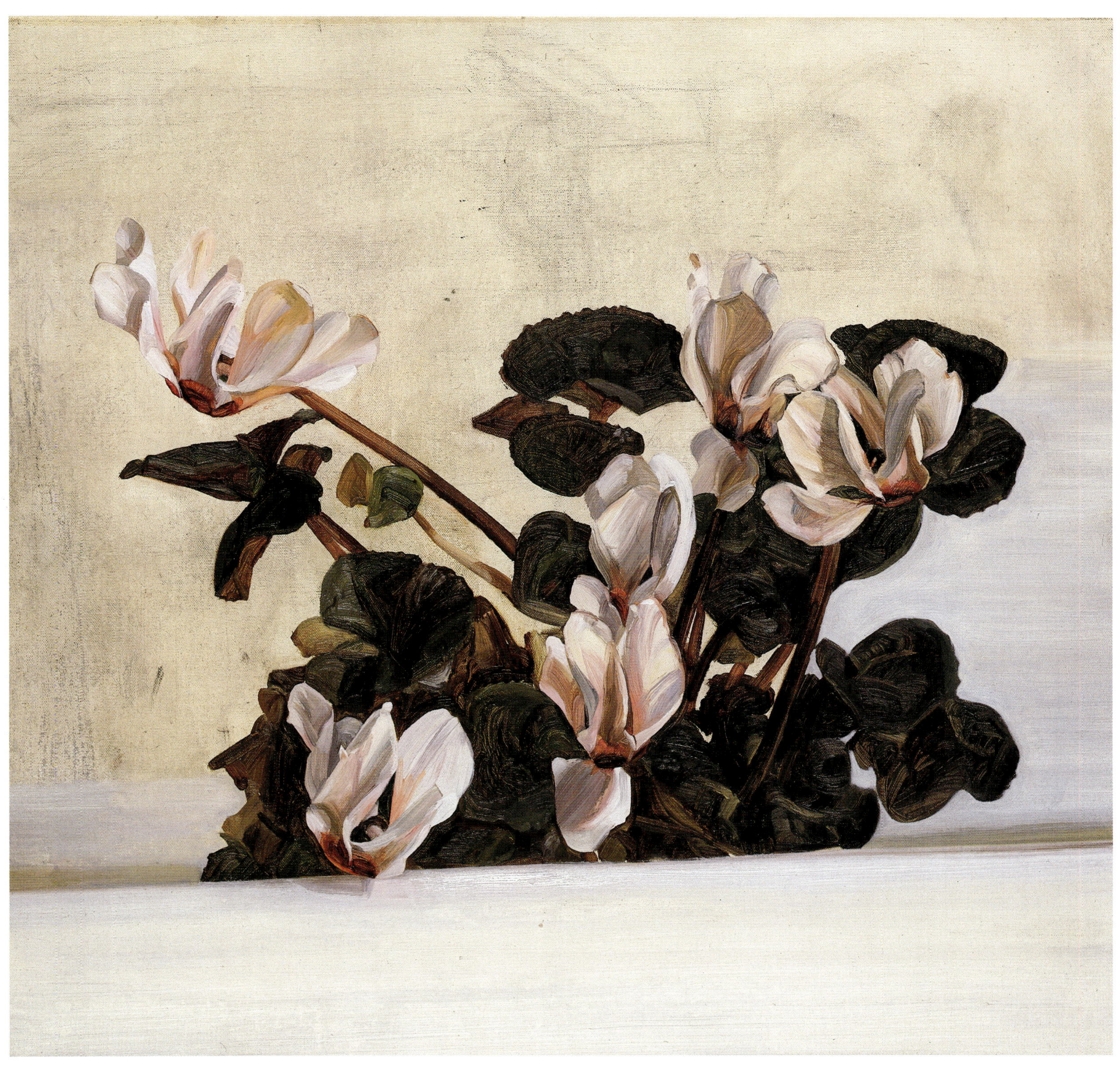

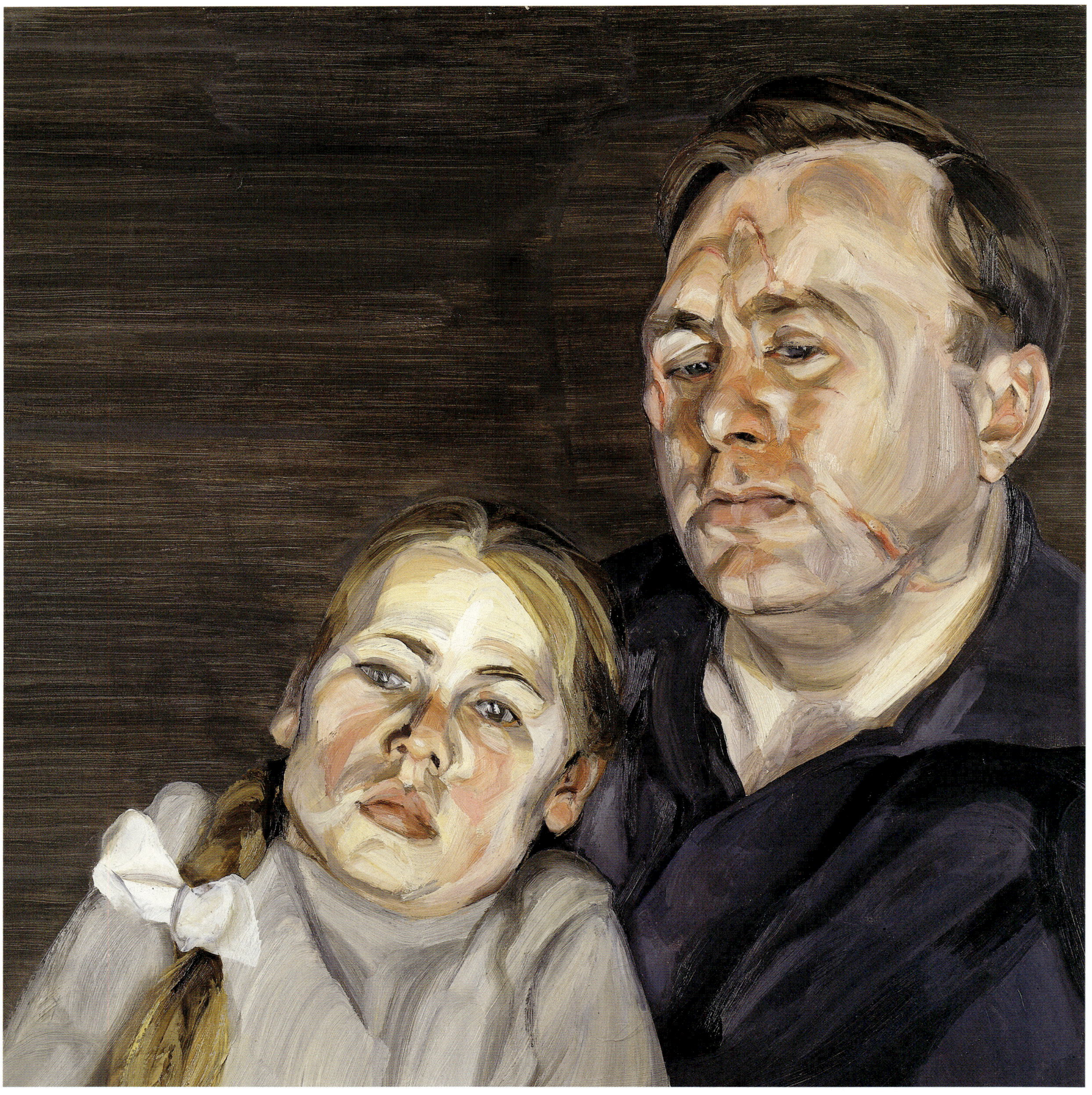

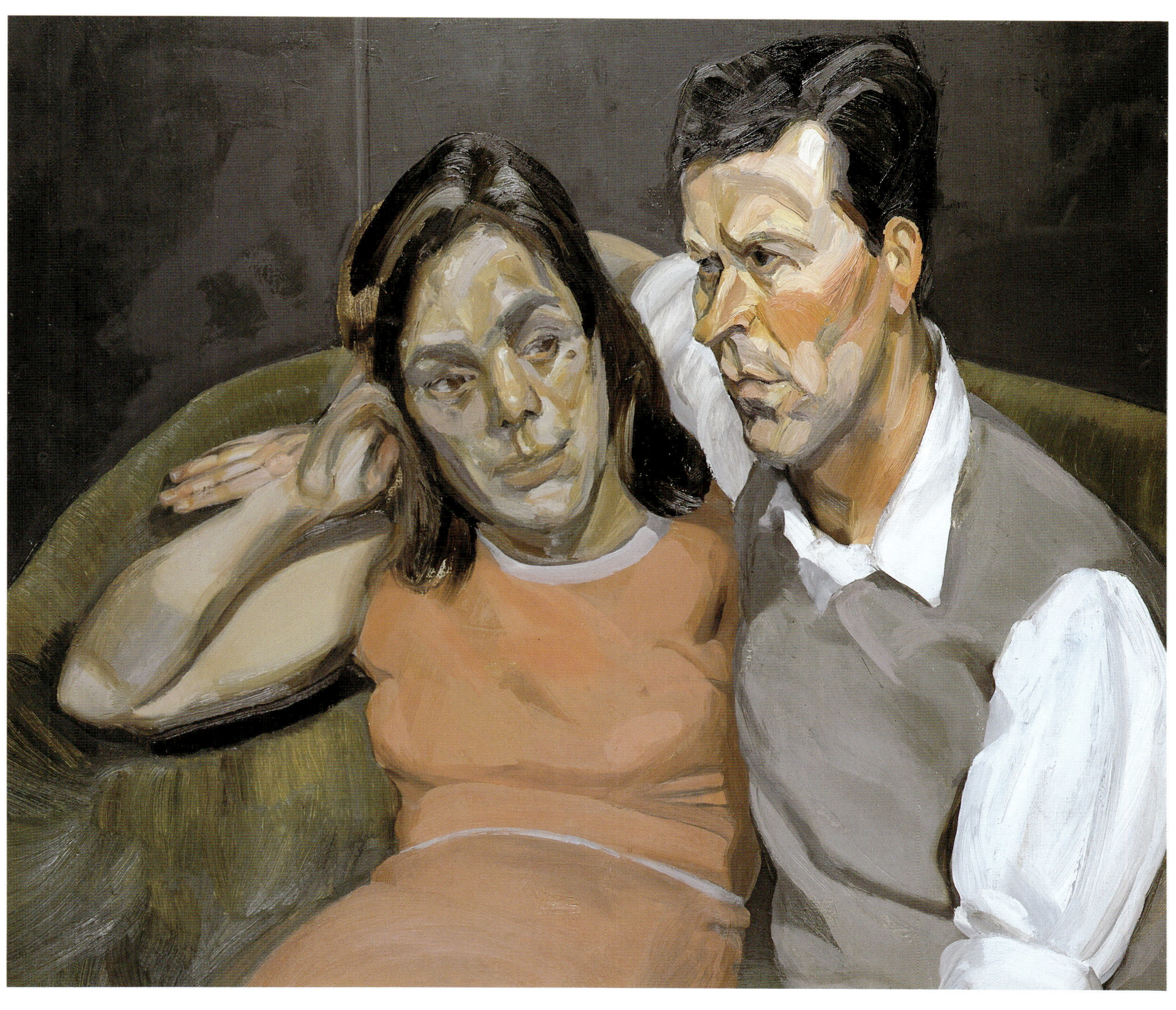

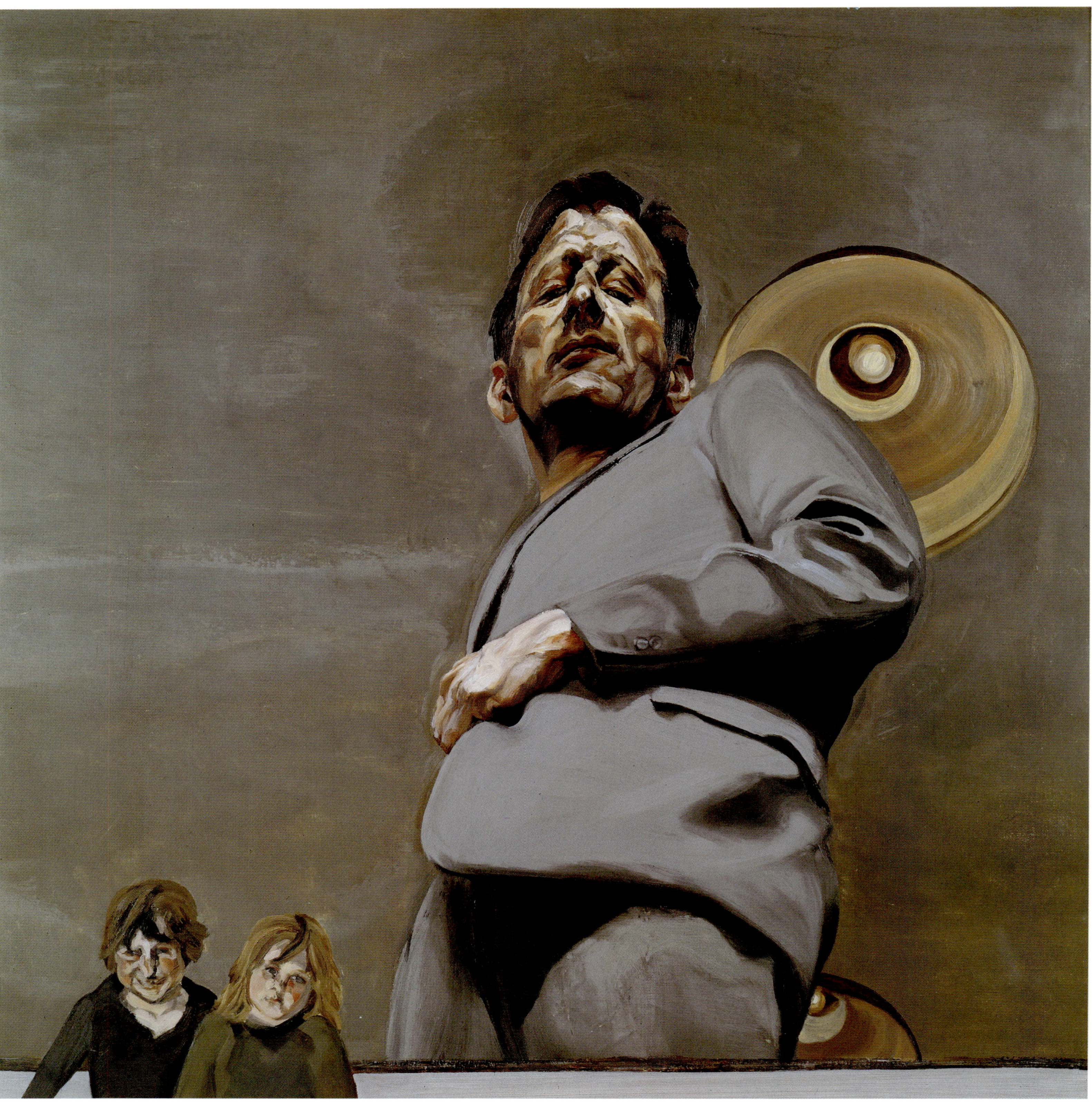

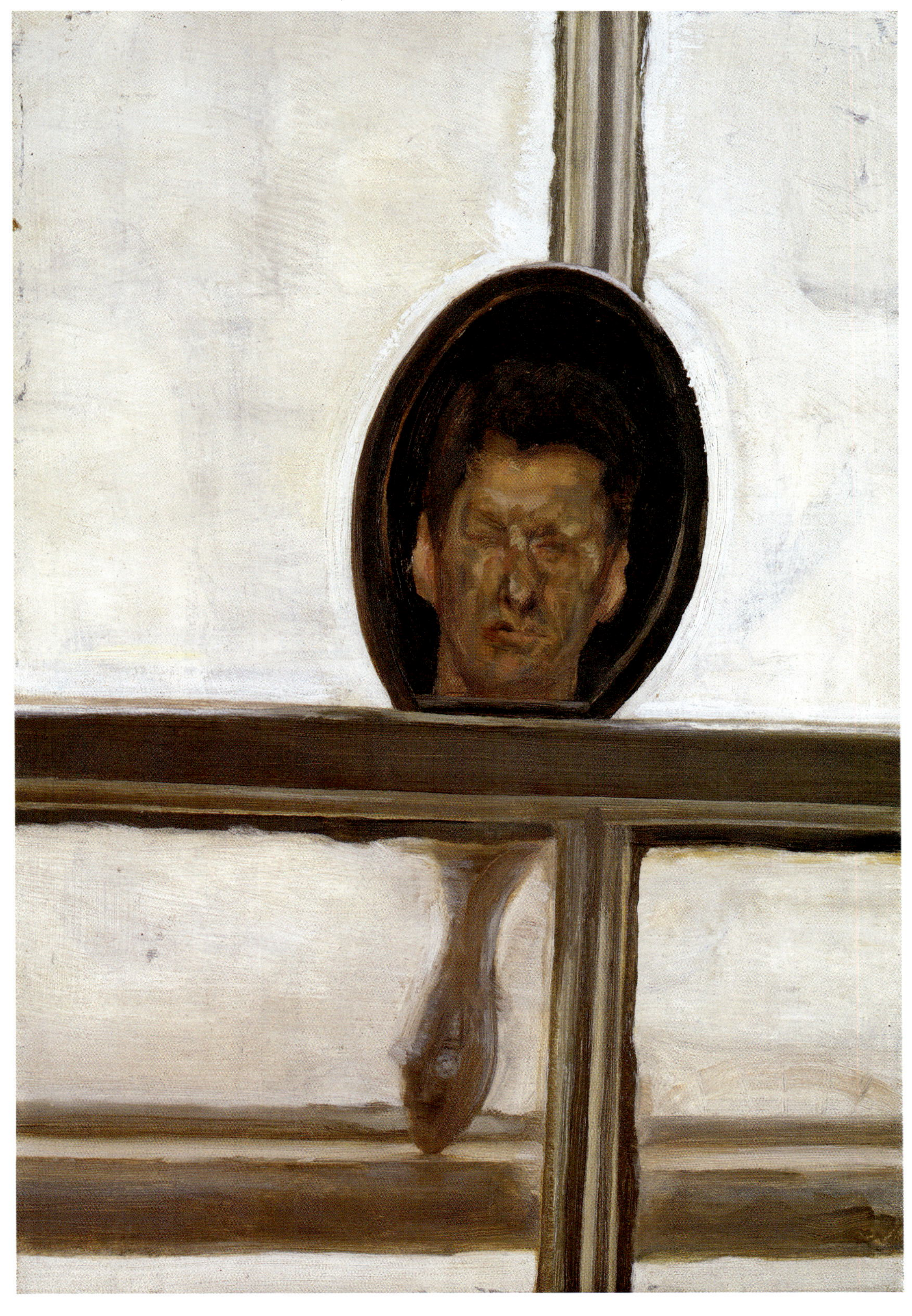

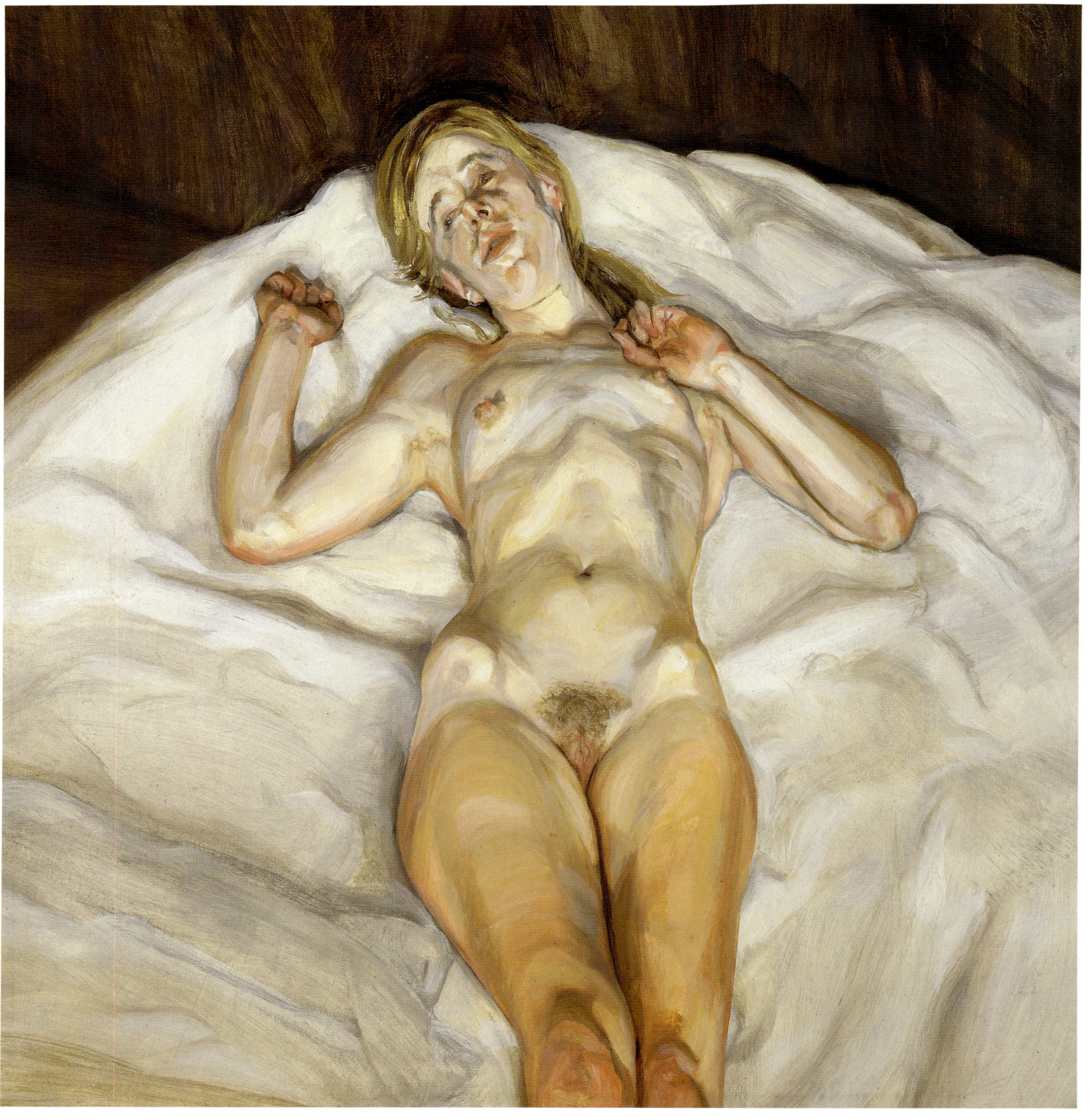

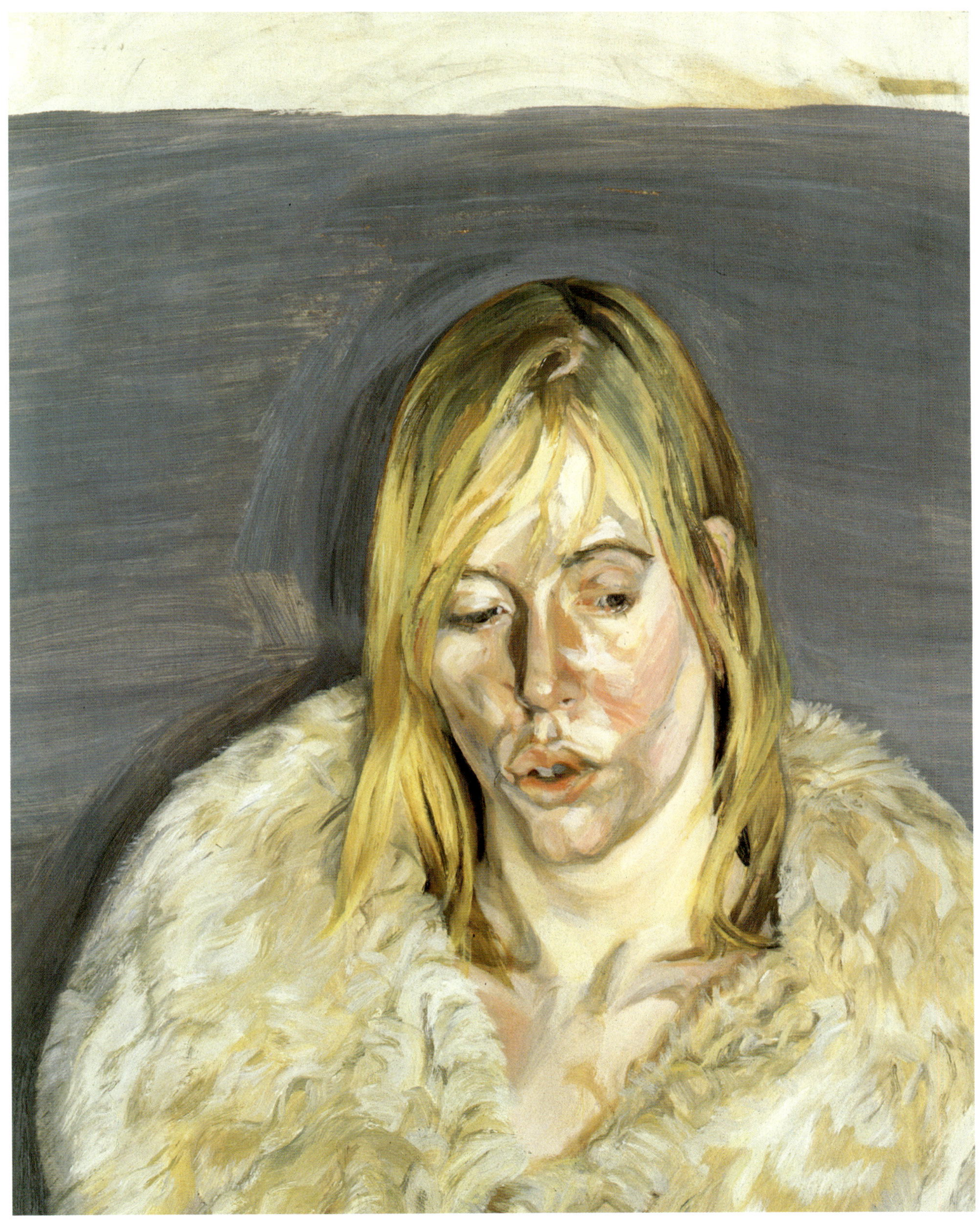

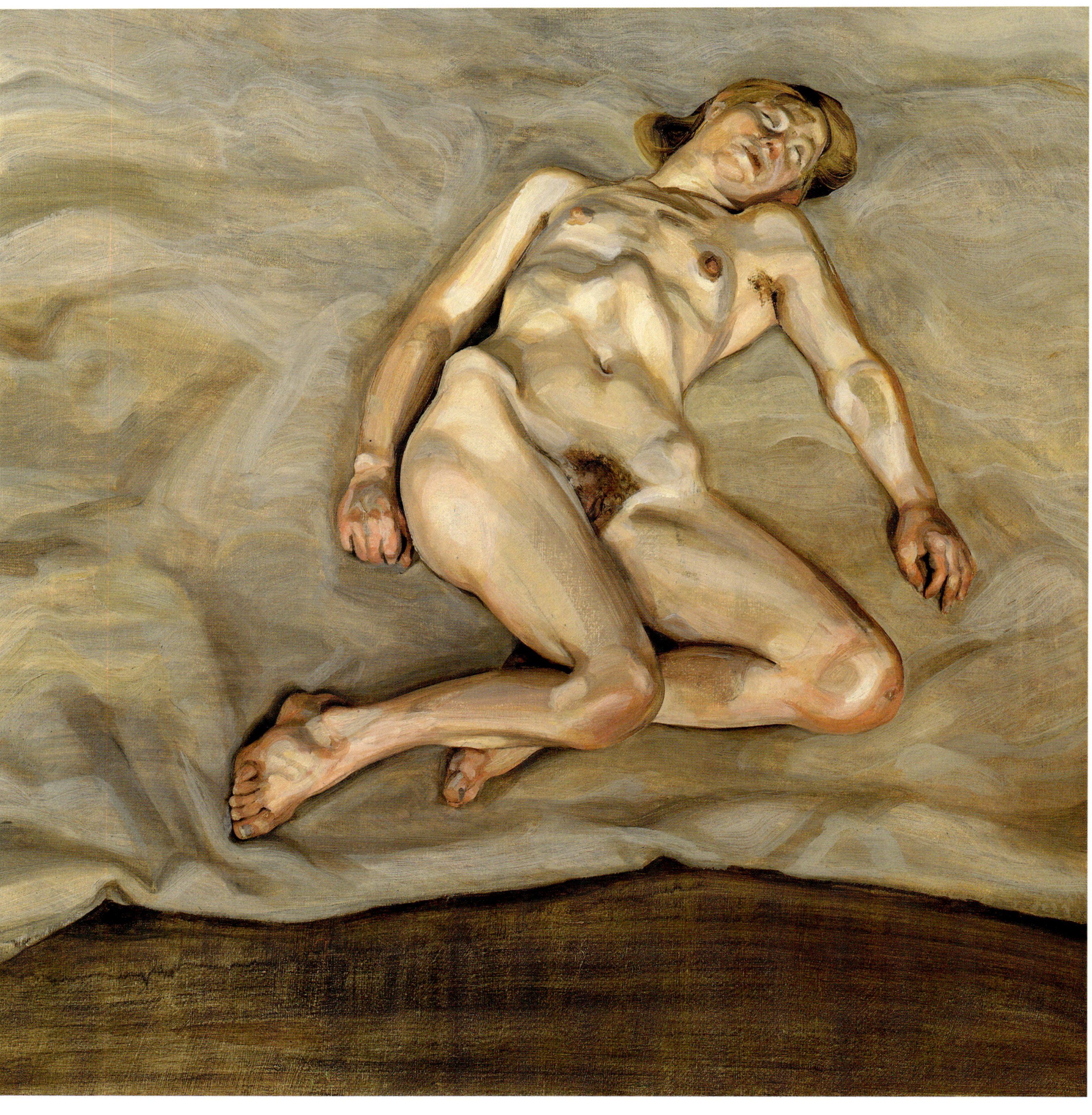

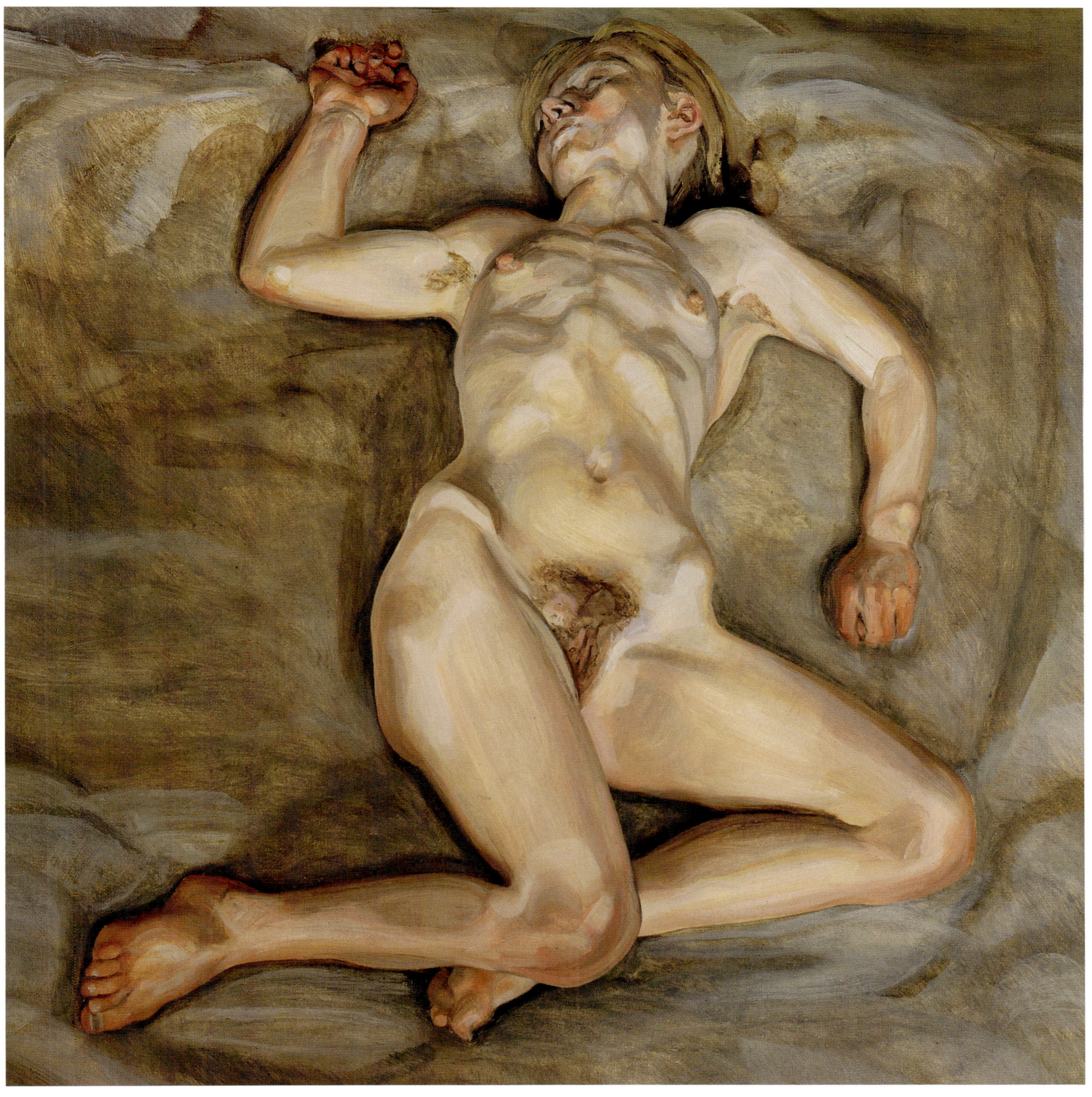

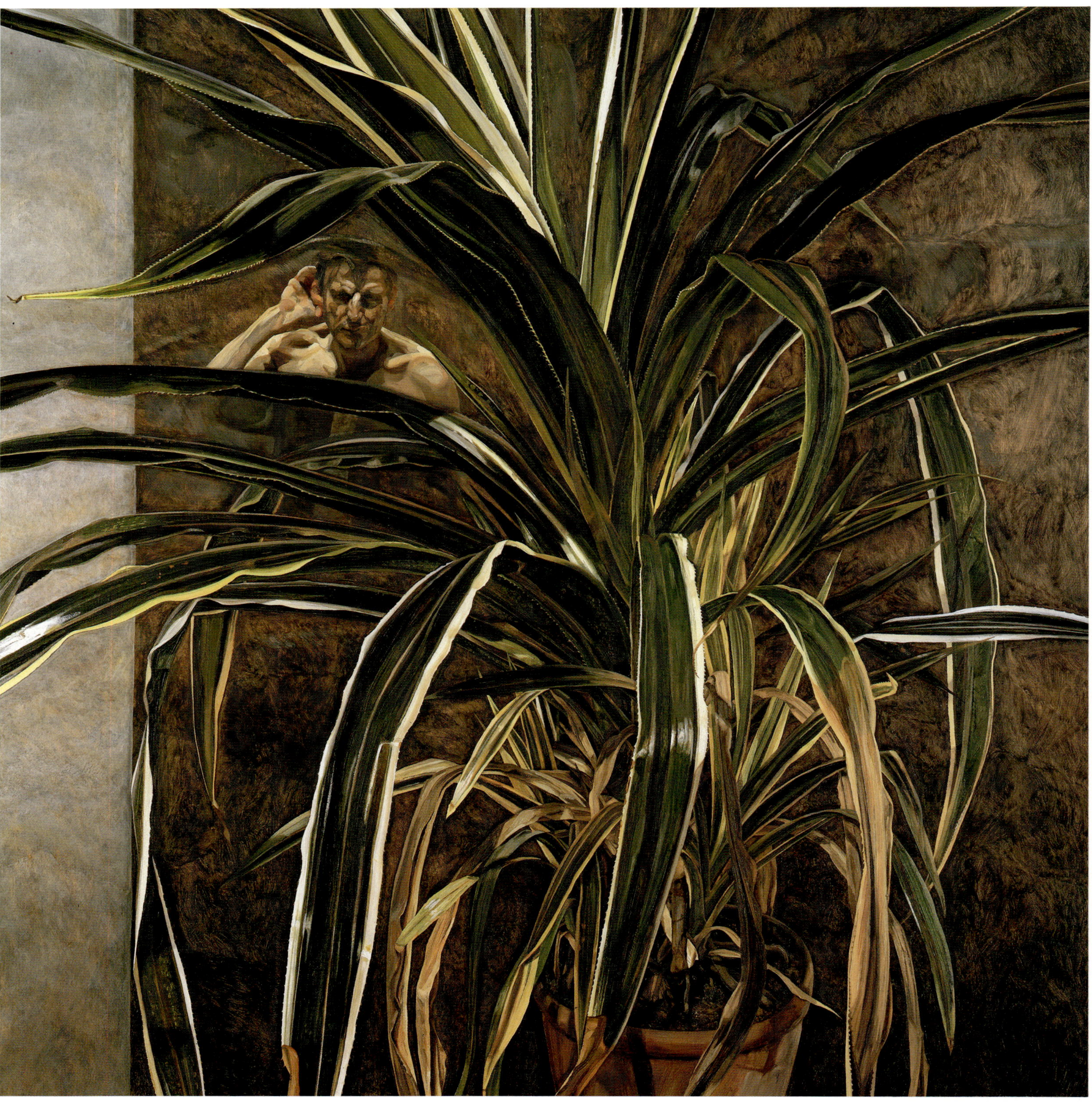

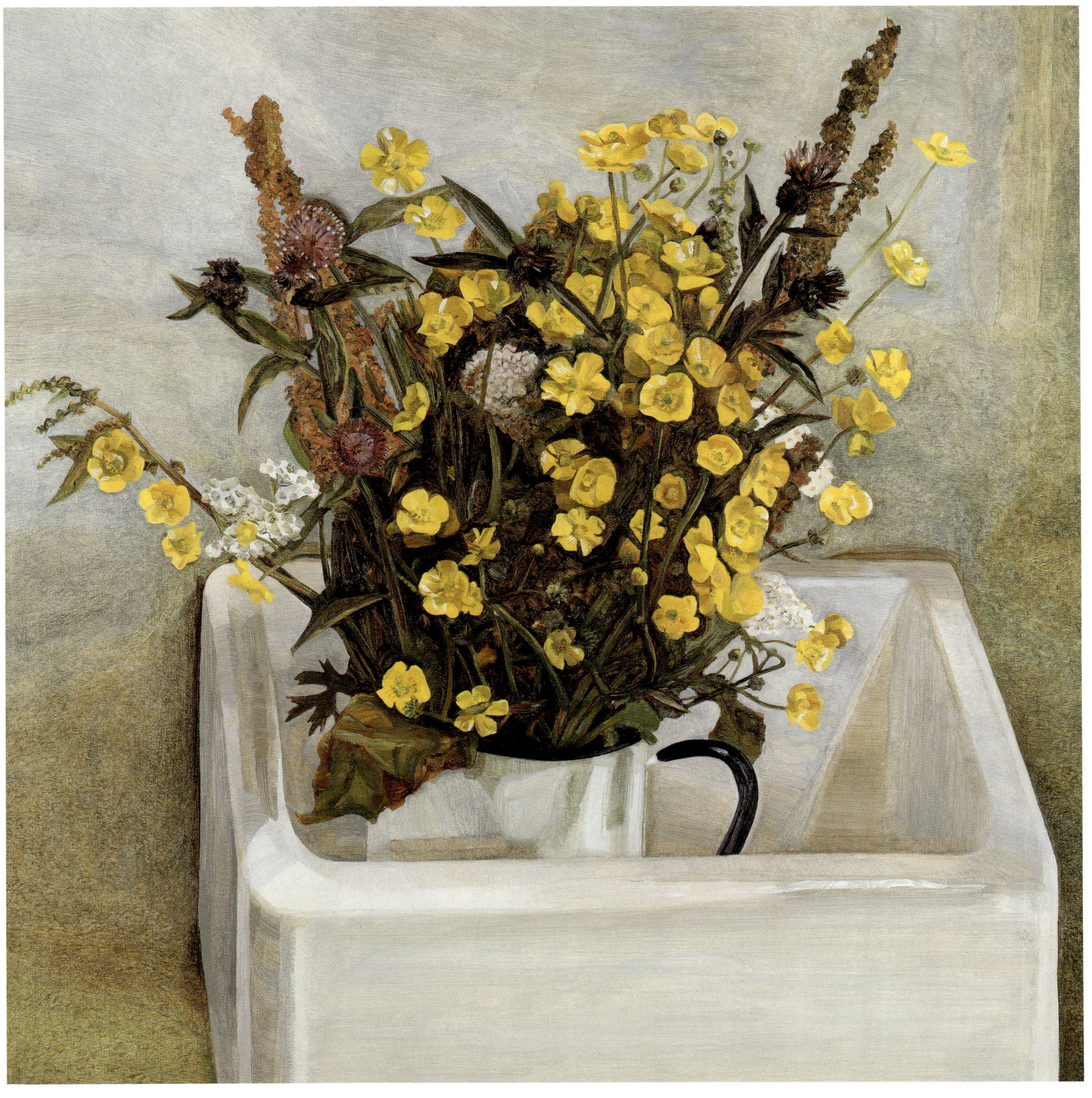

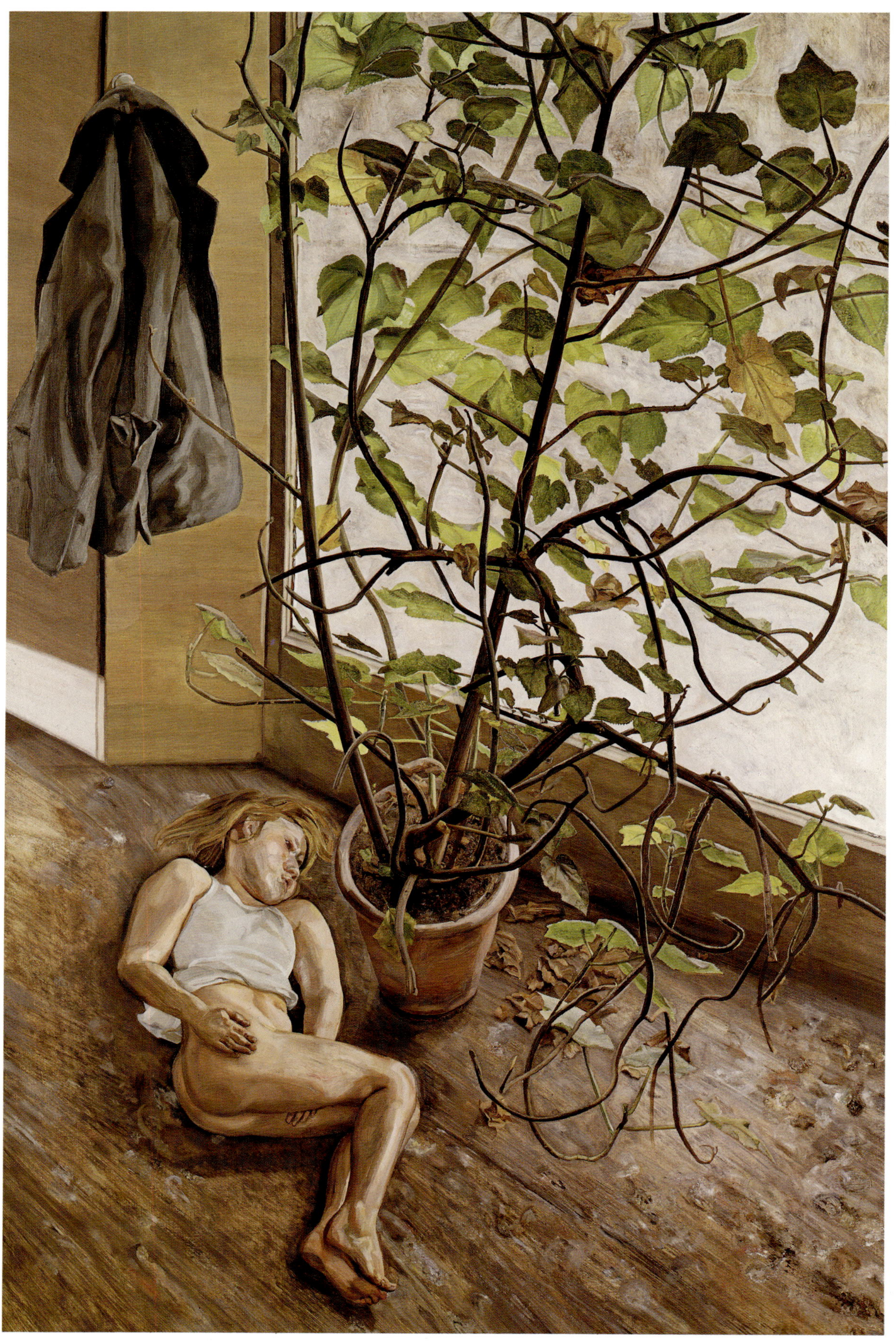

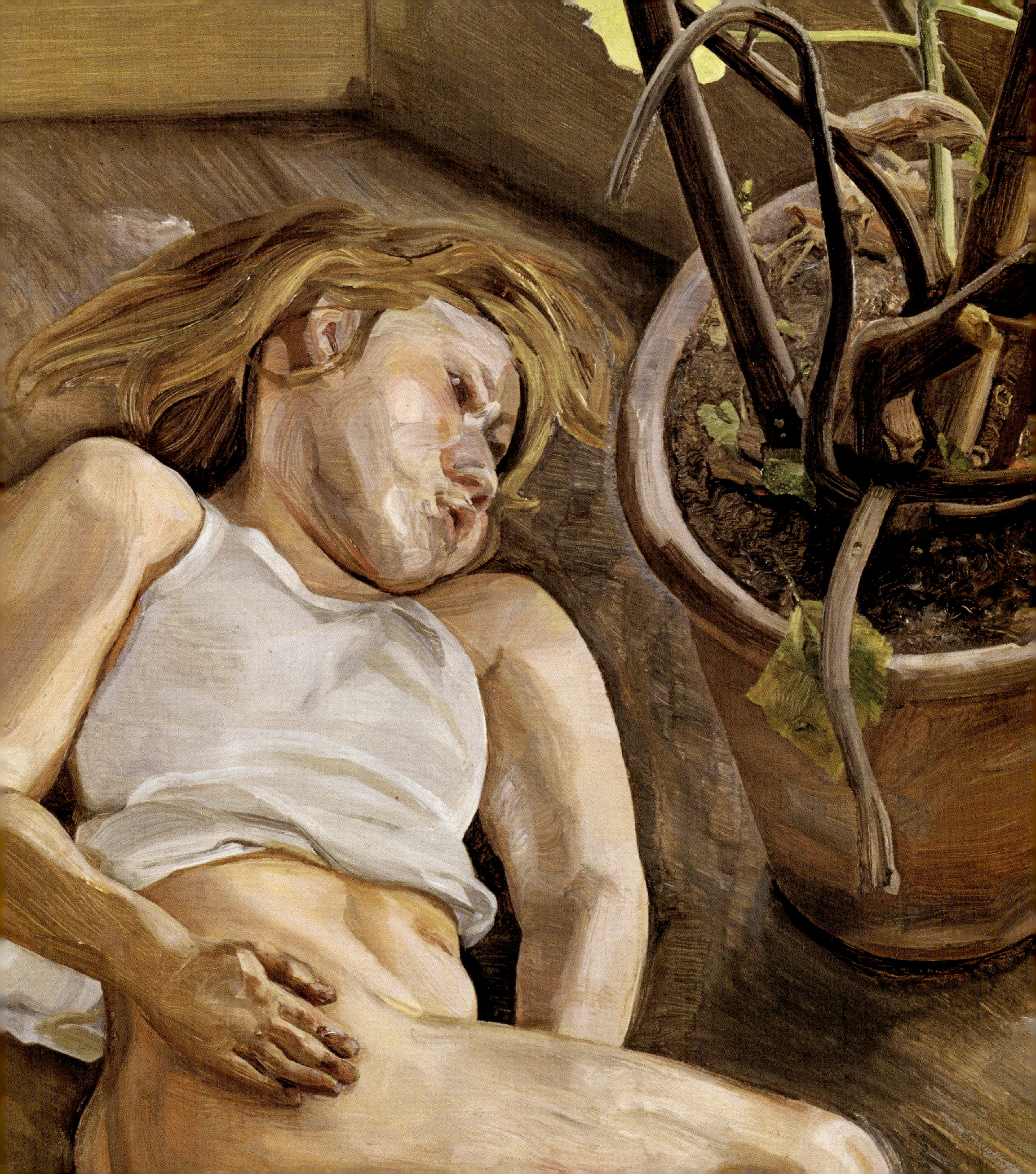

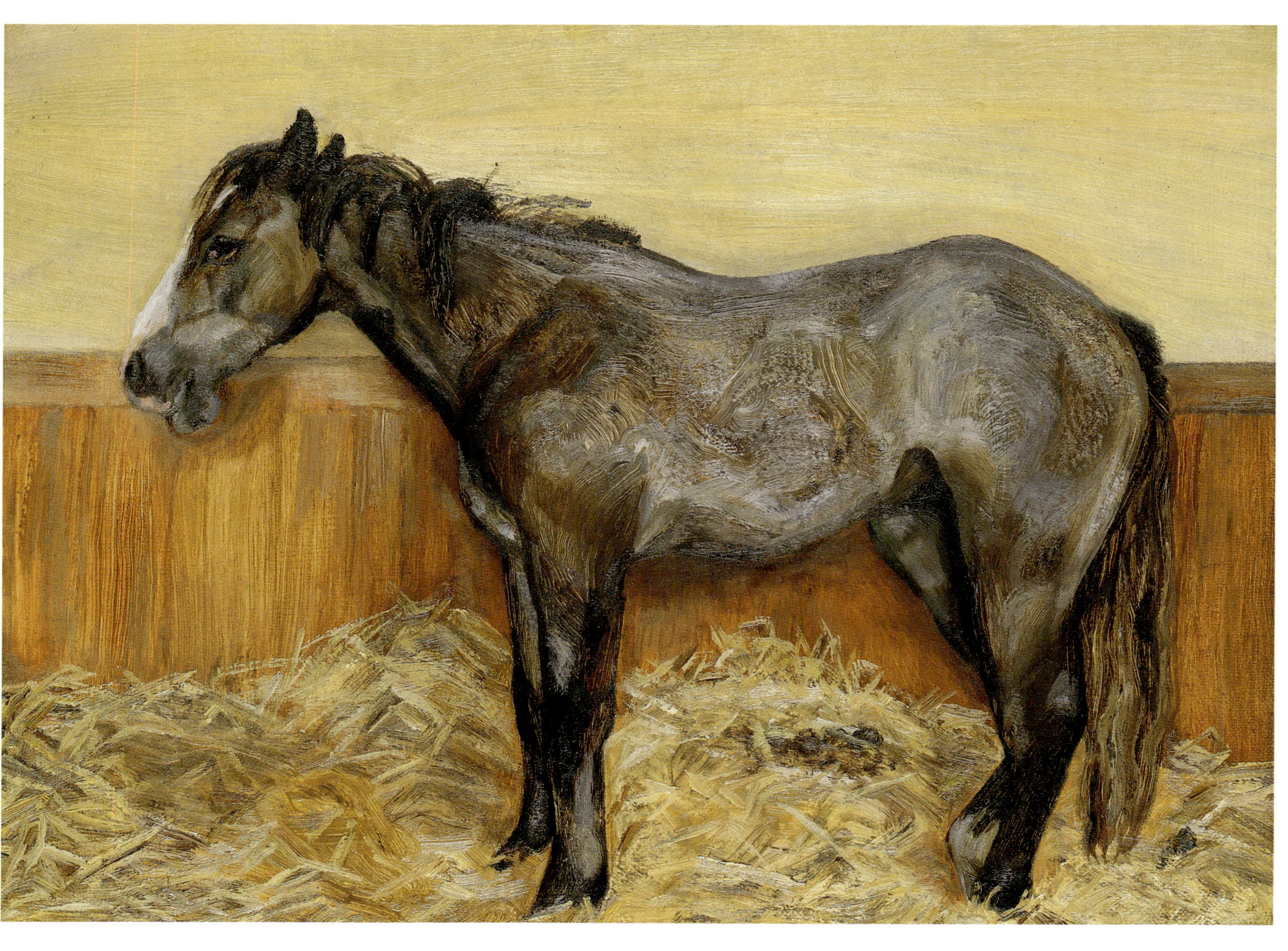

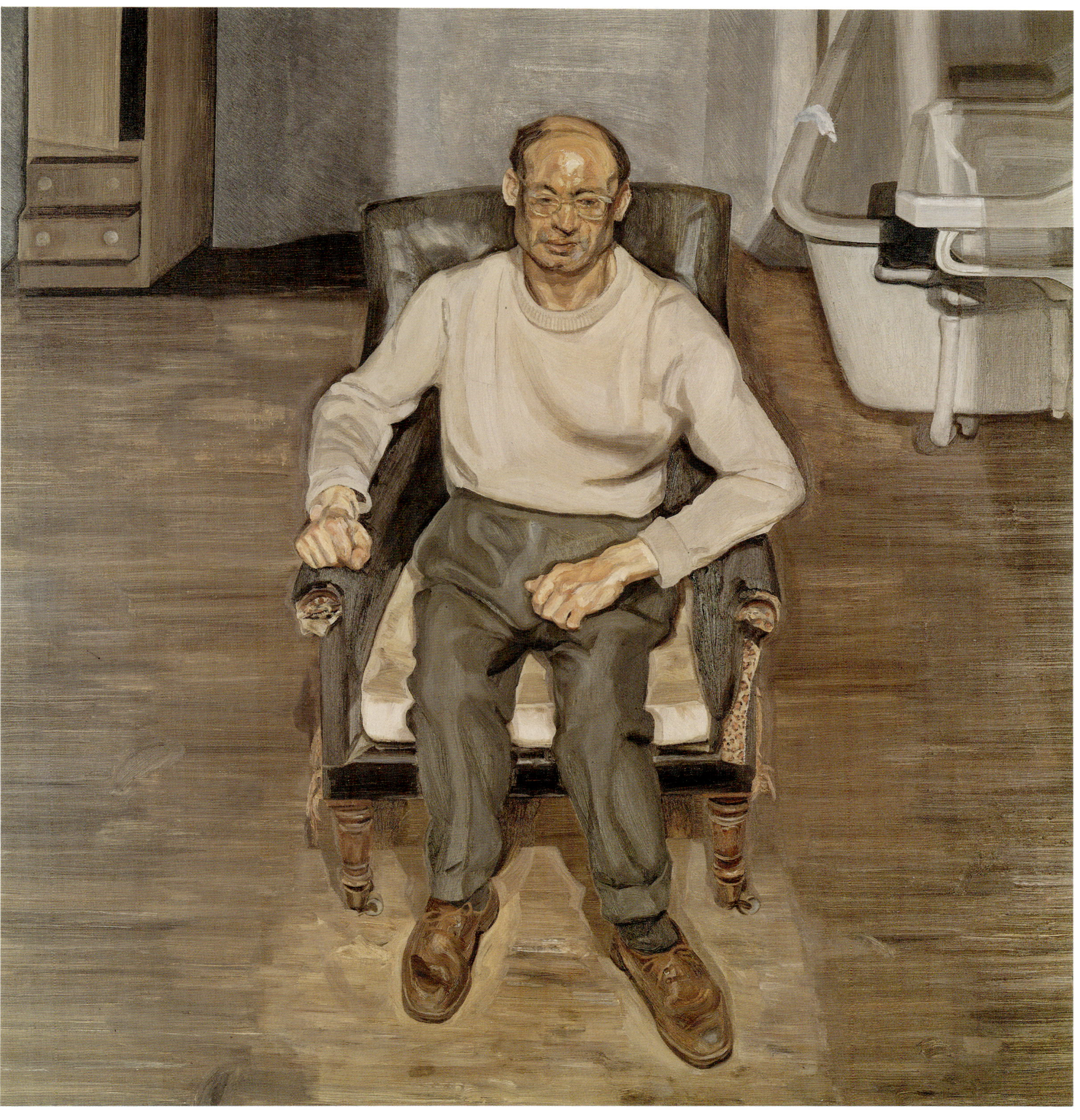

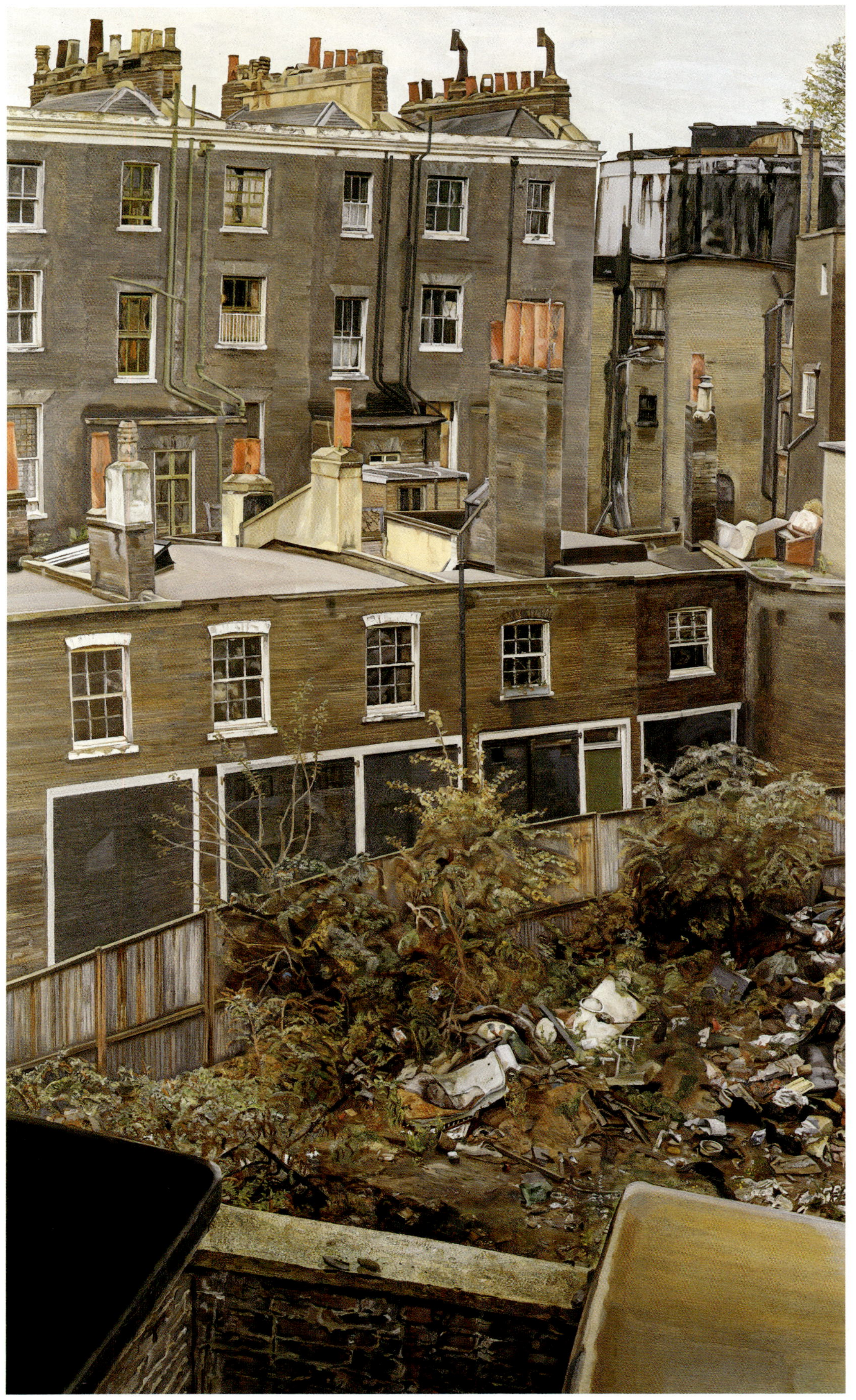

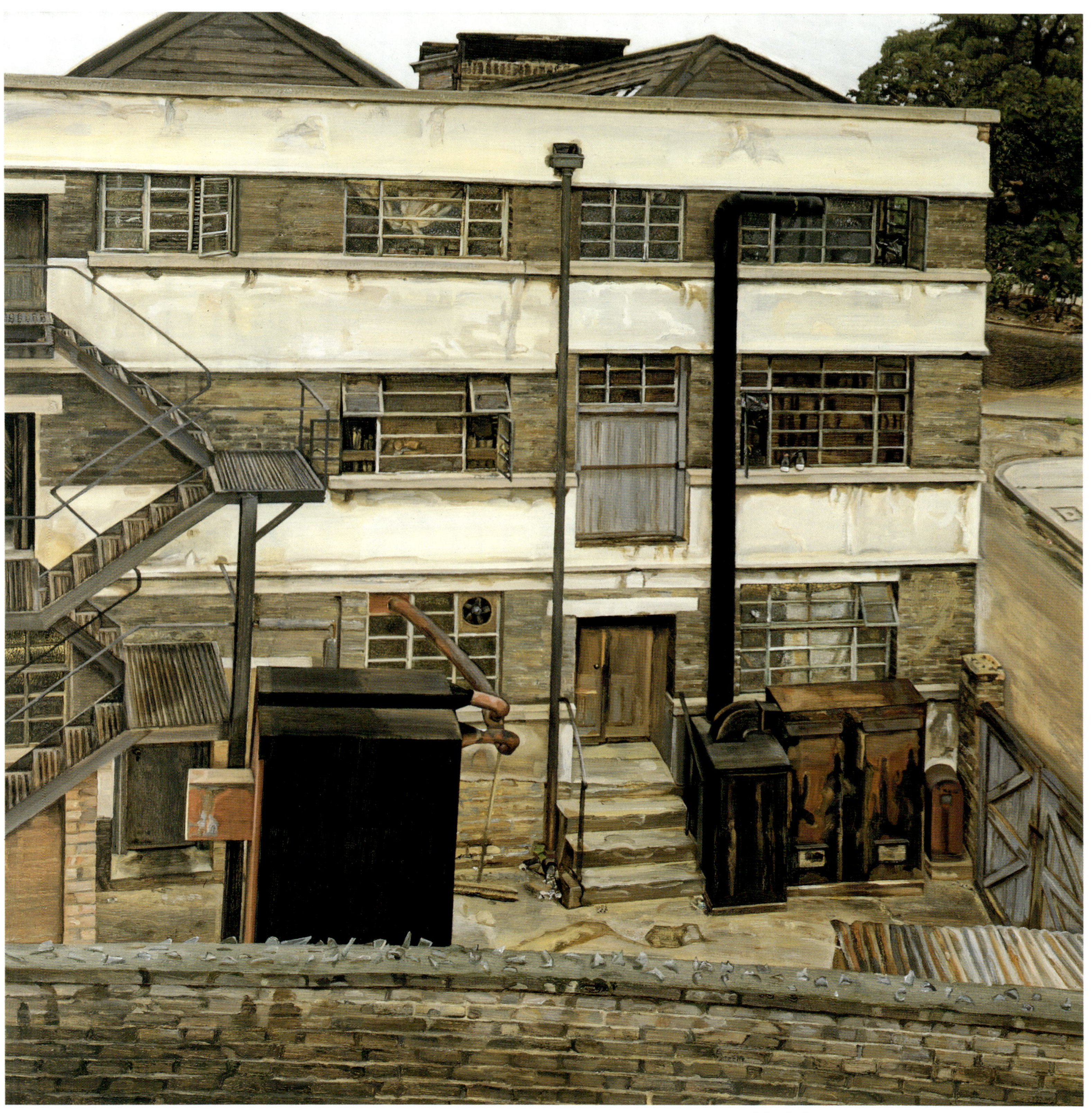

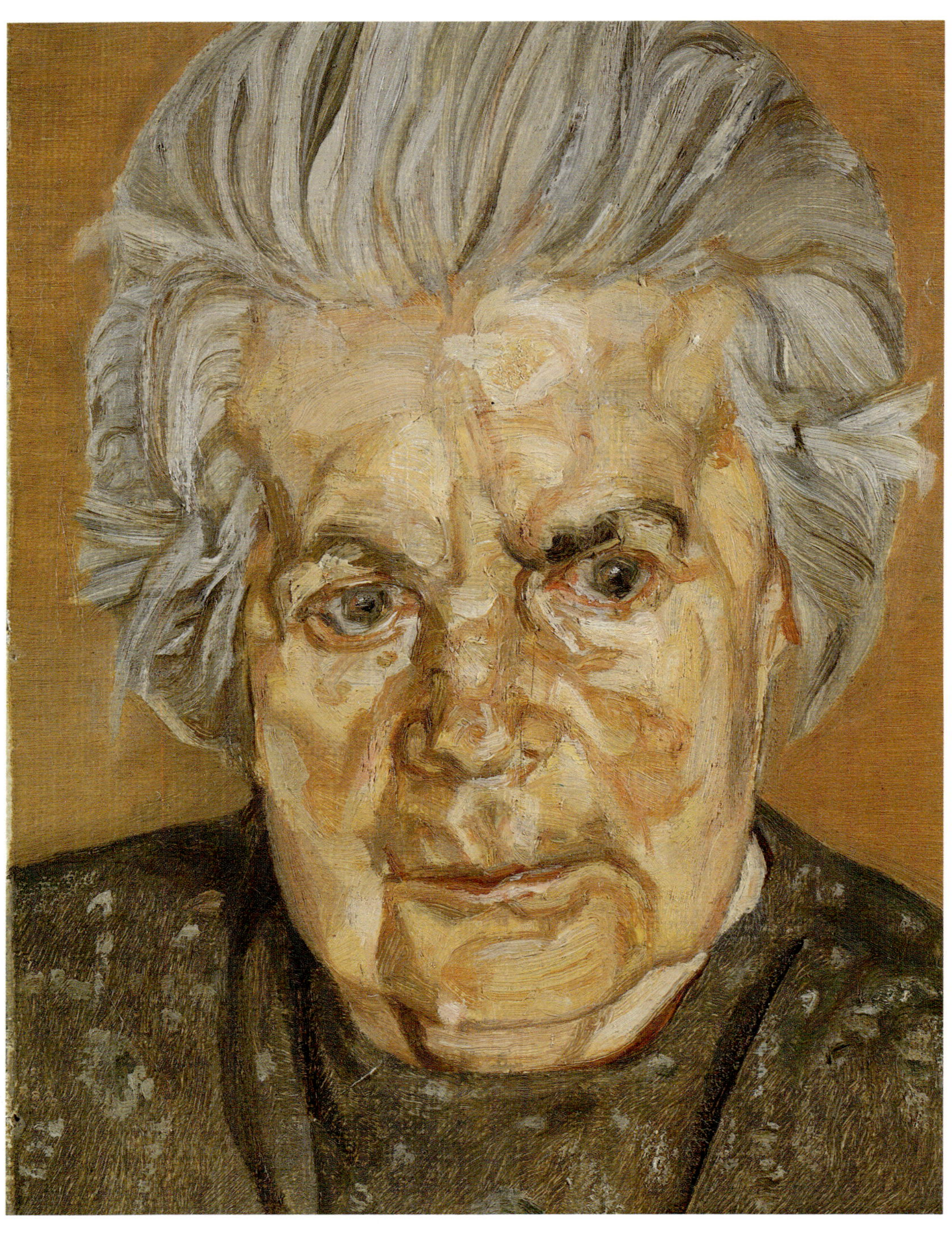

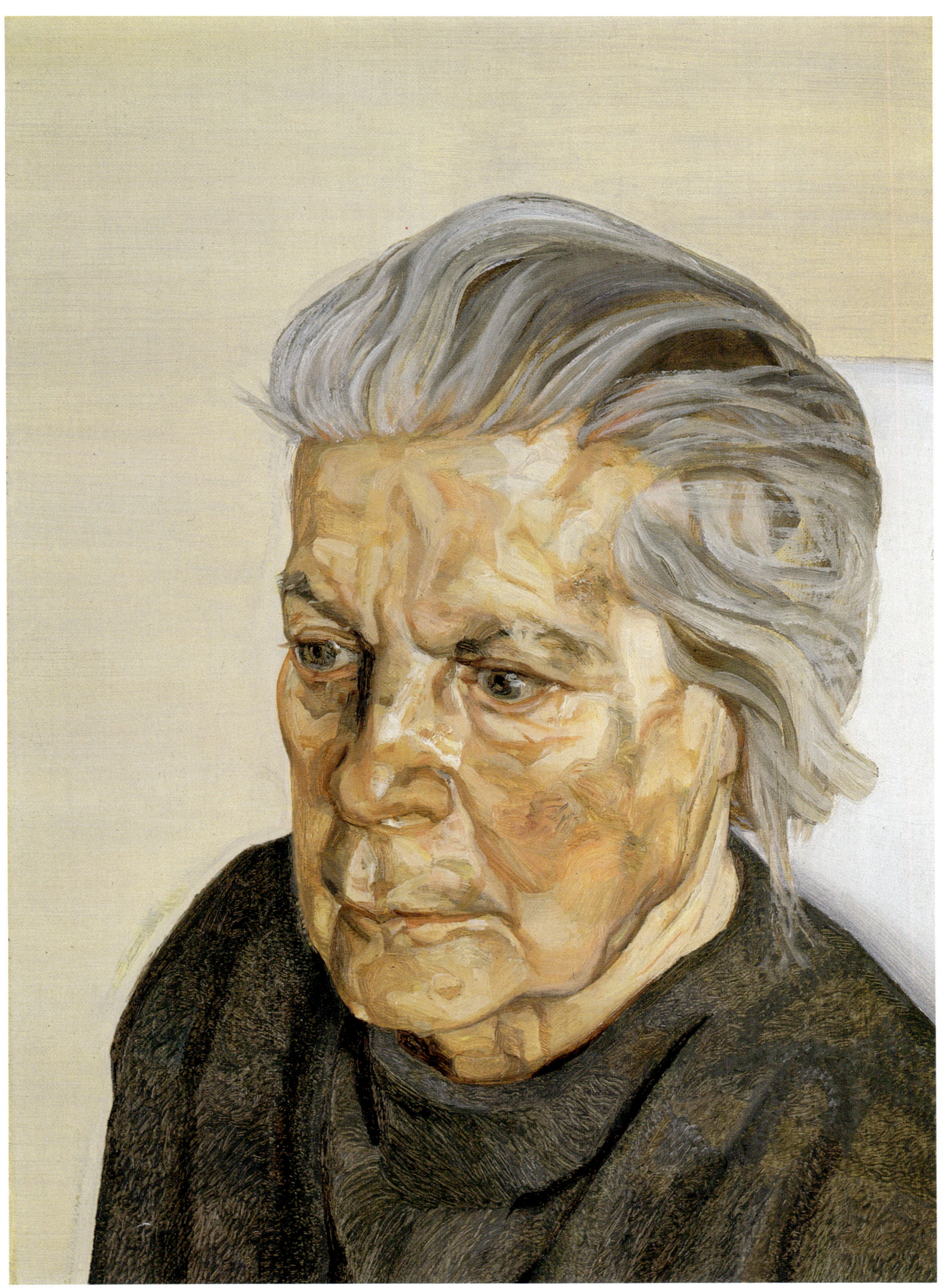

47

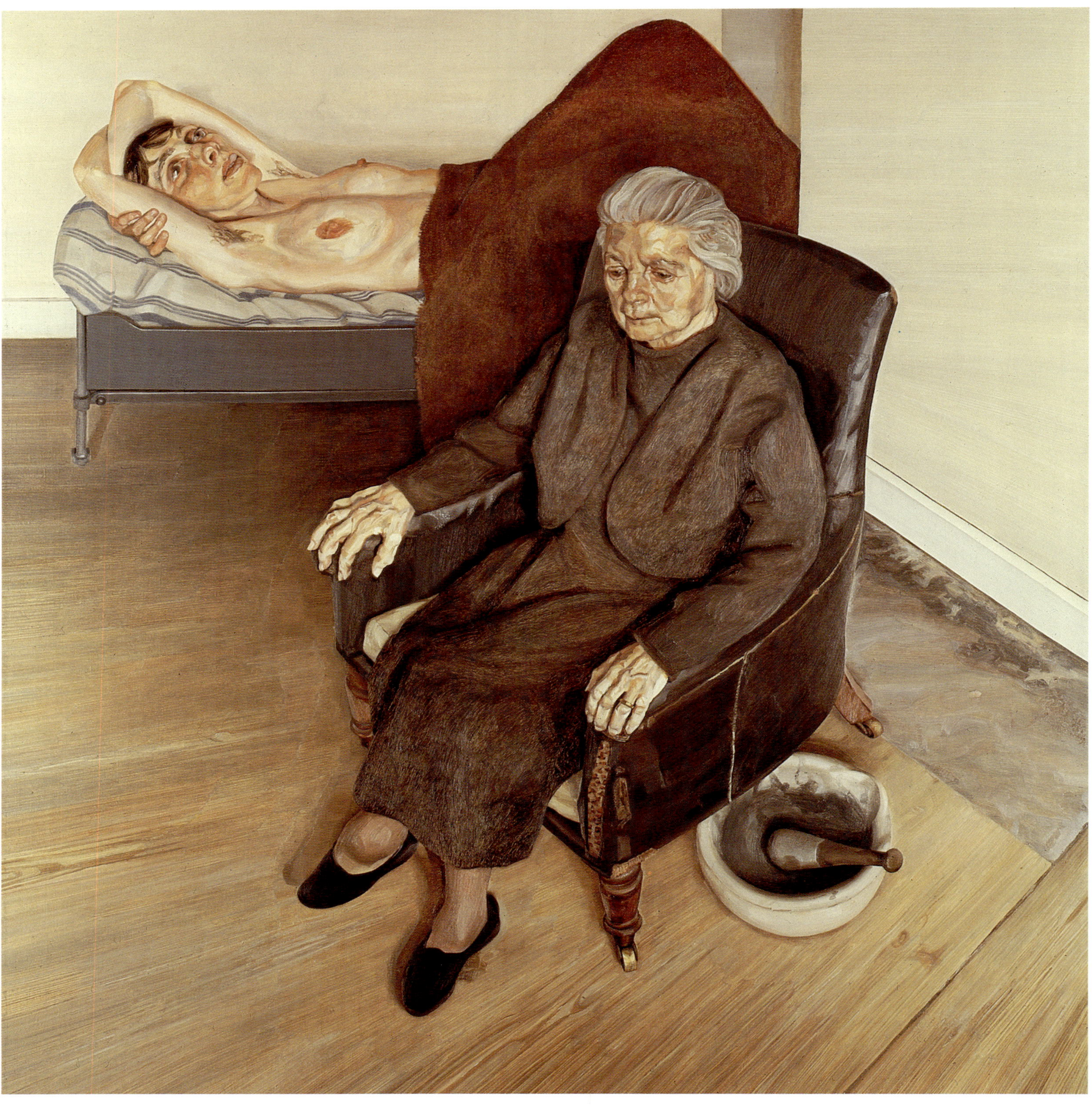

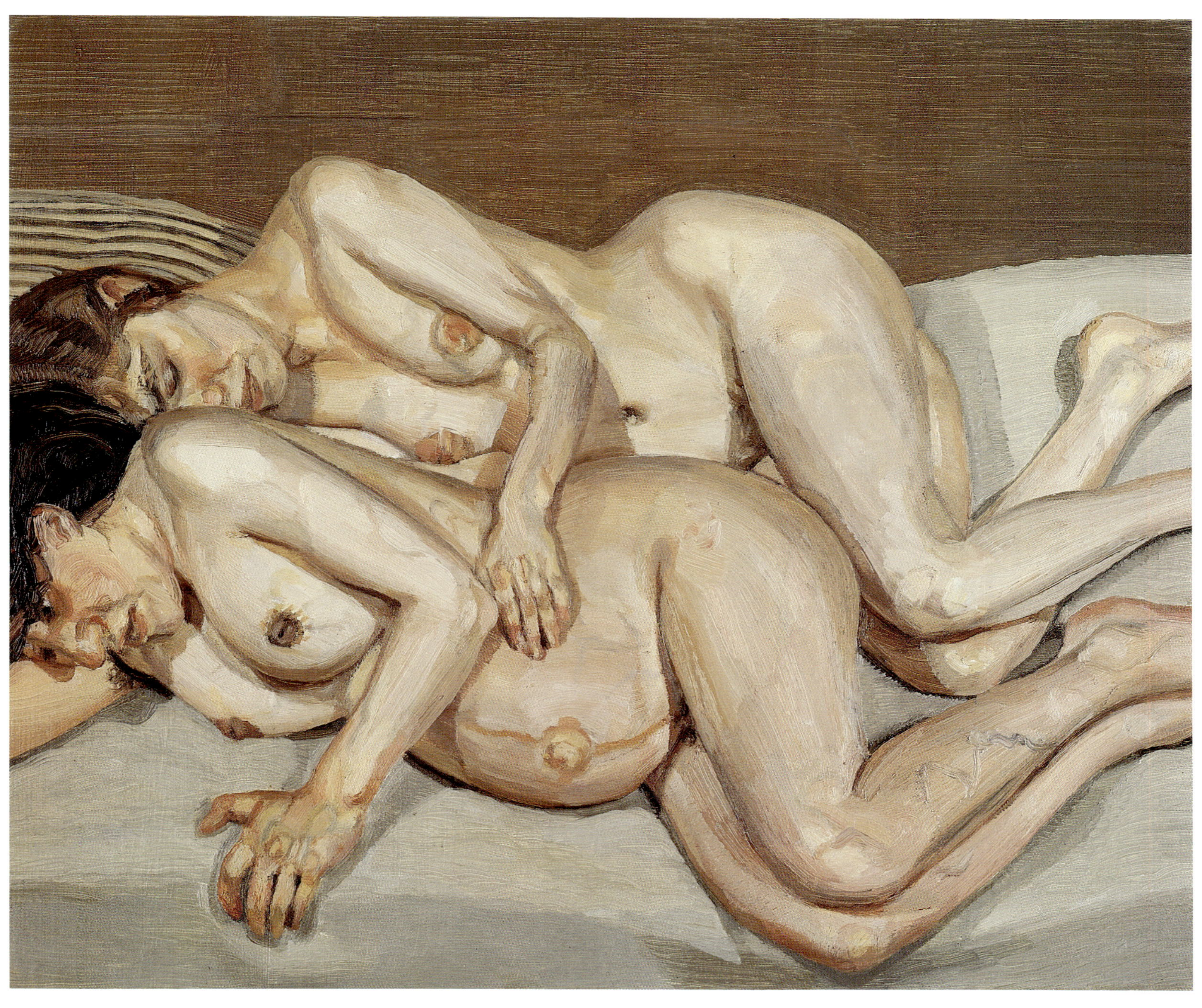

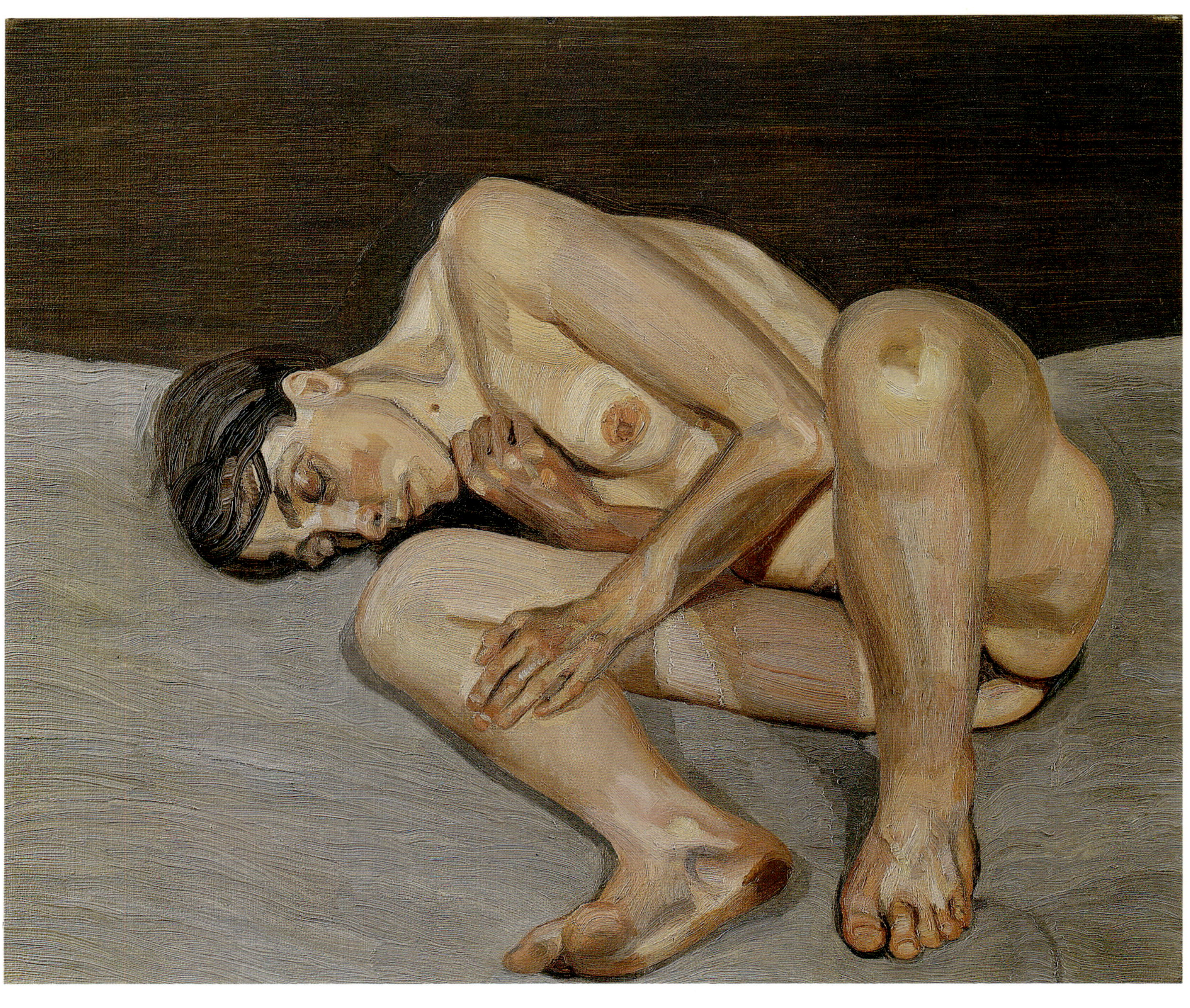

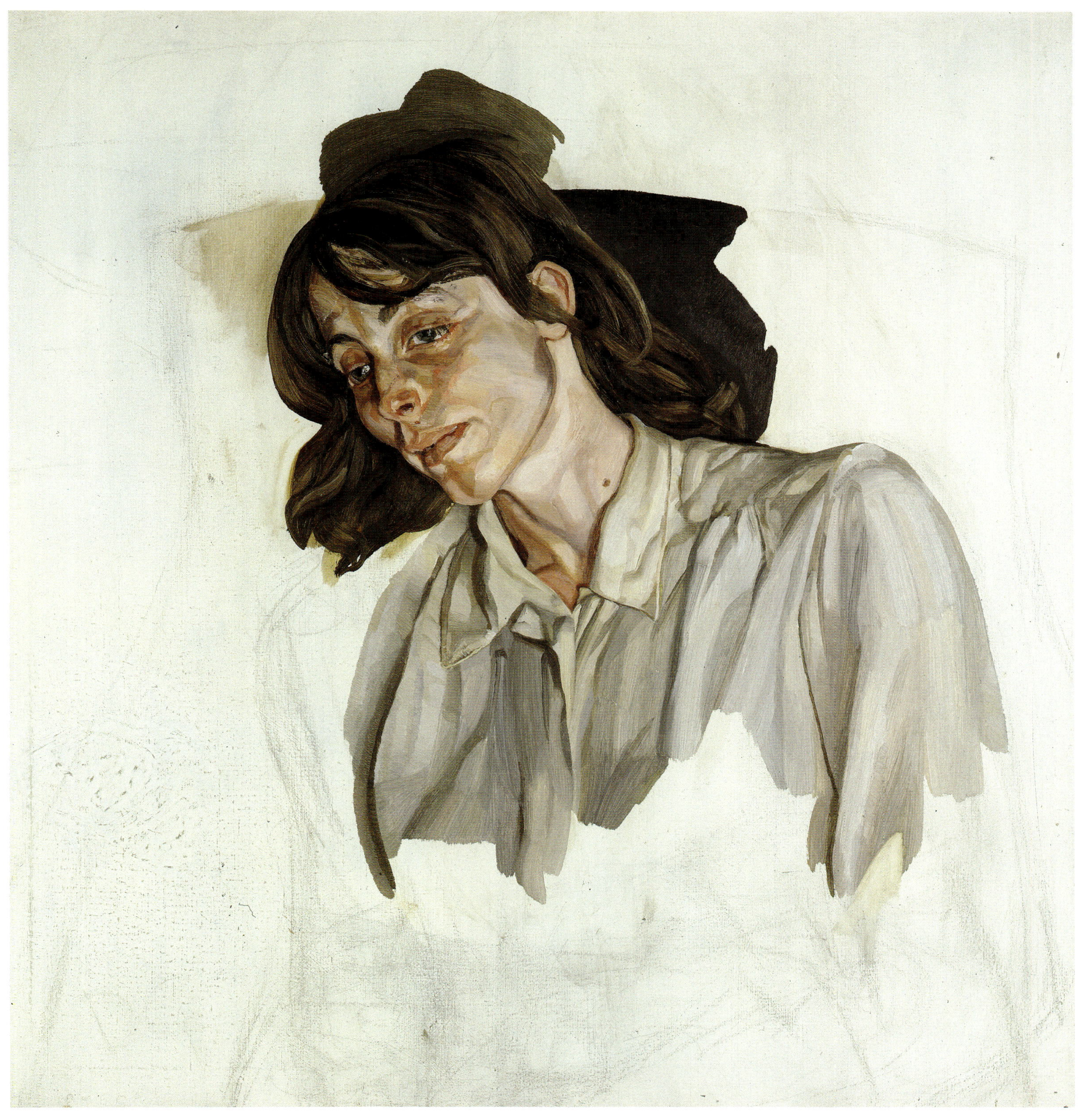

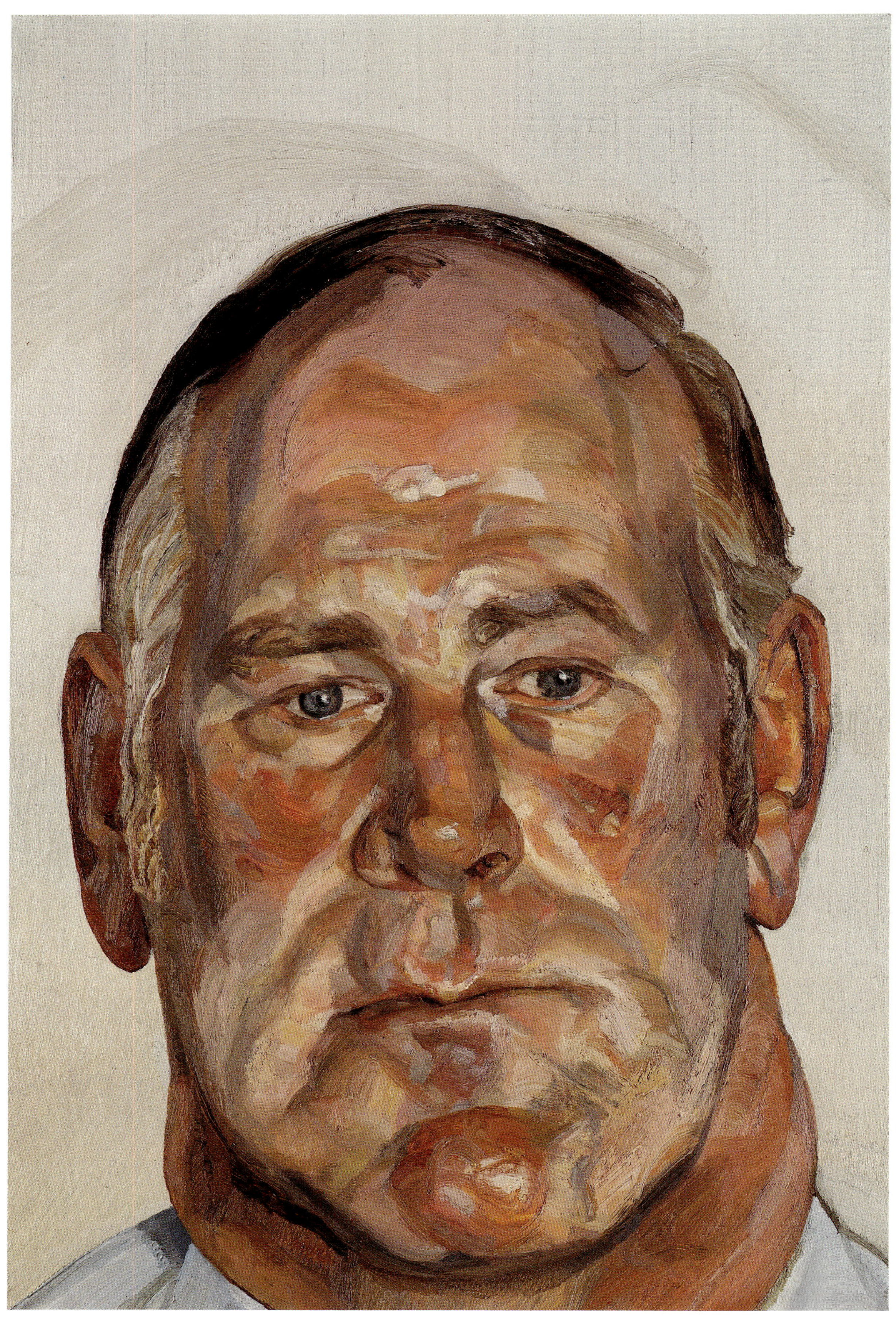

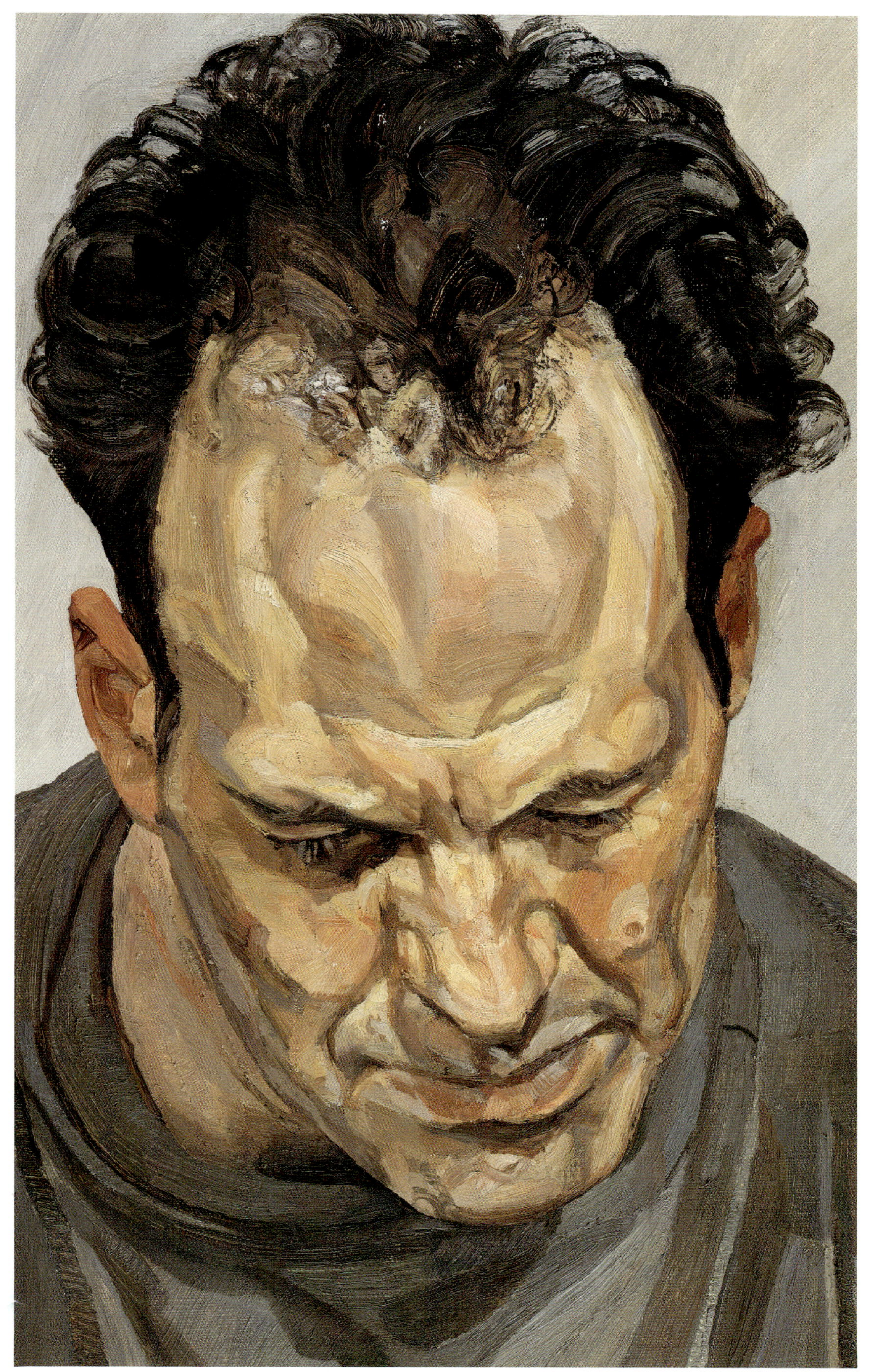

53

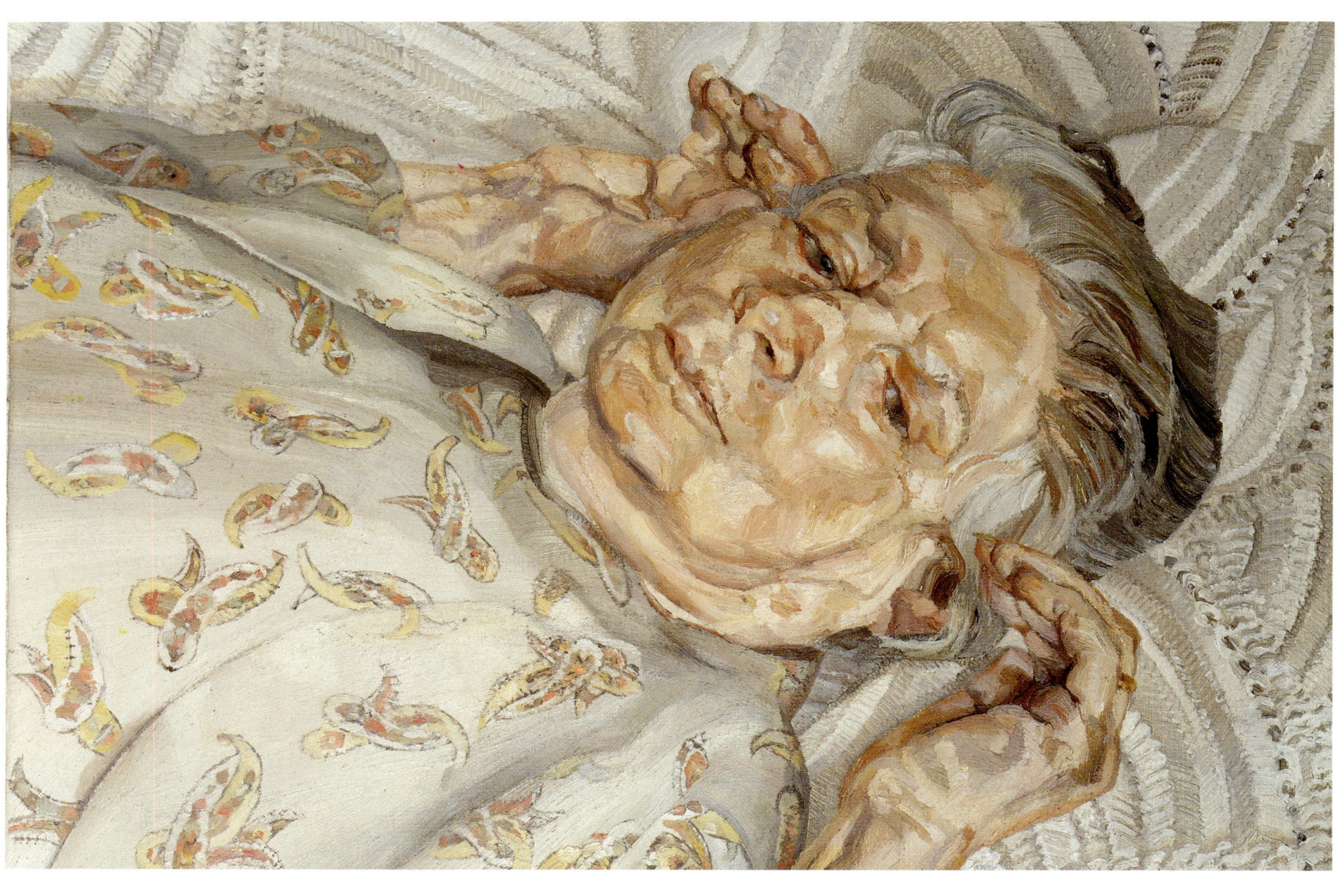

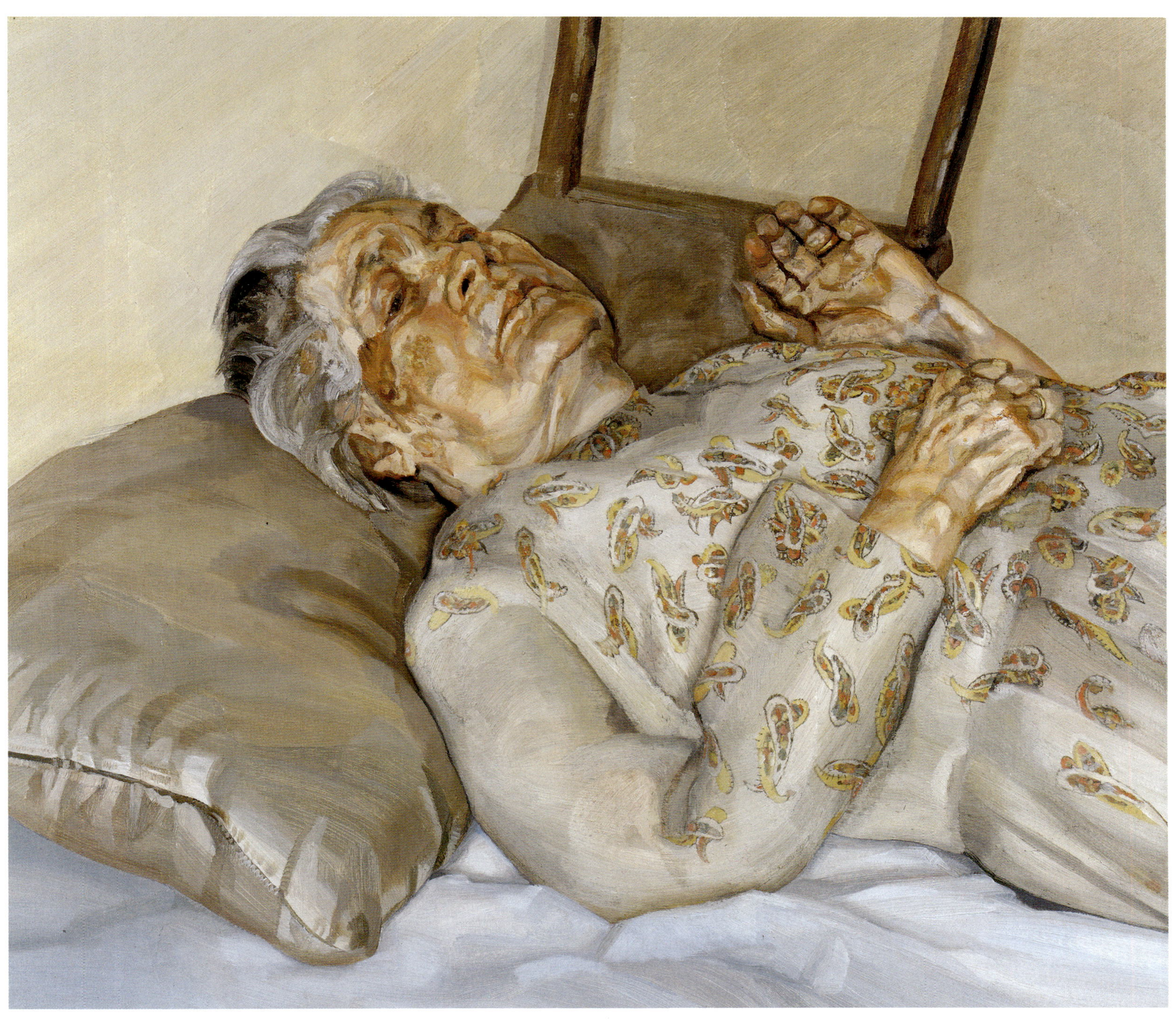

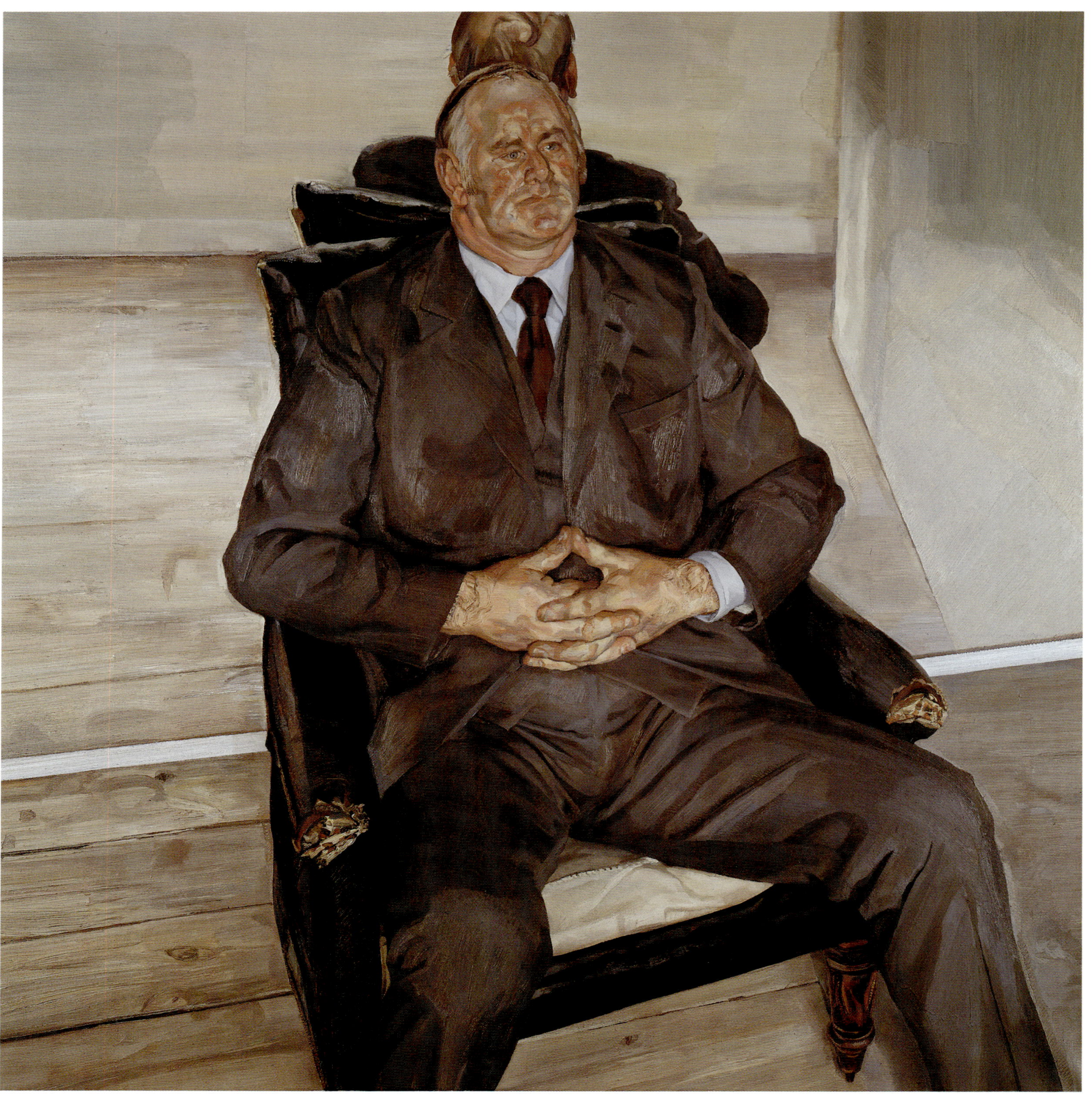

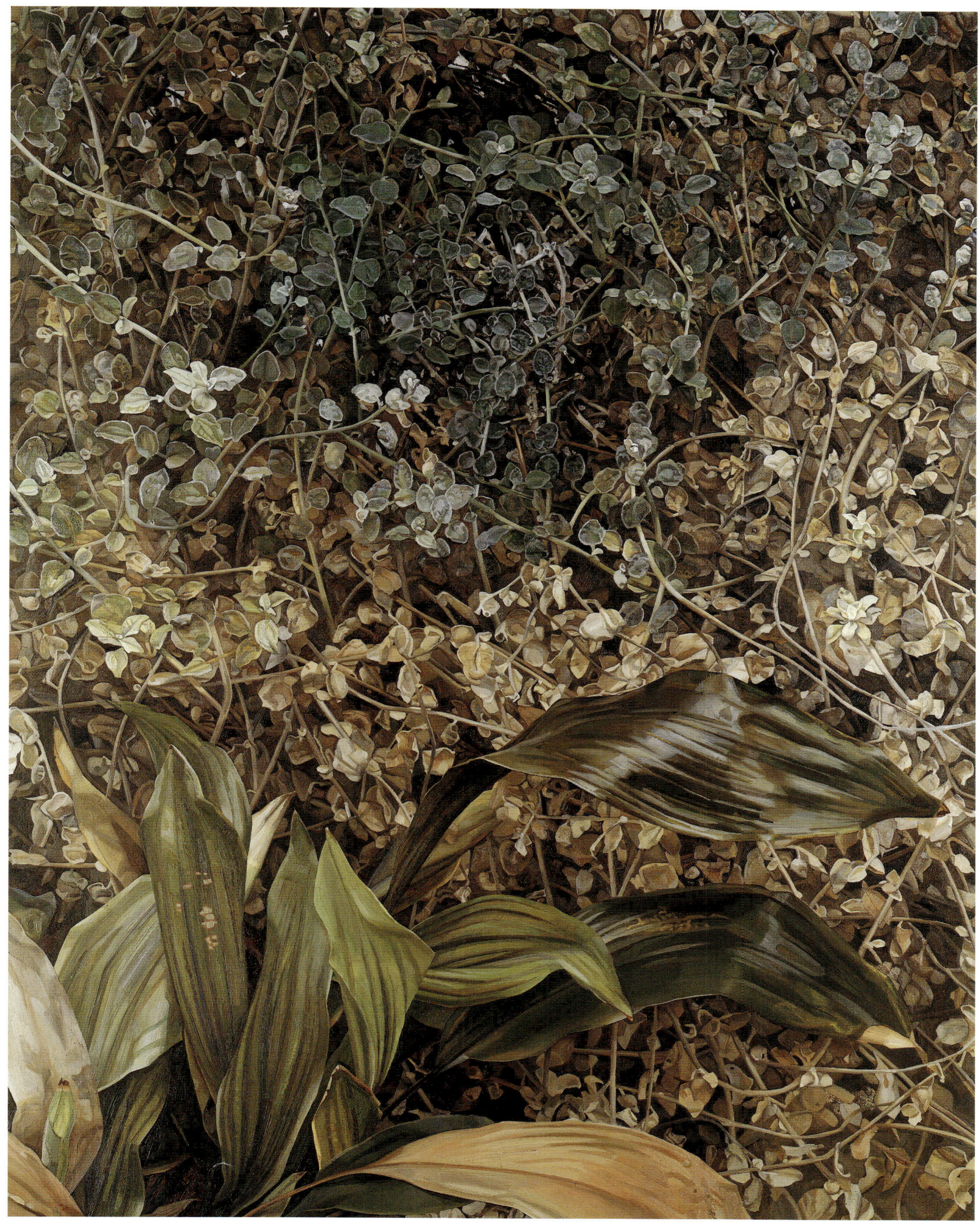

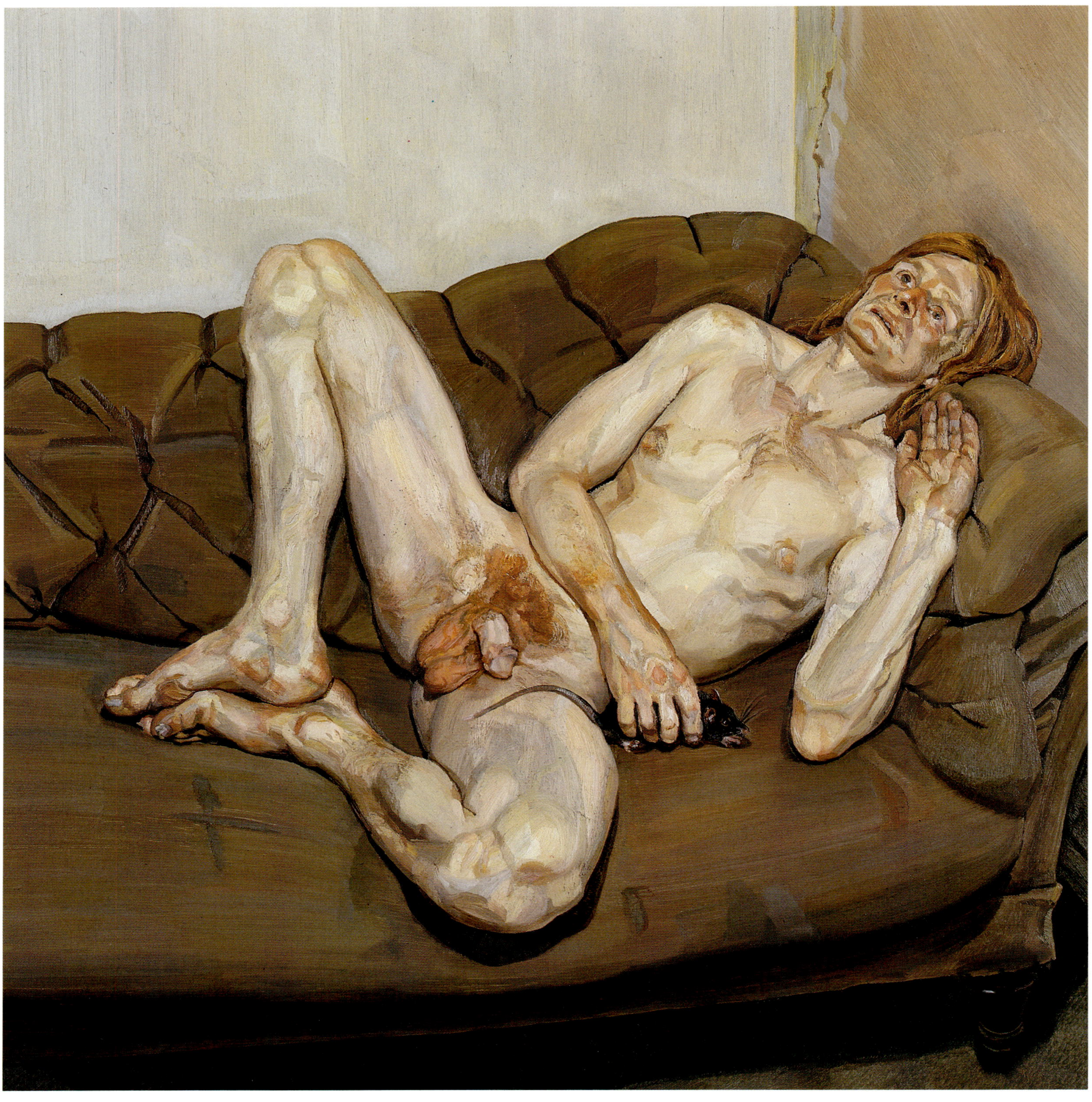

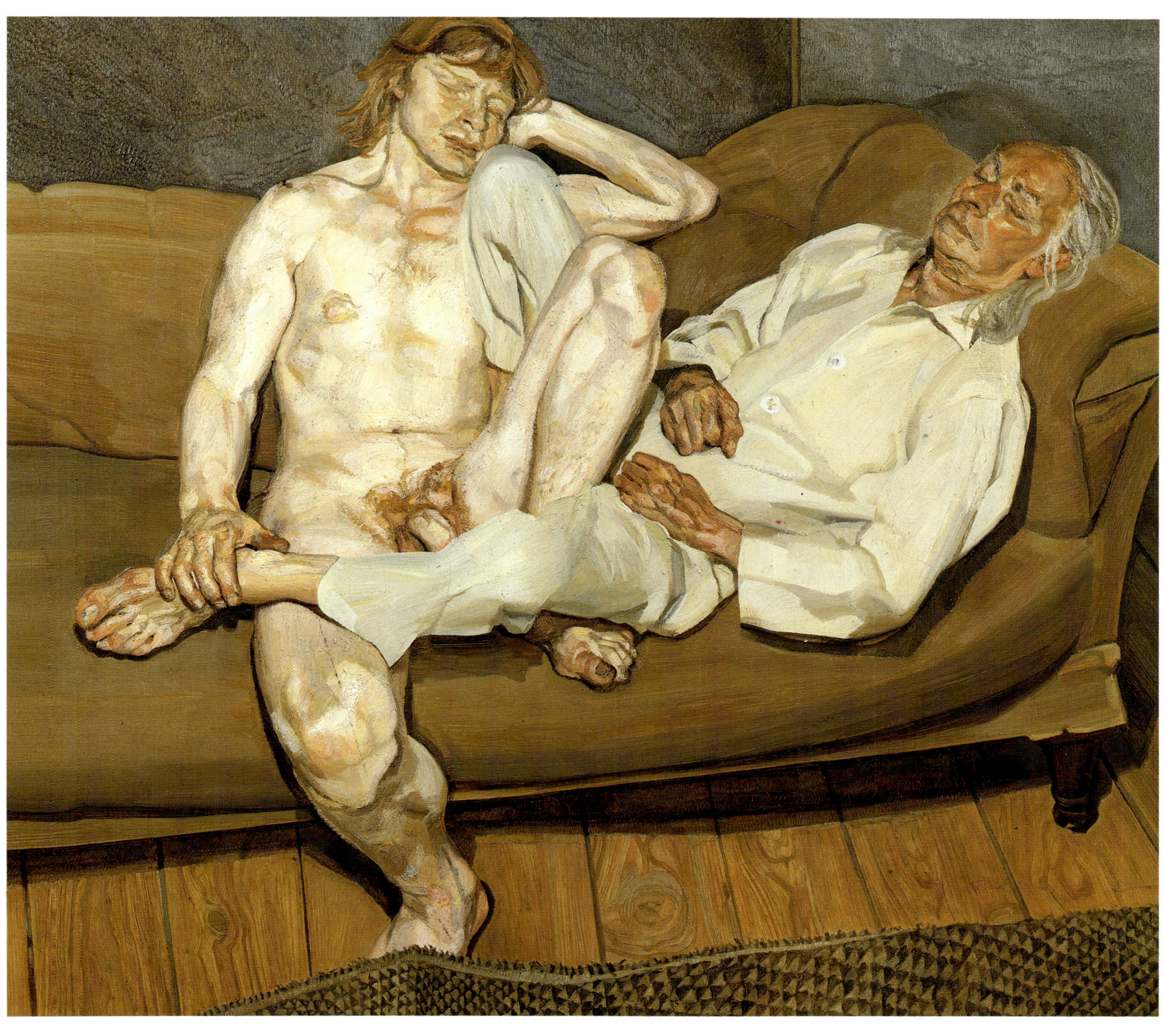

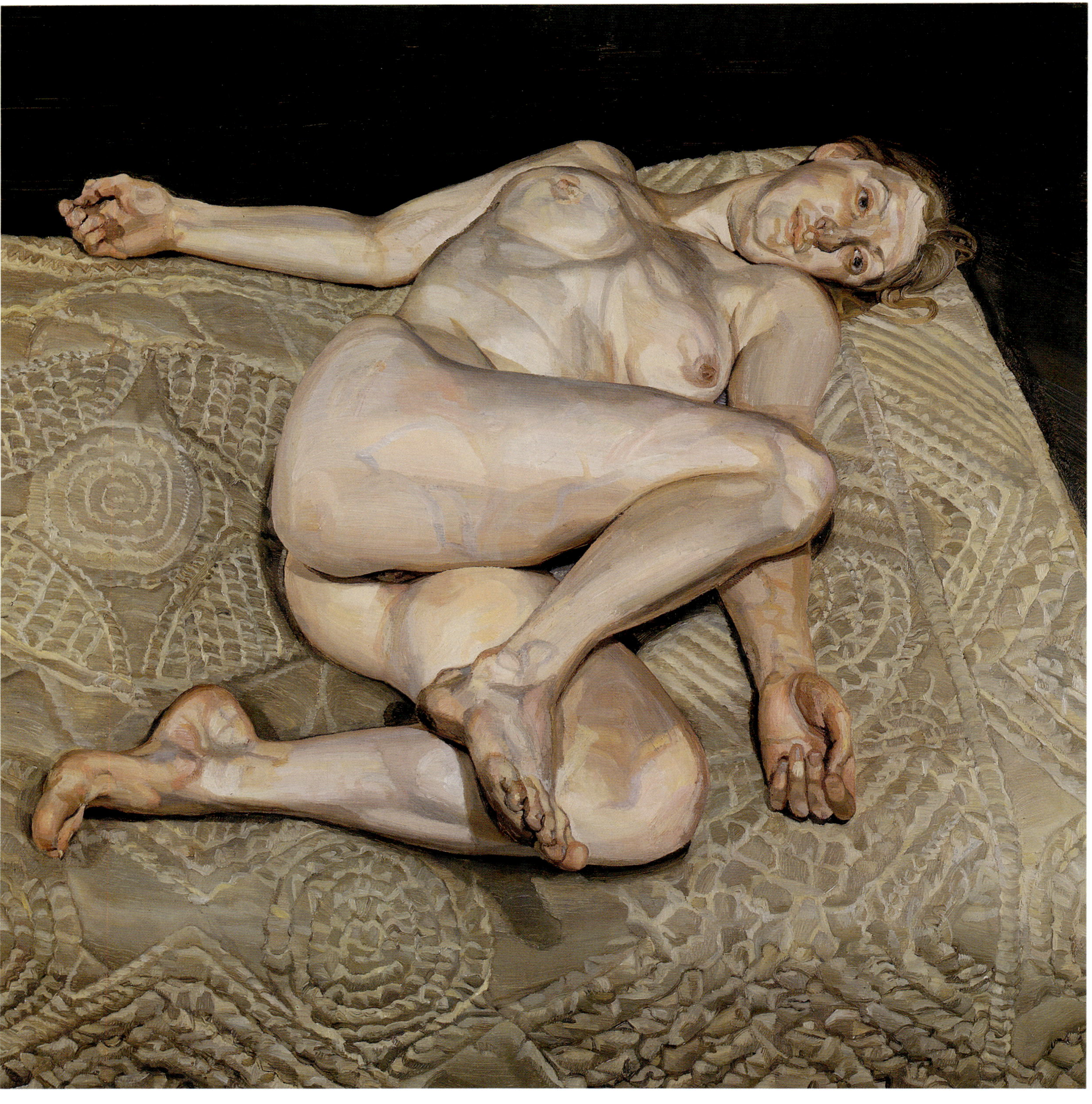

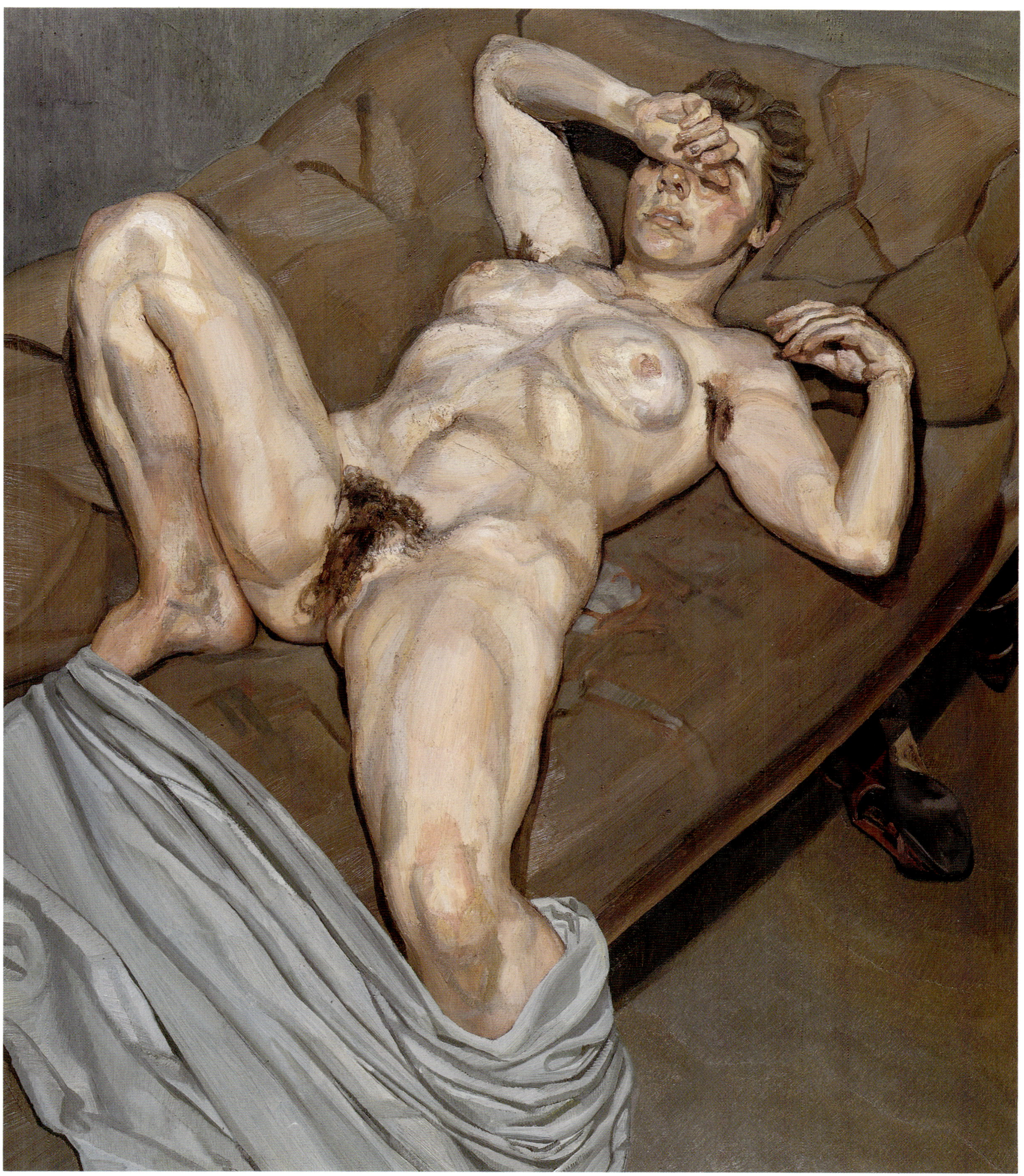

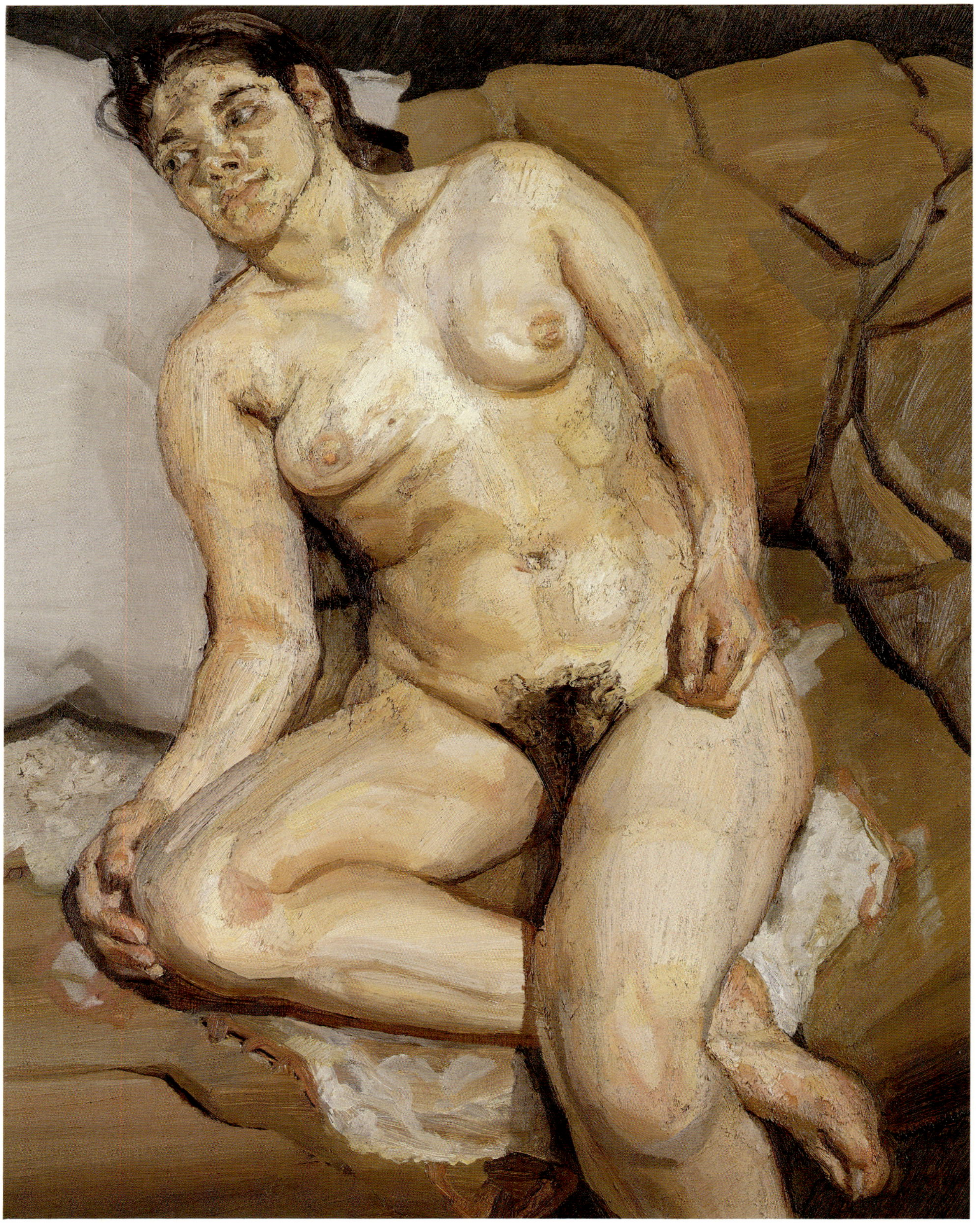

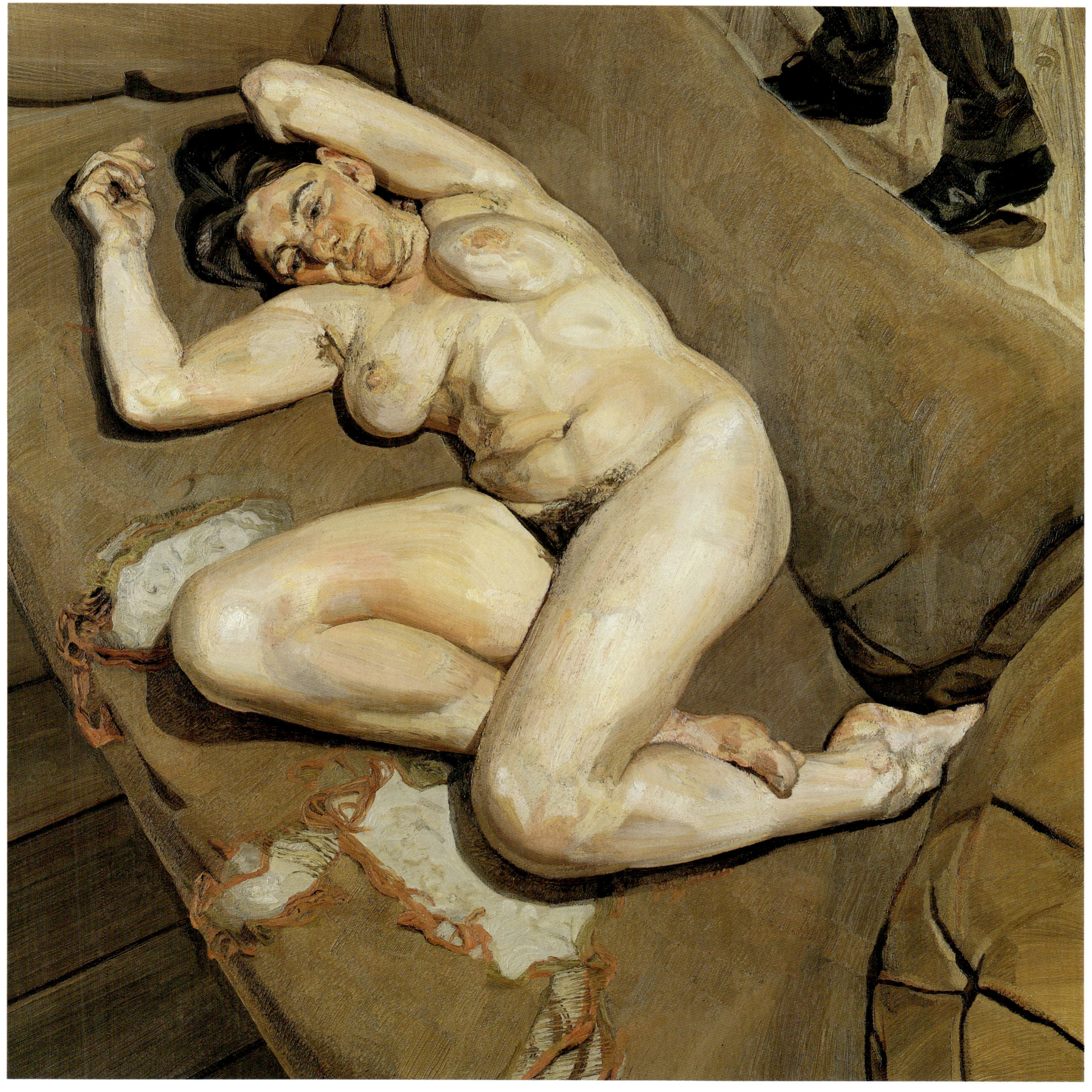

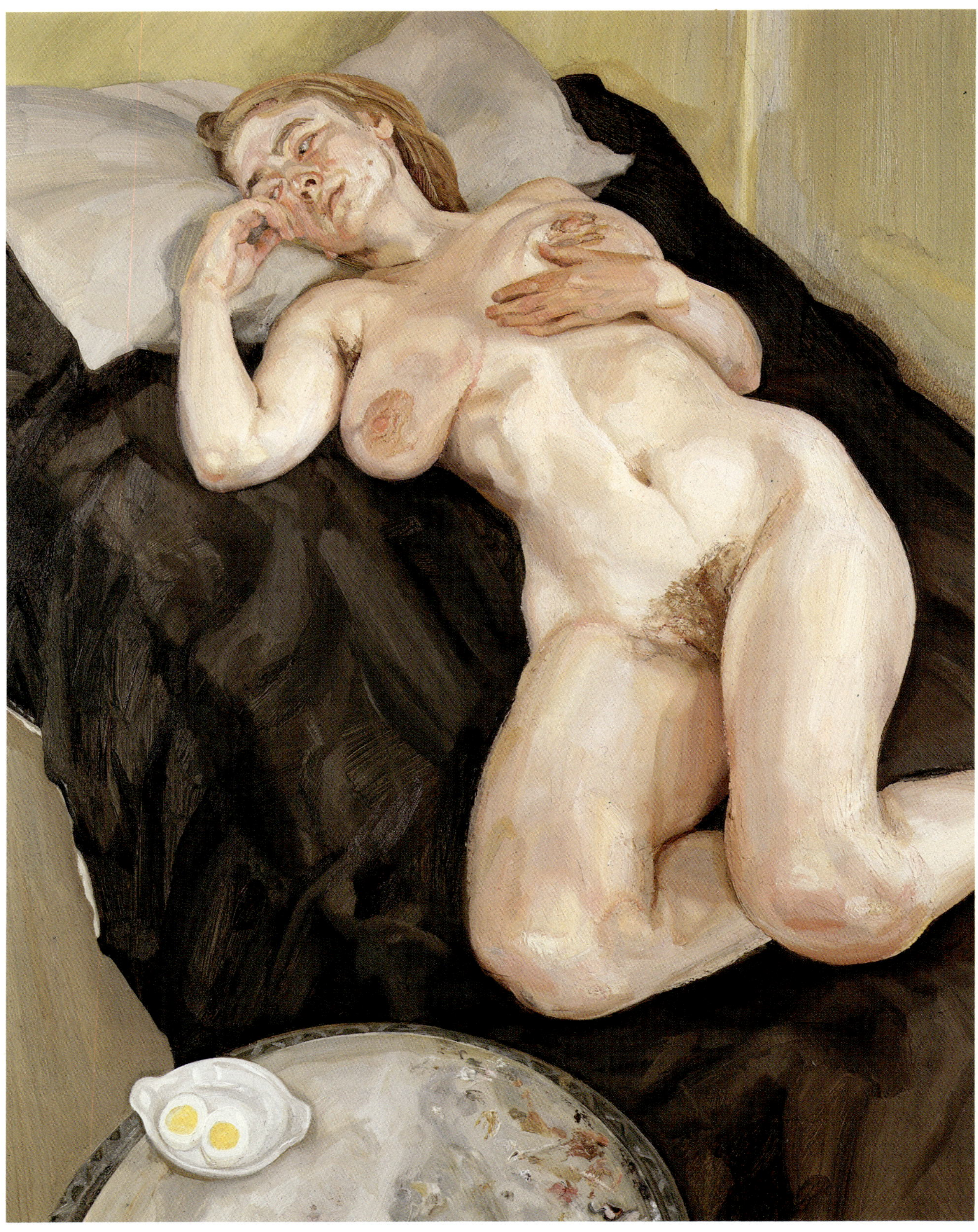

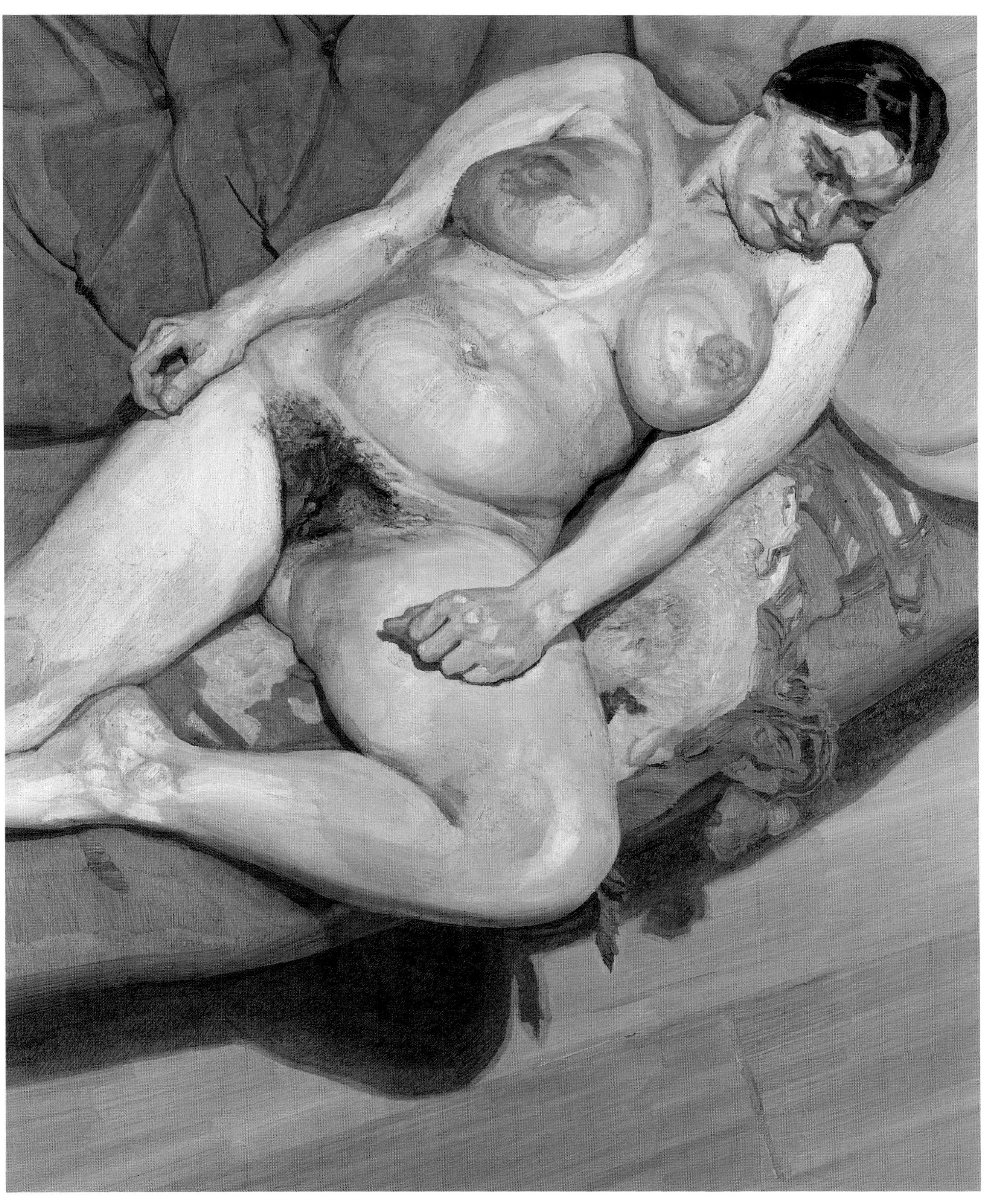

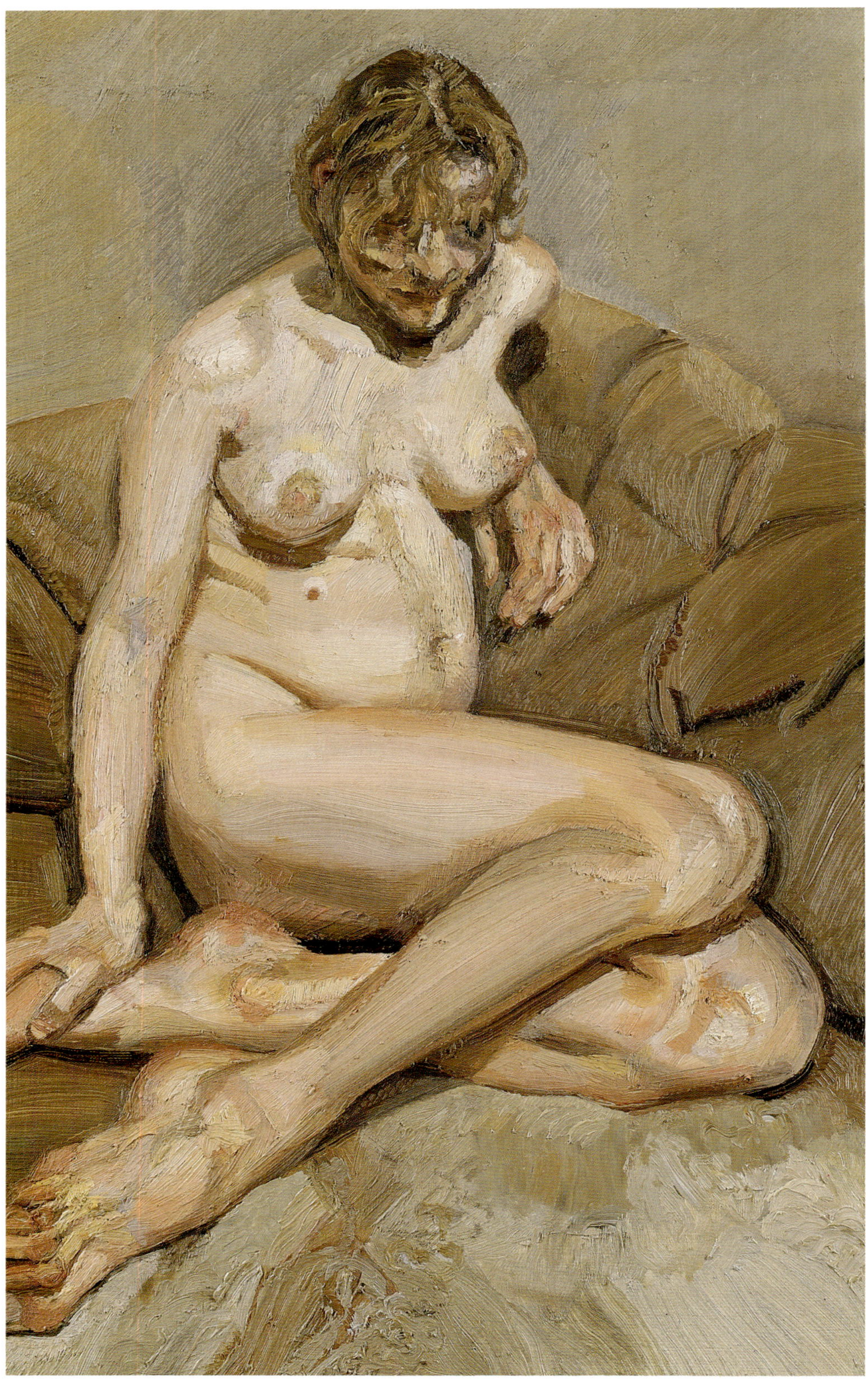

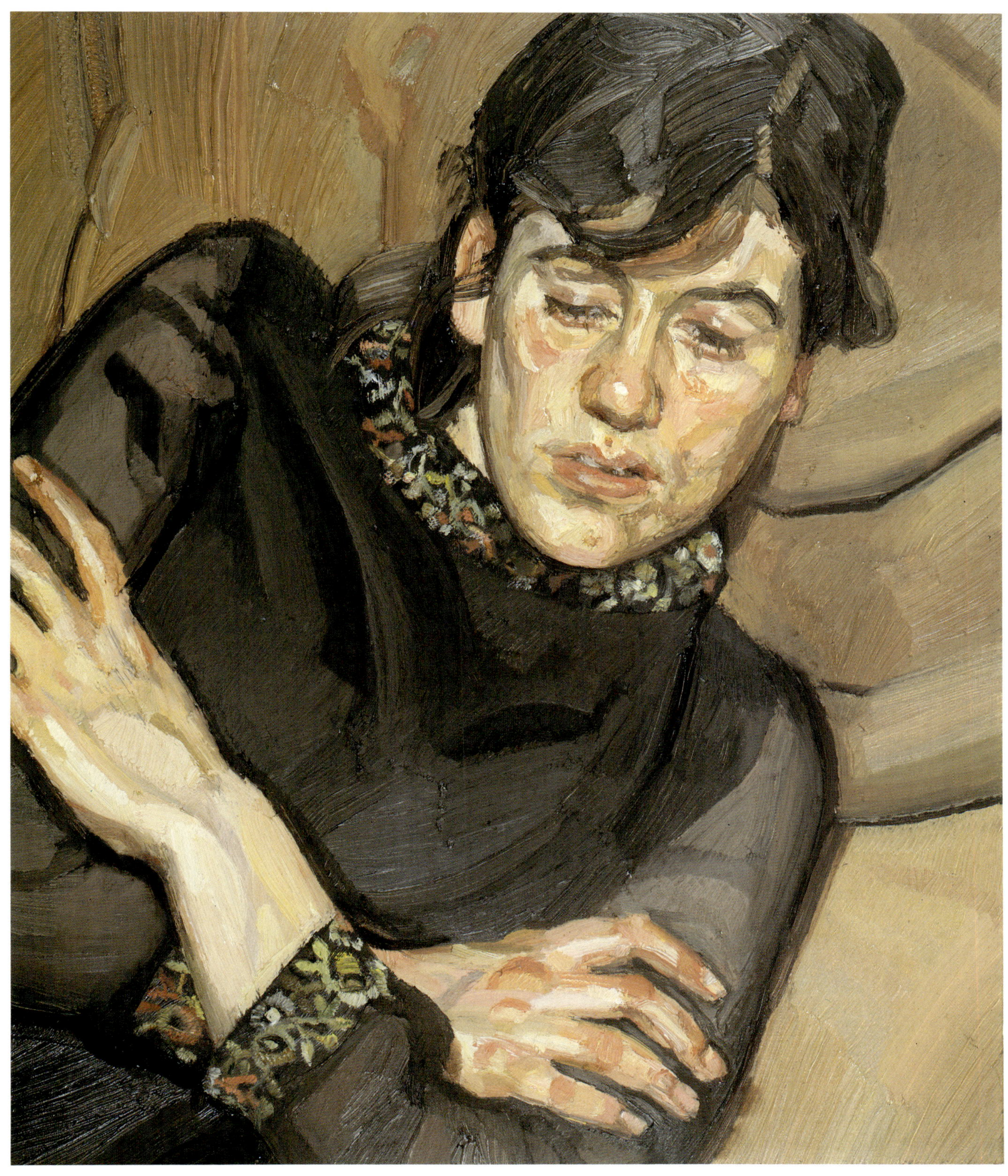

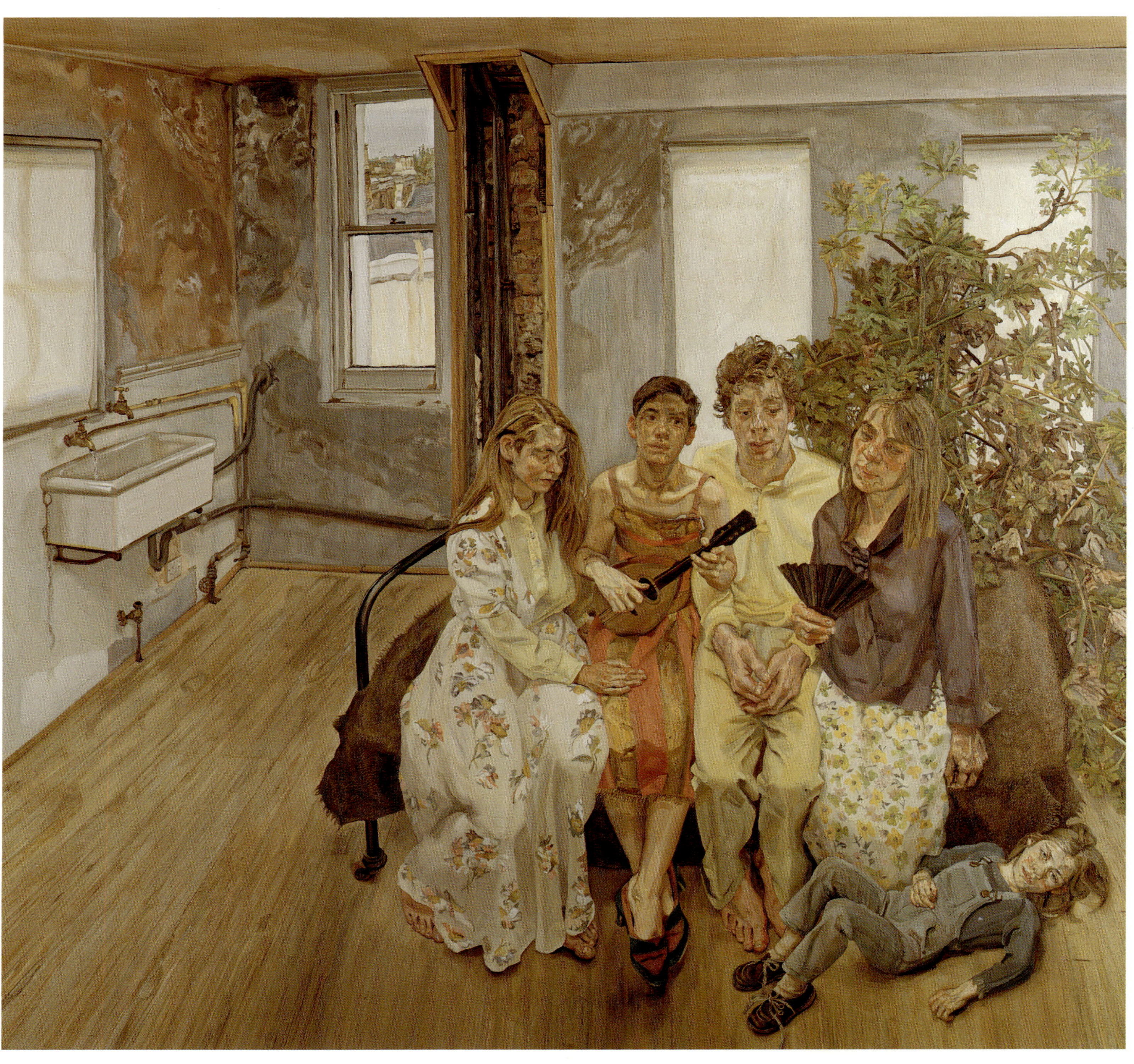

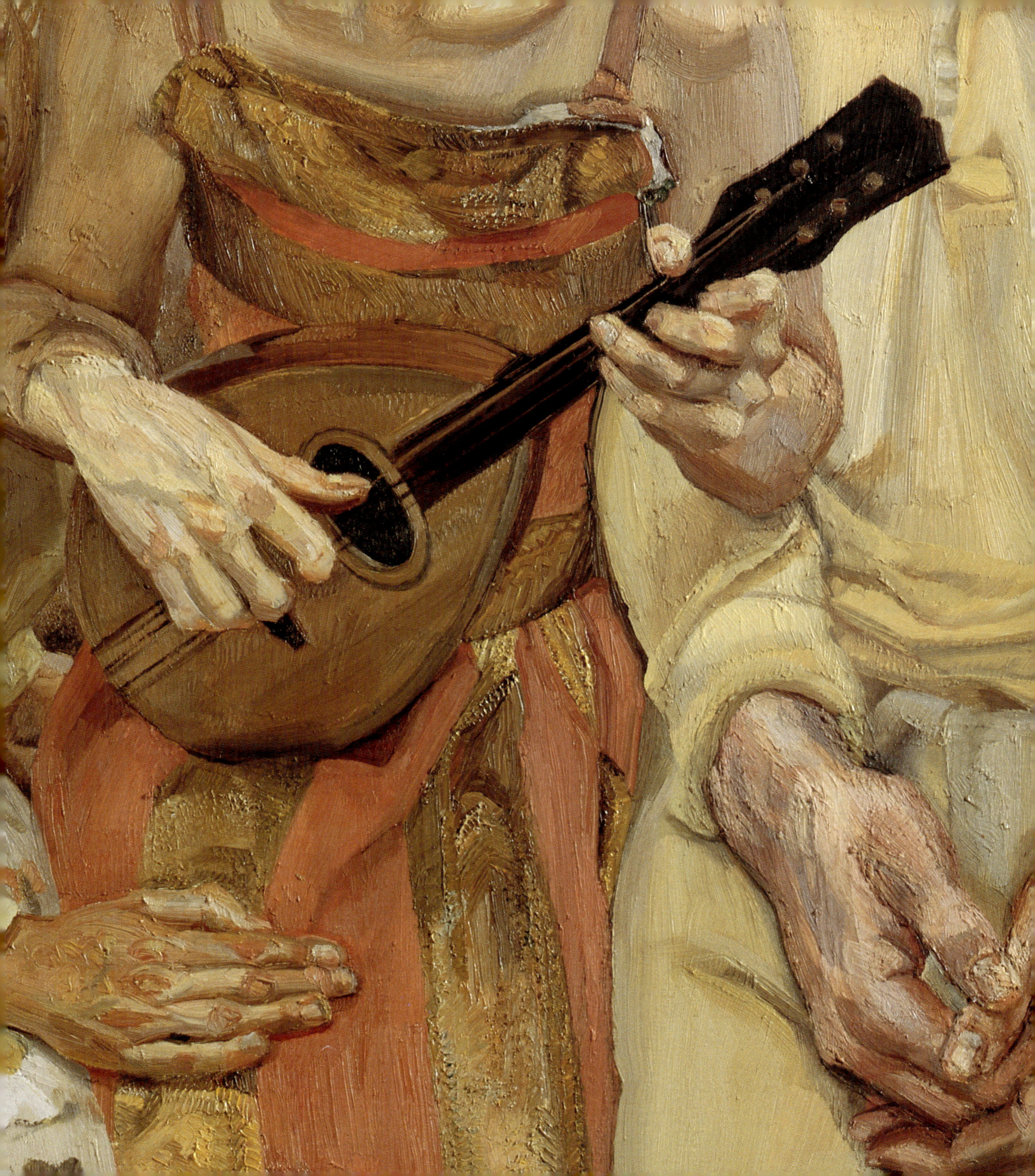

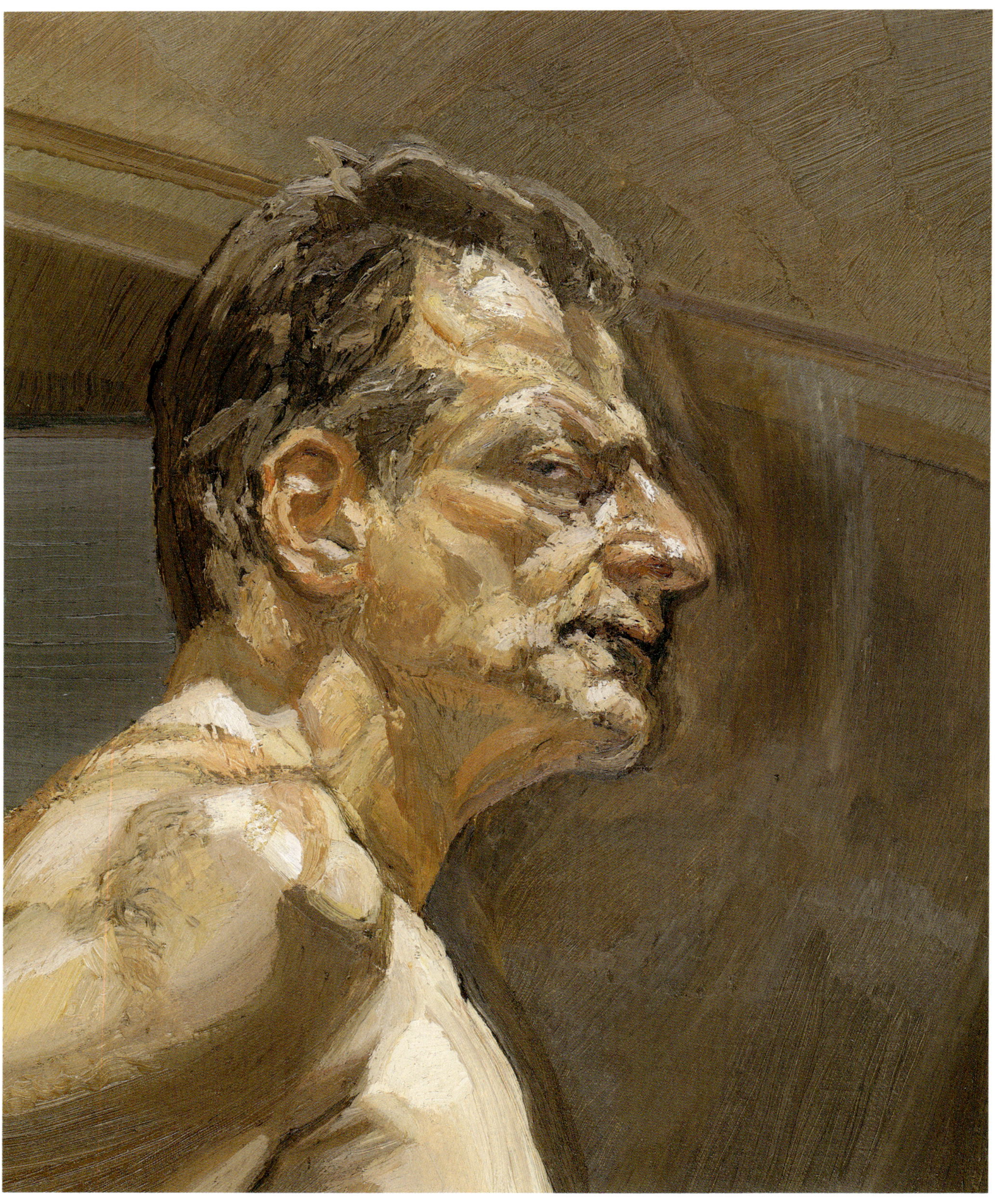

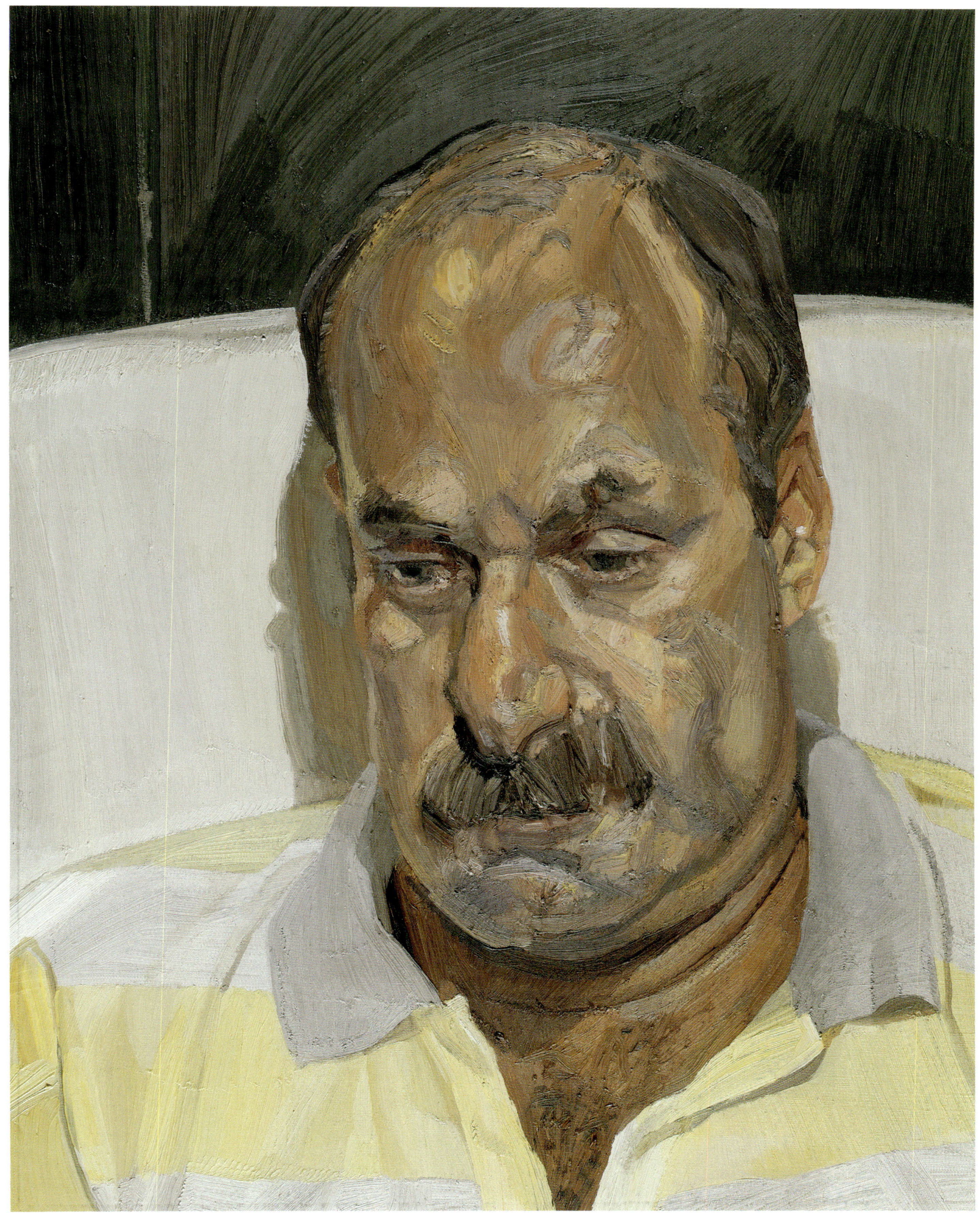

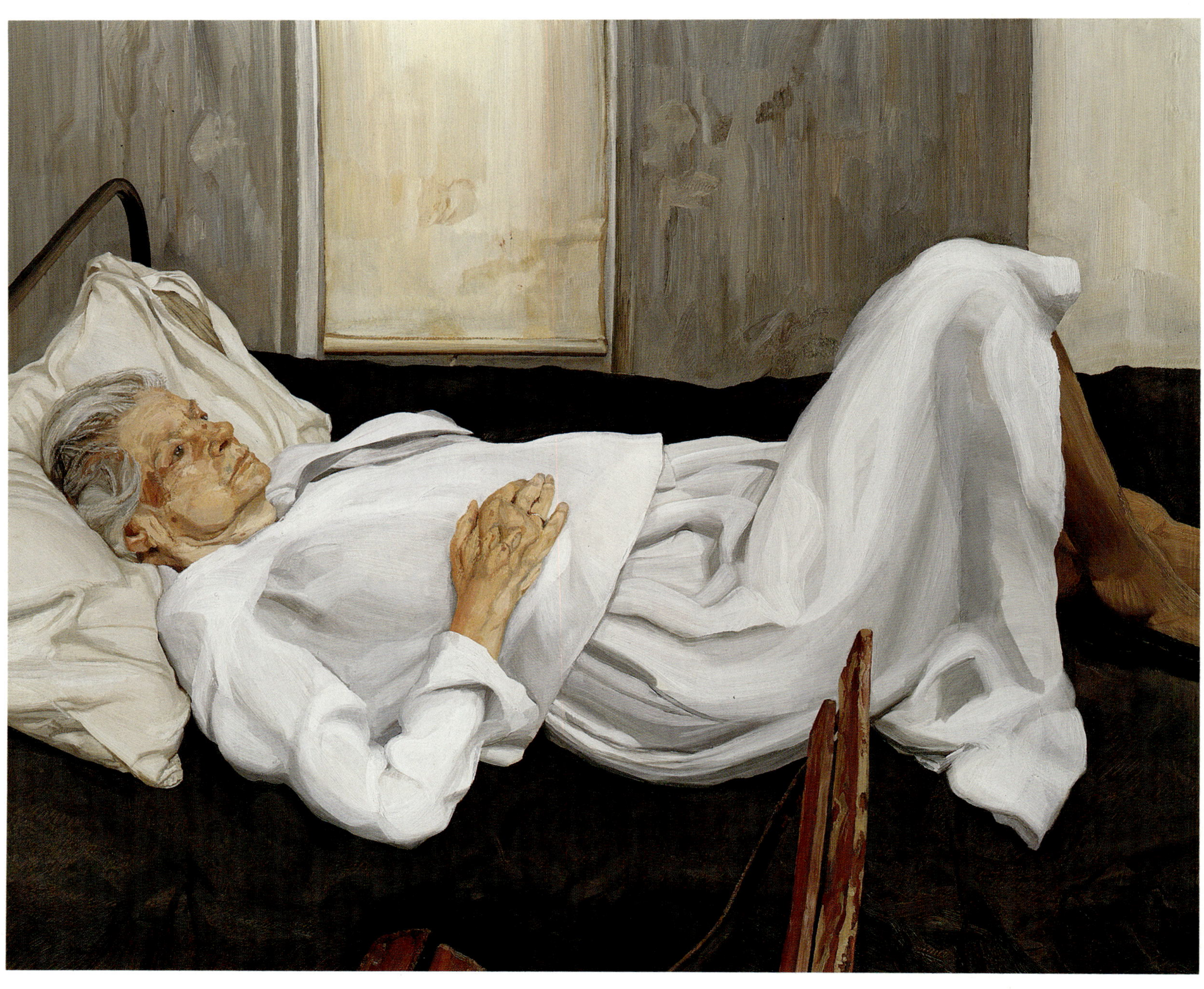

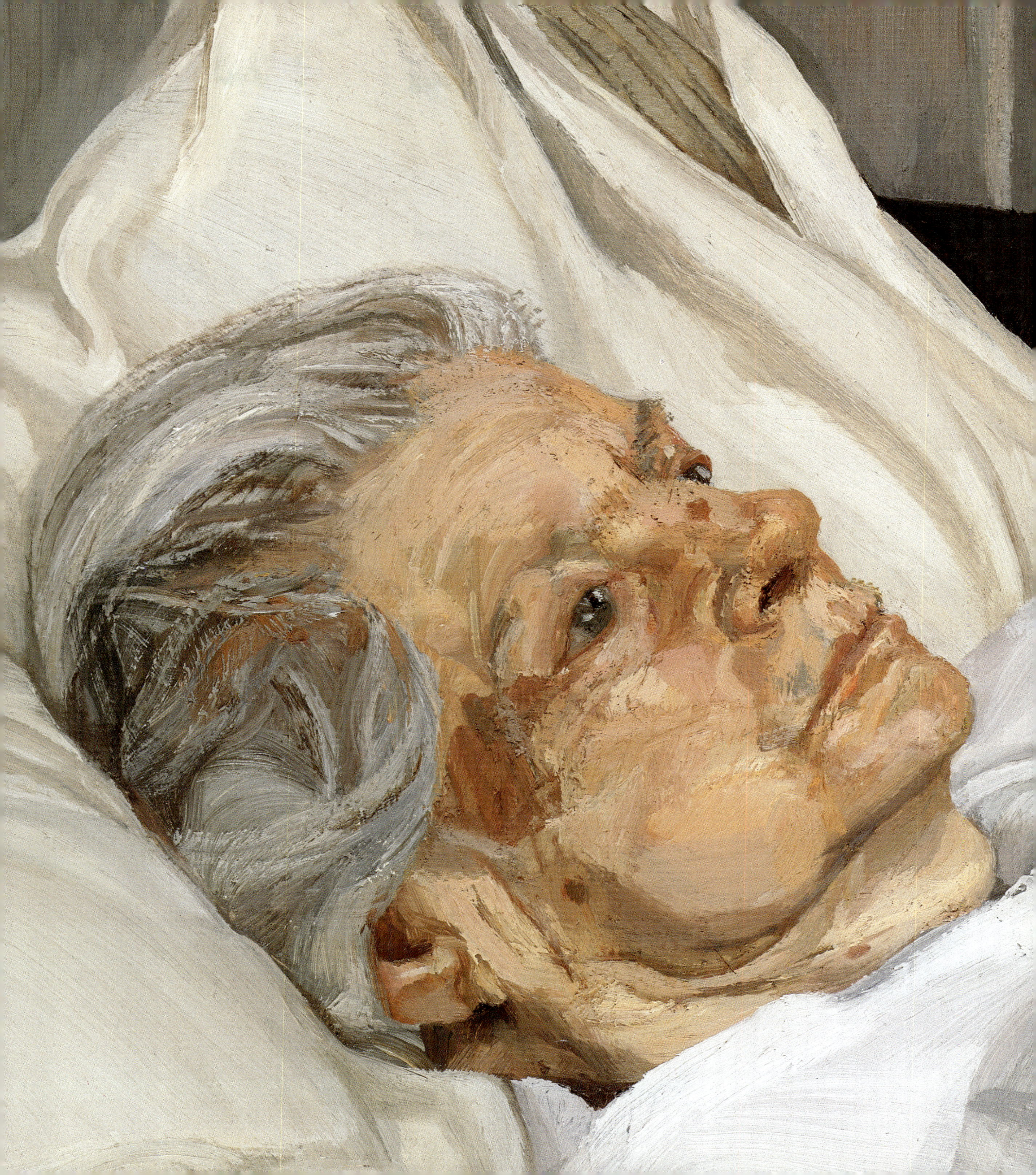

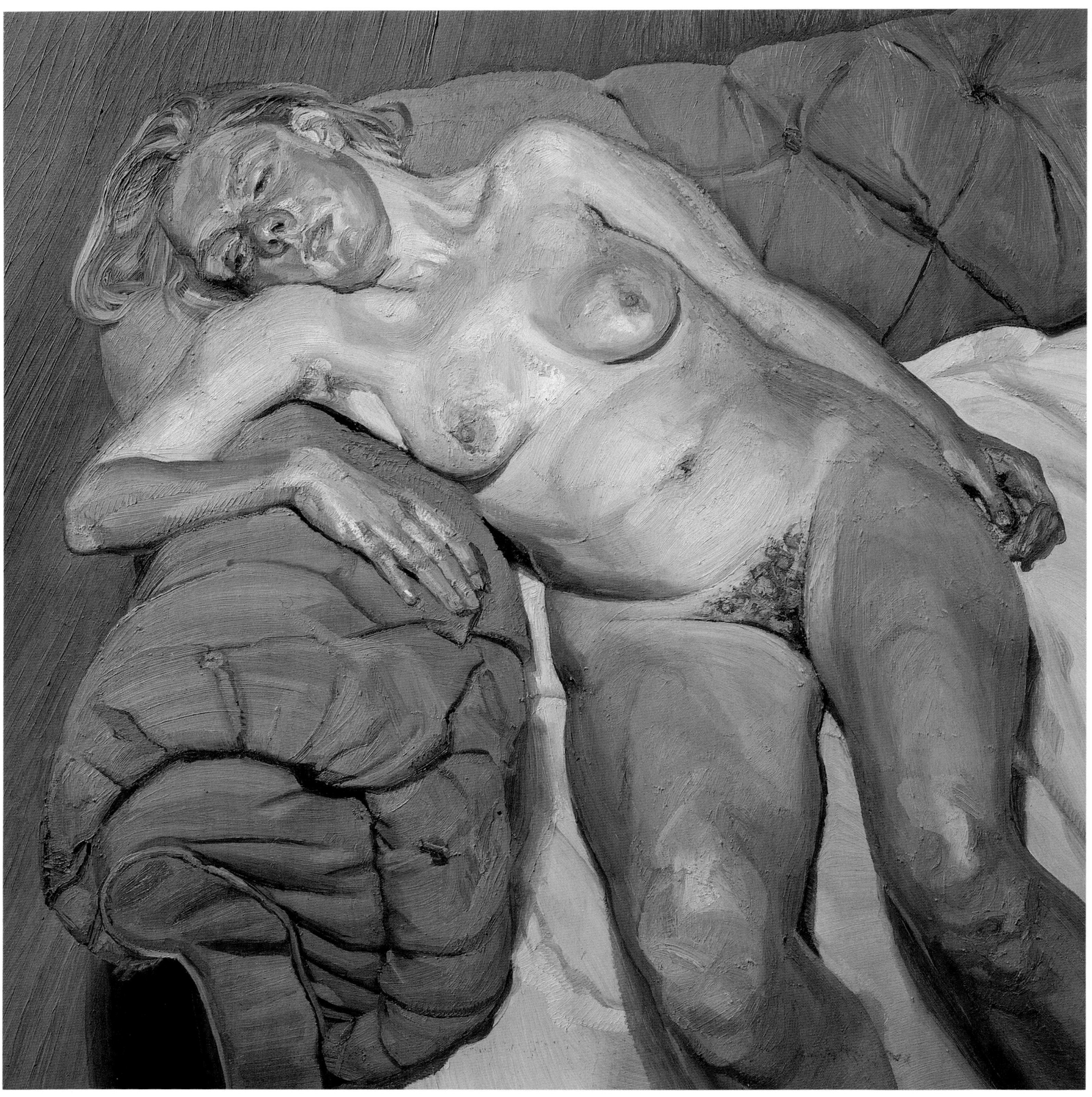

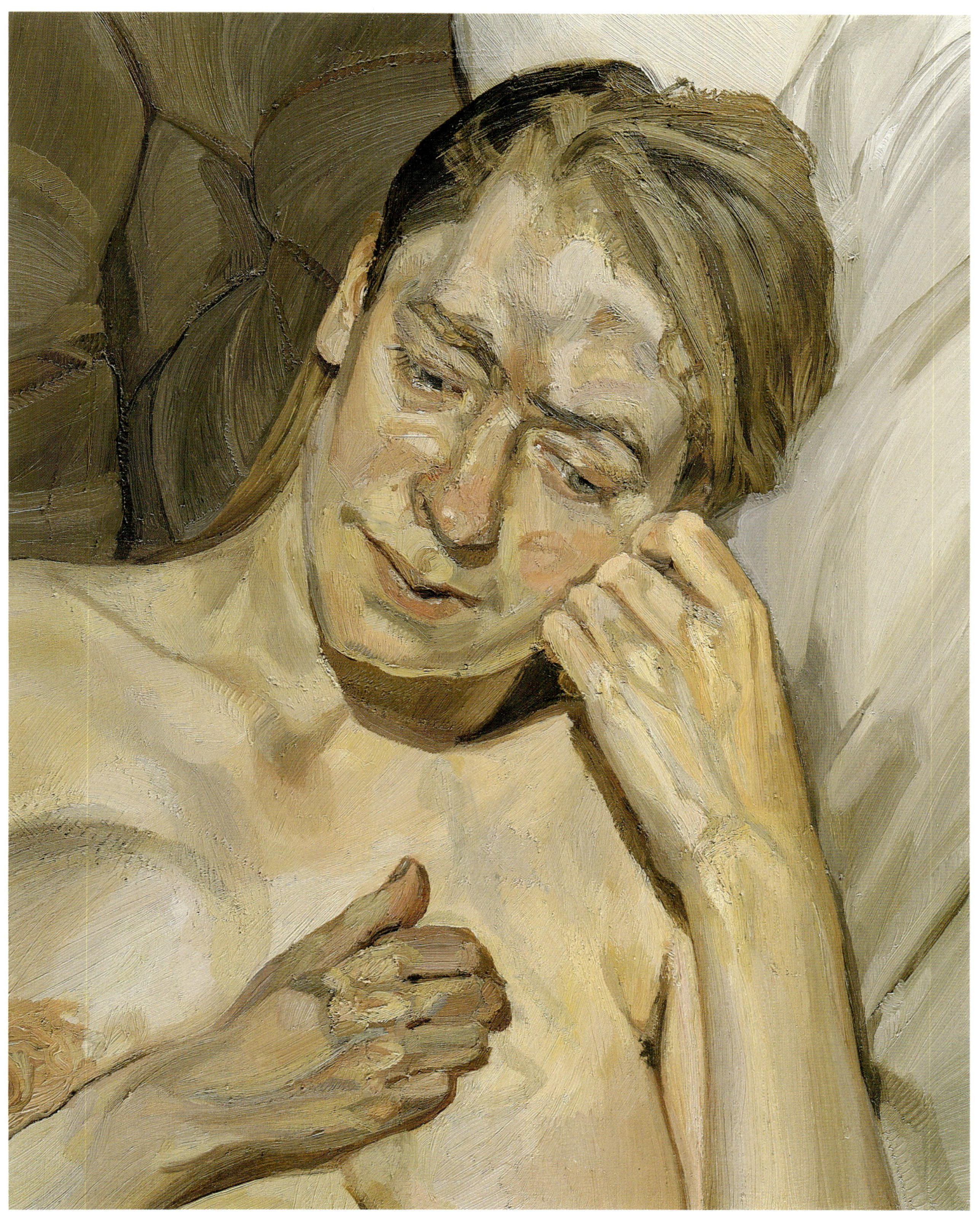

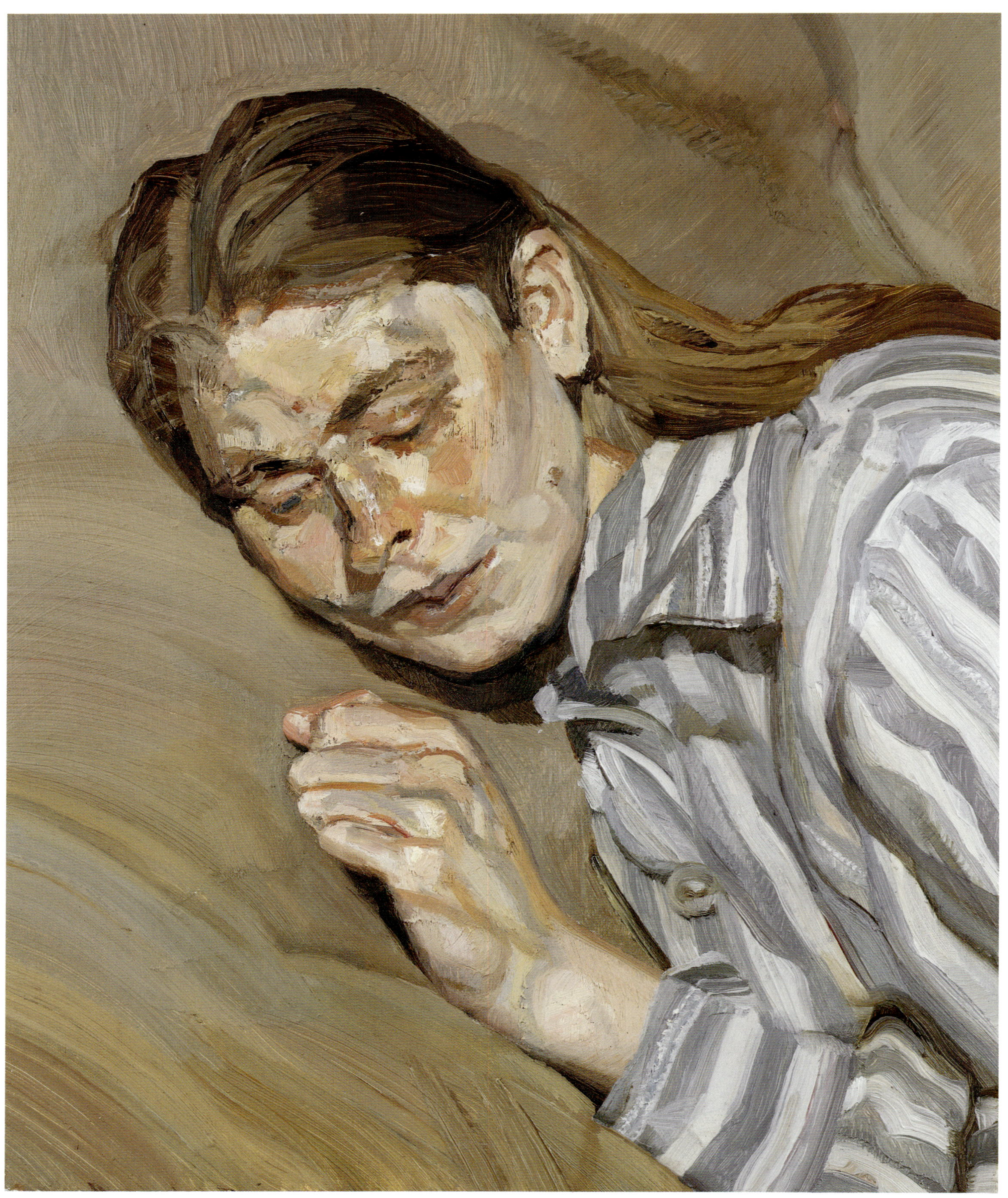

74

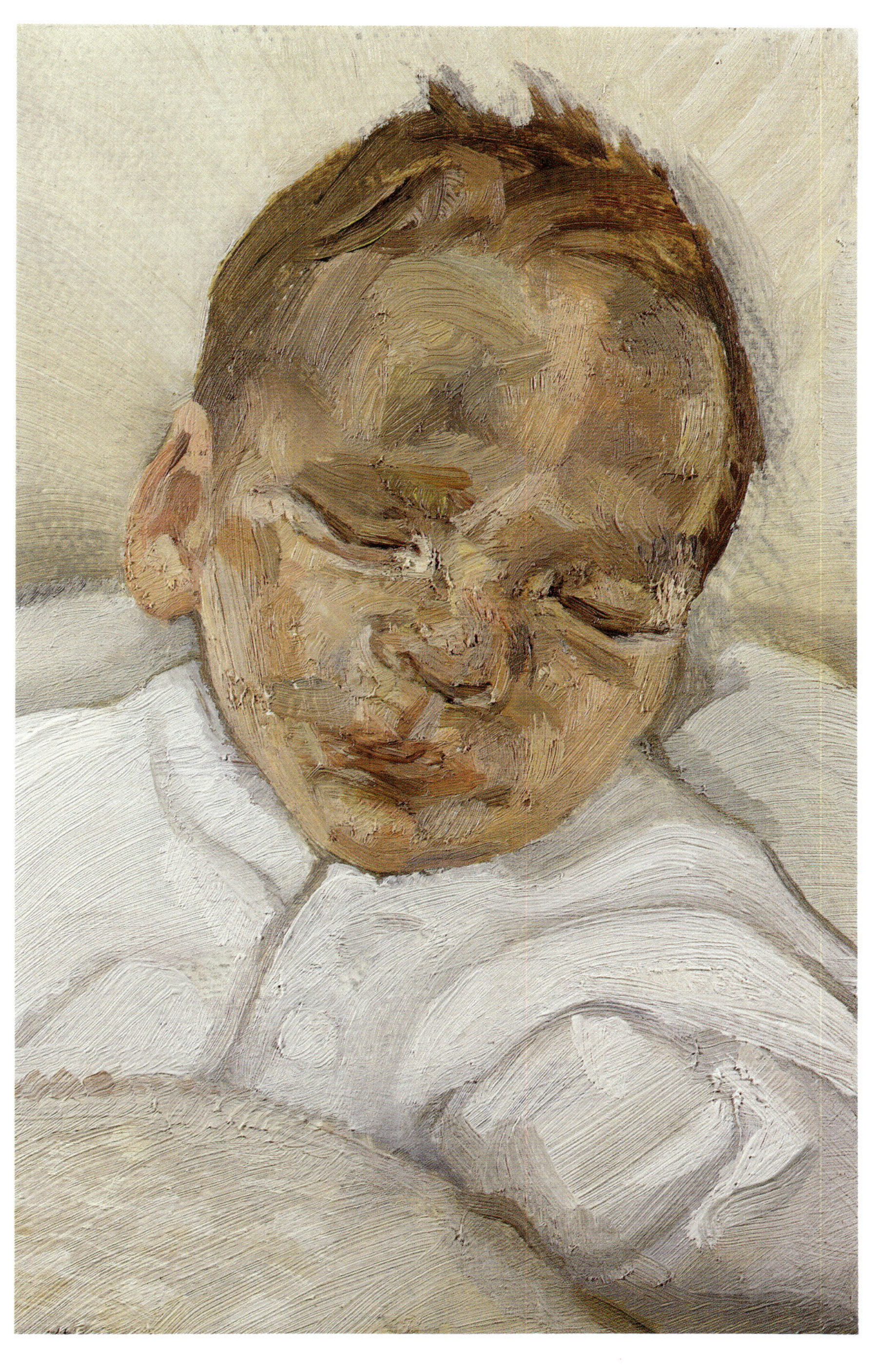

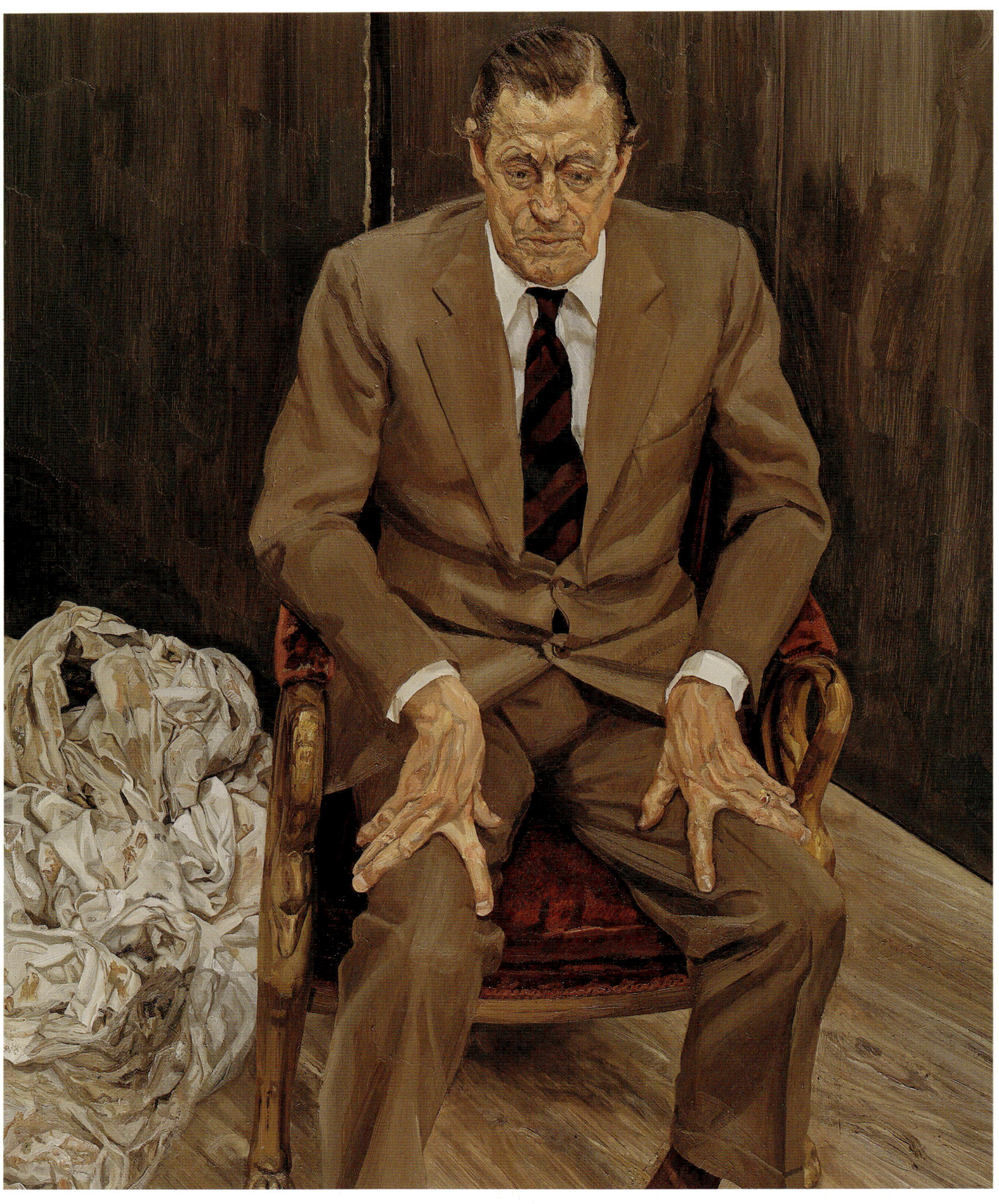

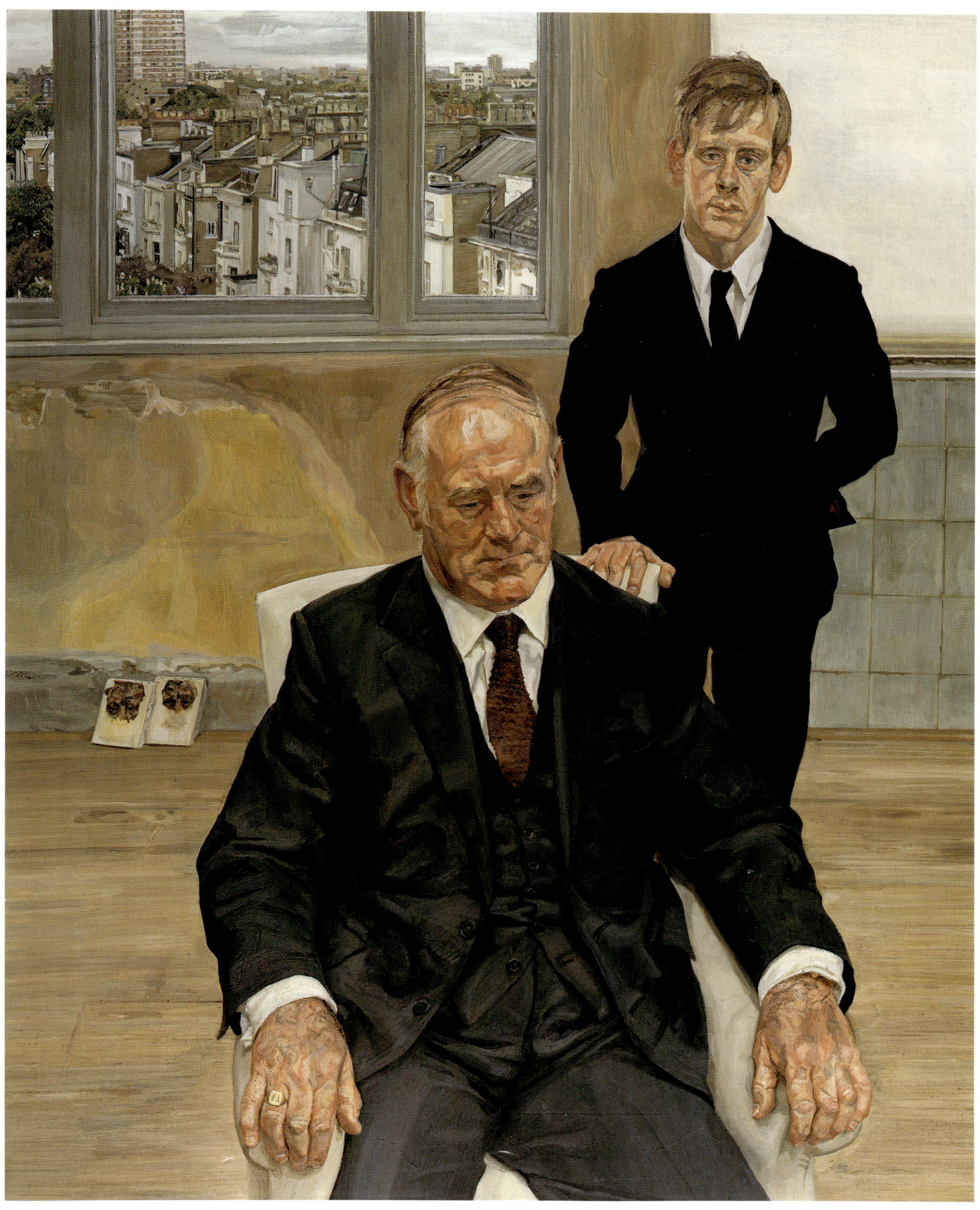

77

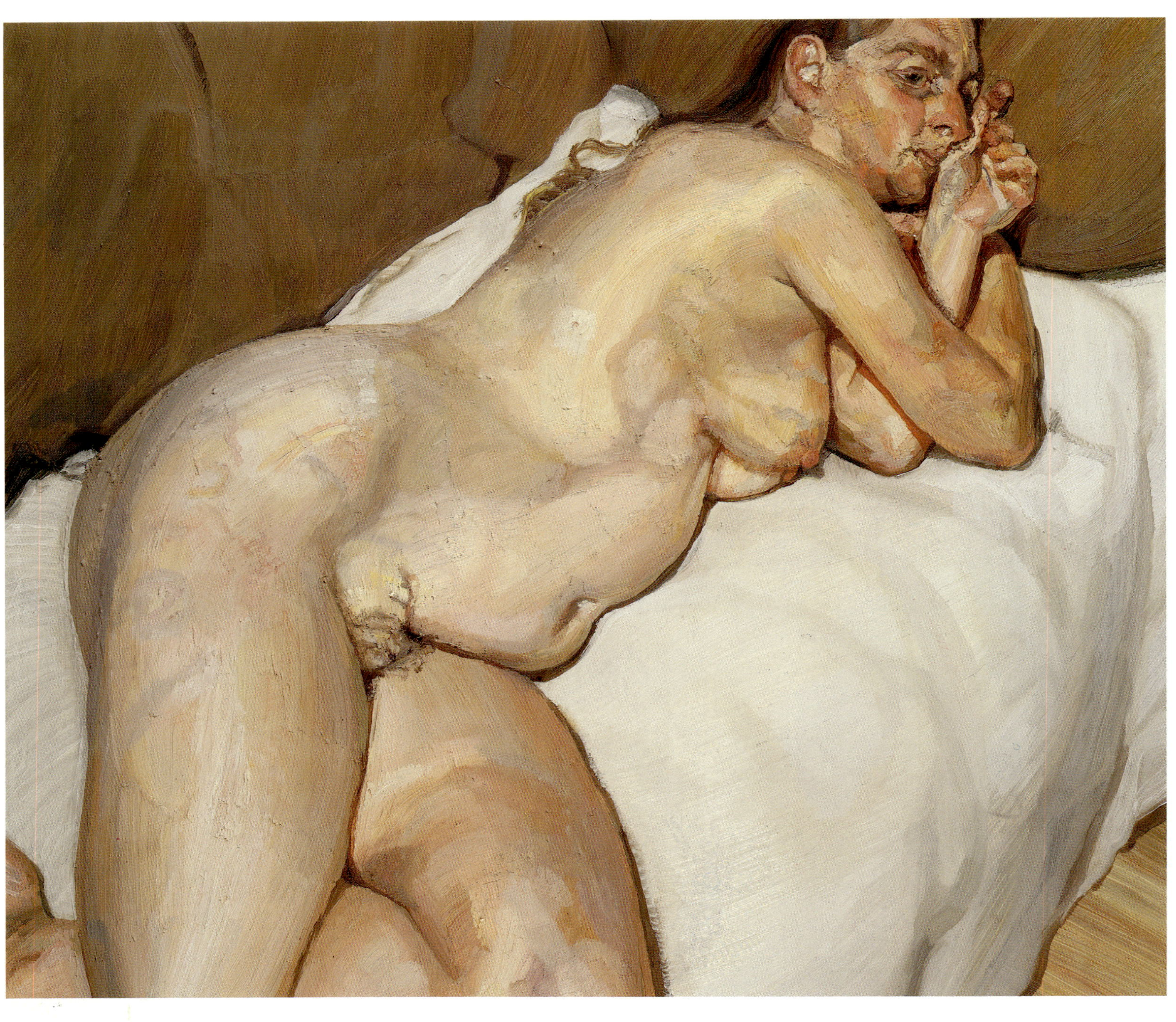

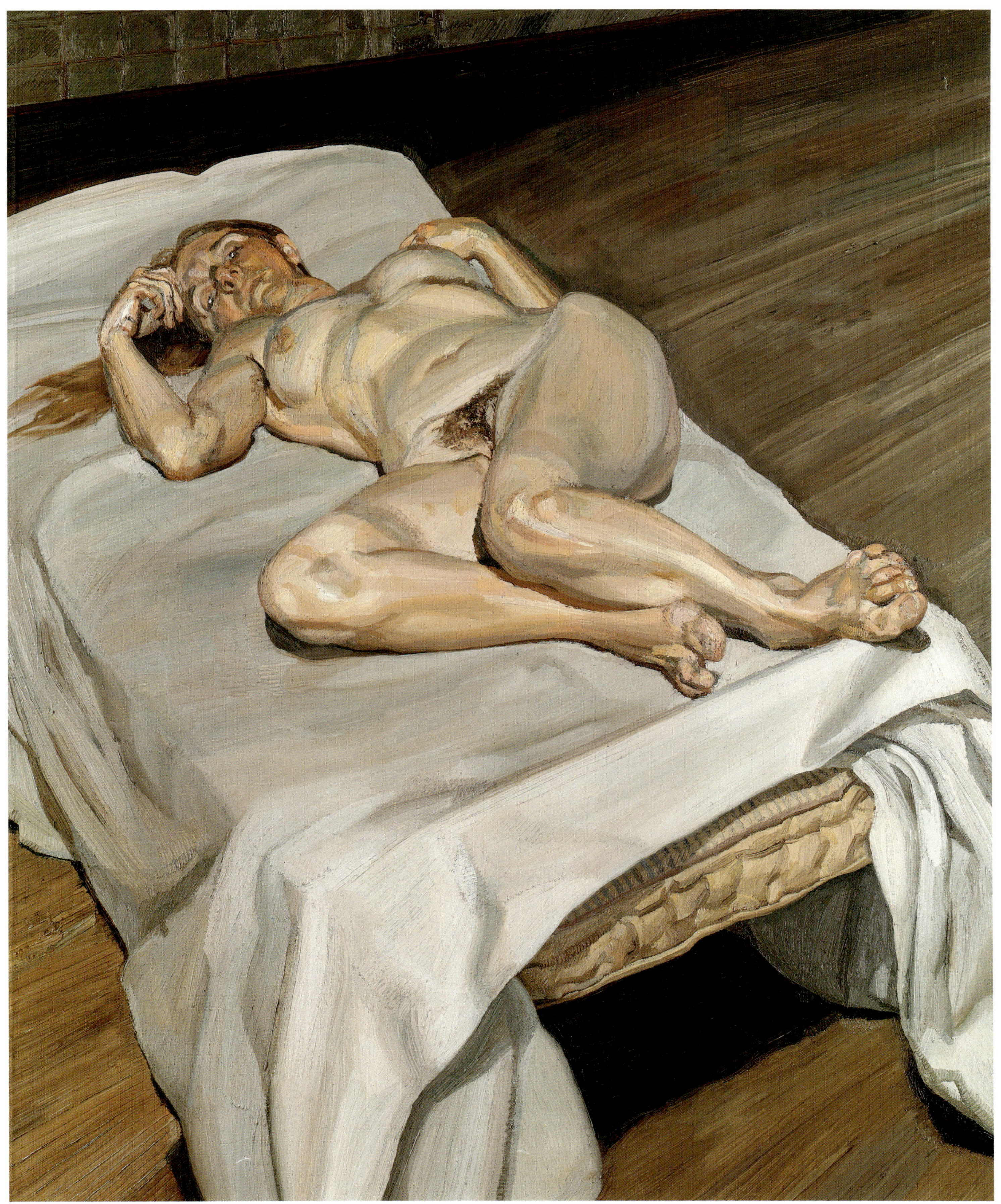

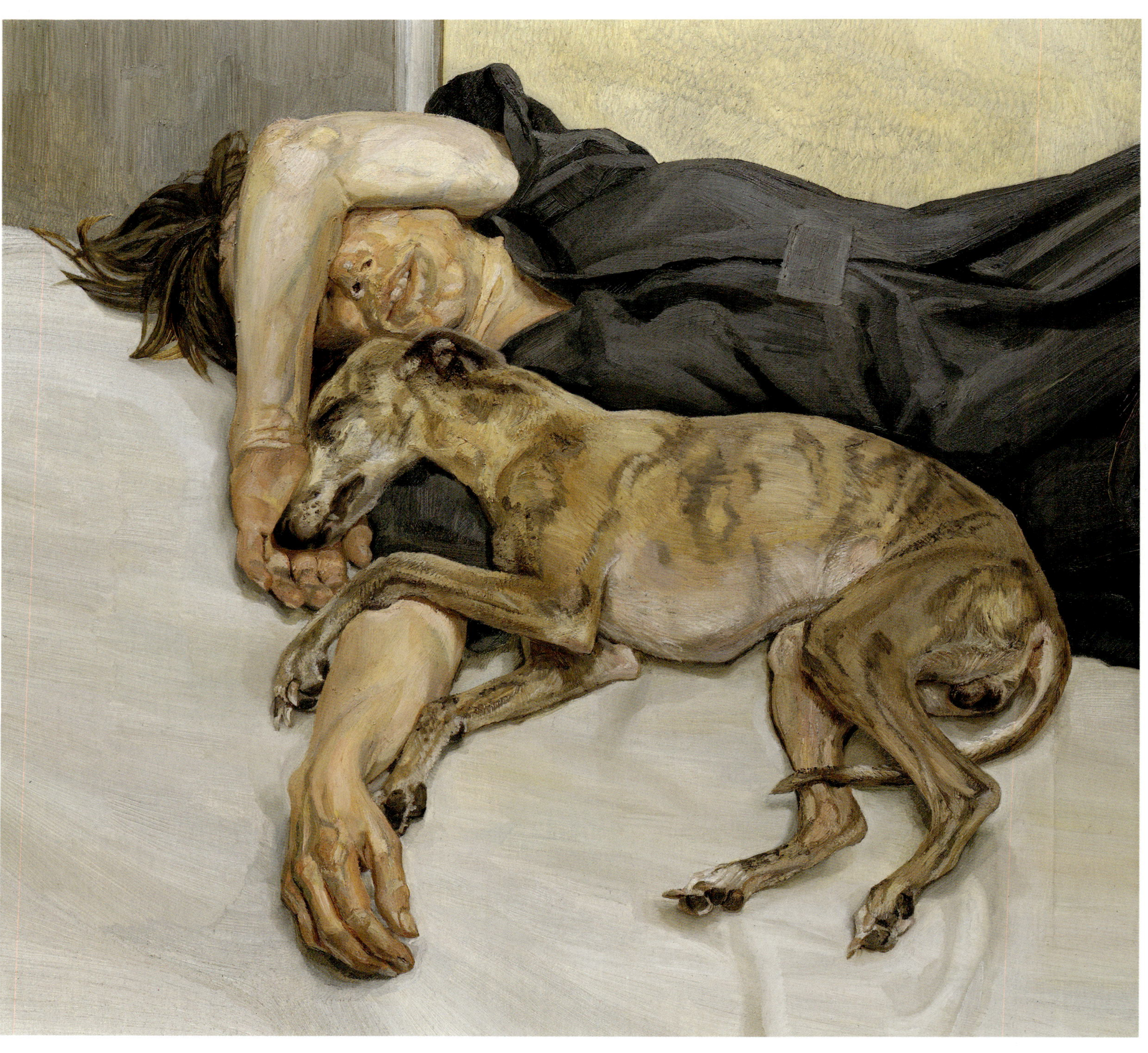

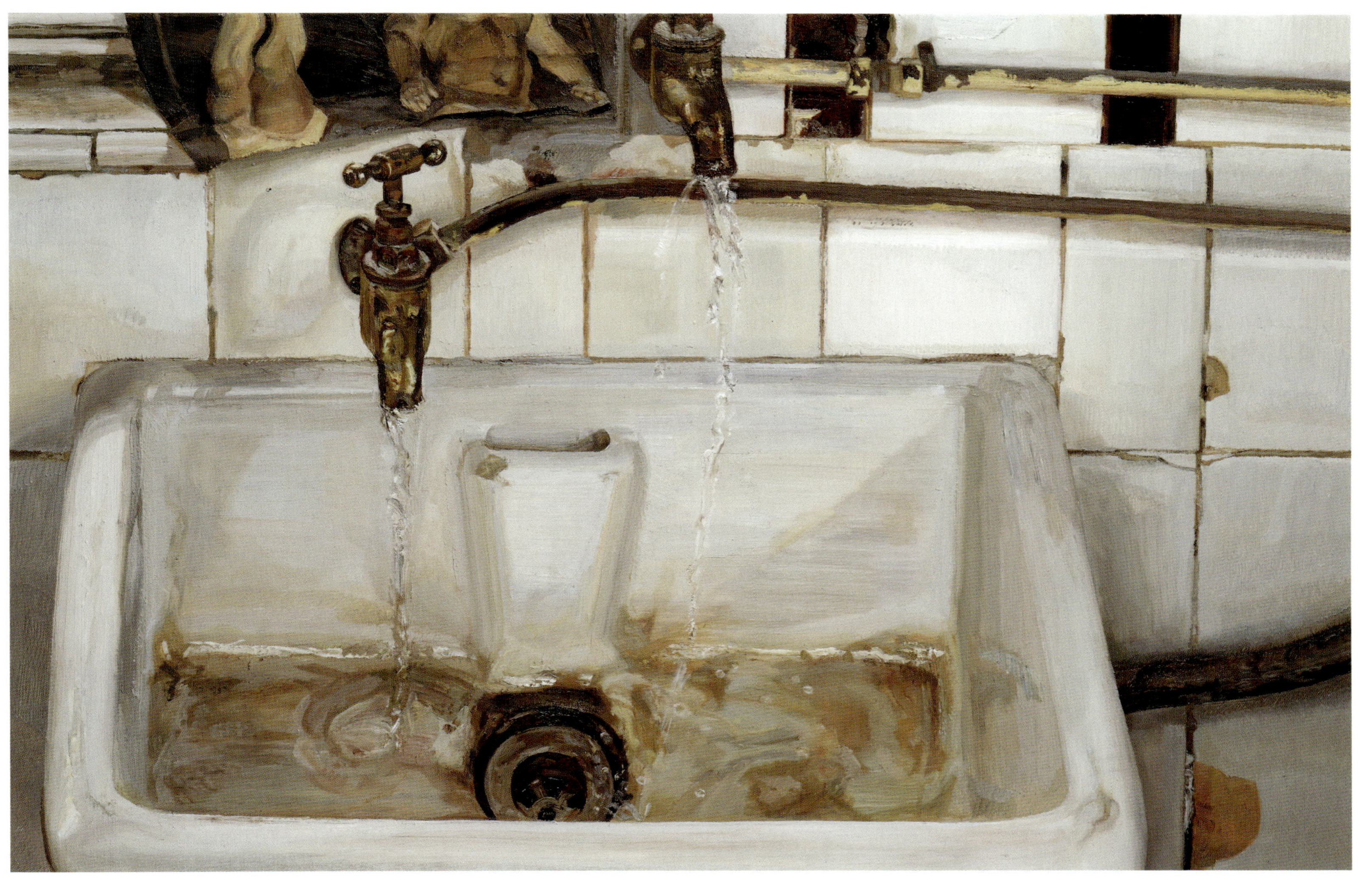

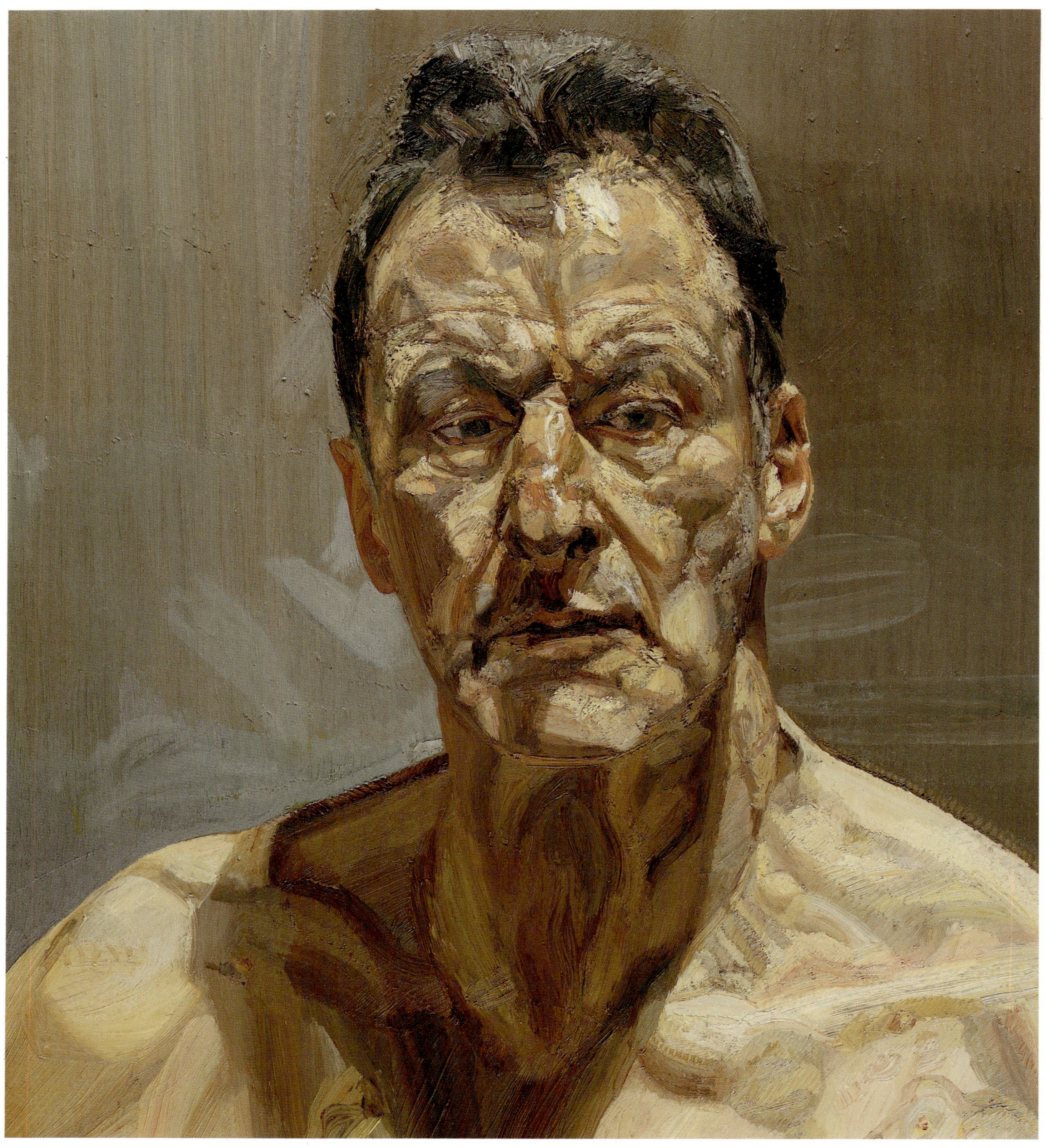

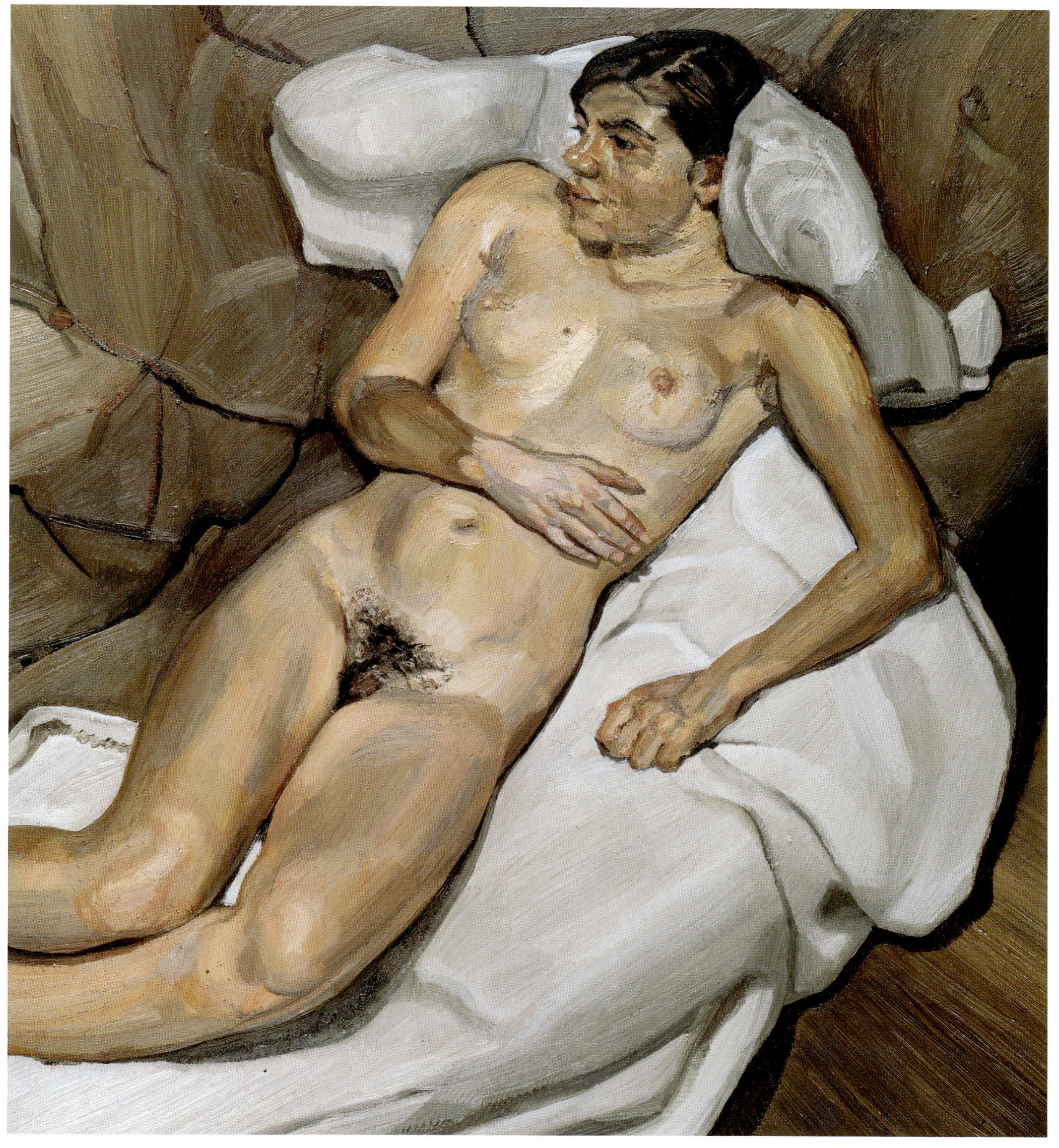

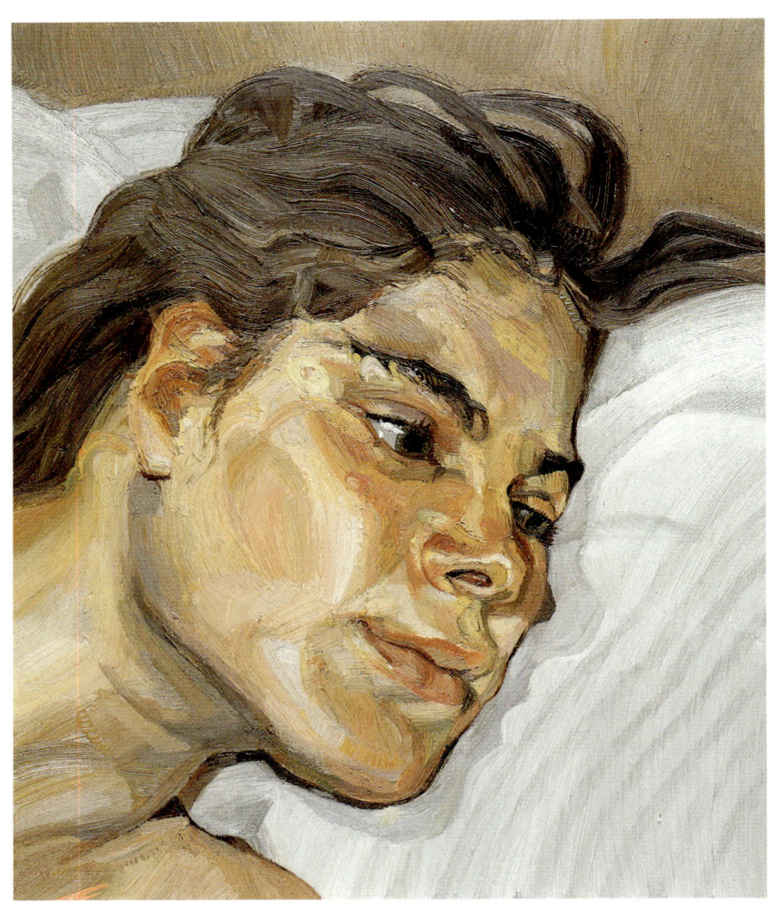

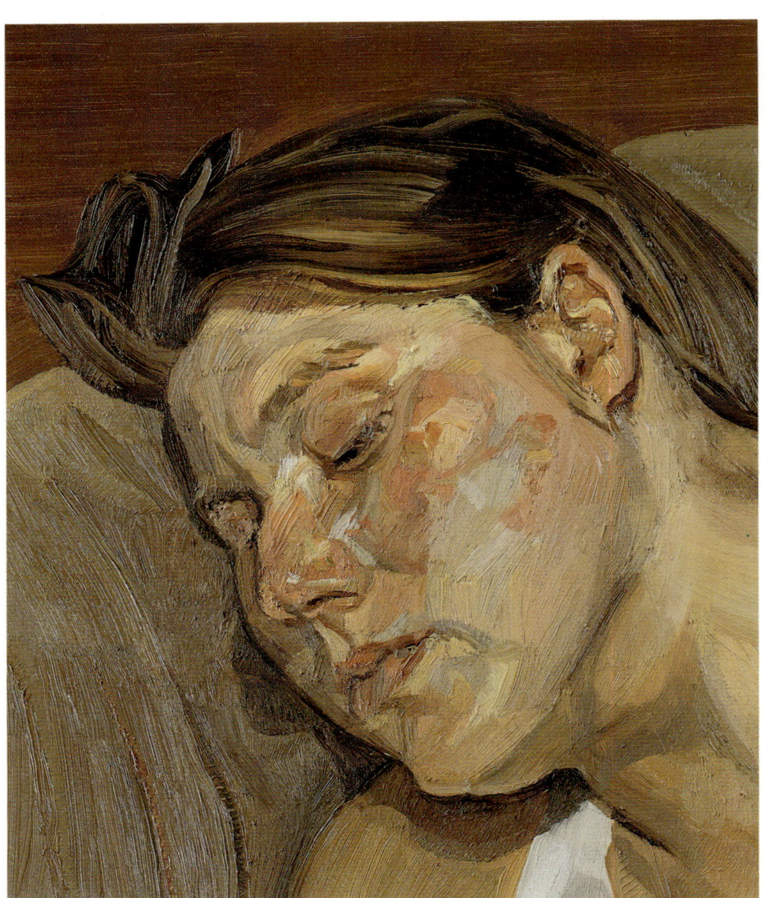

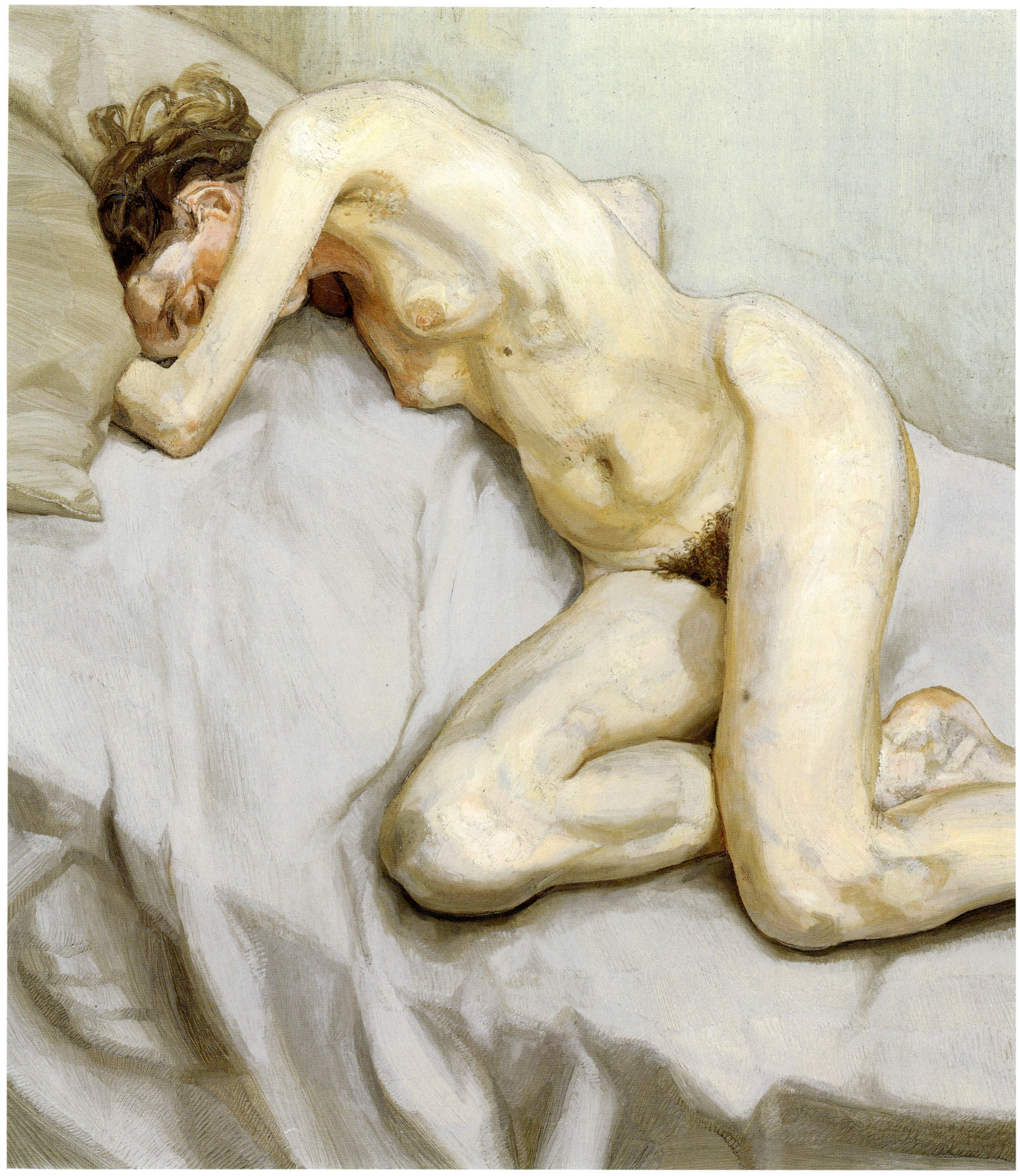

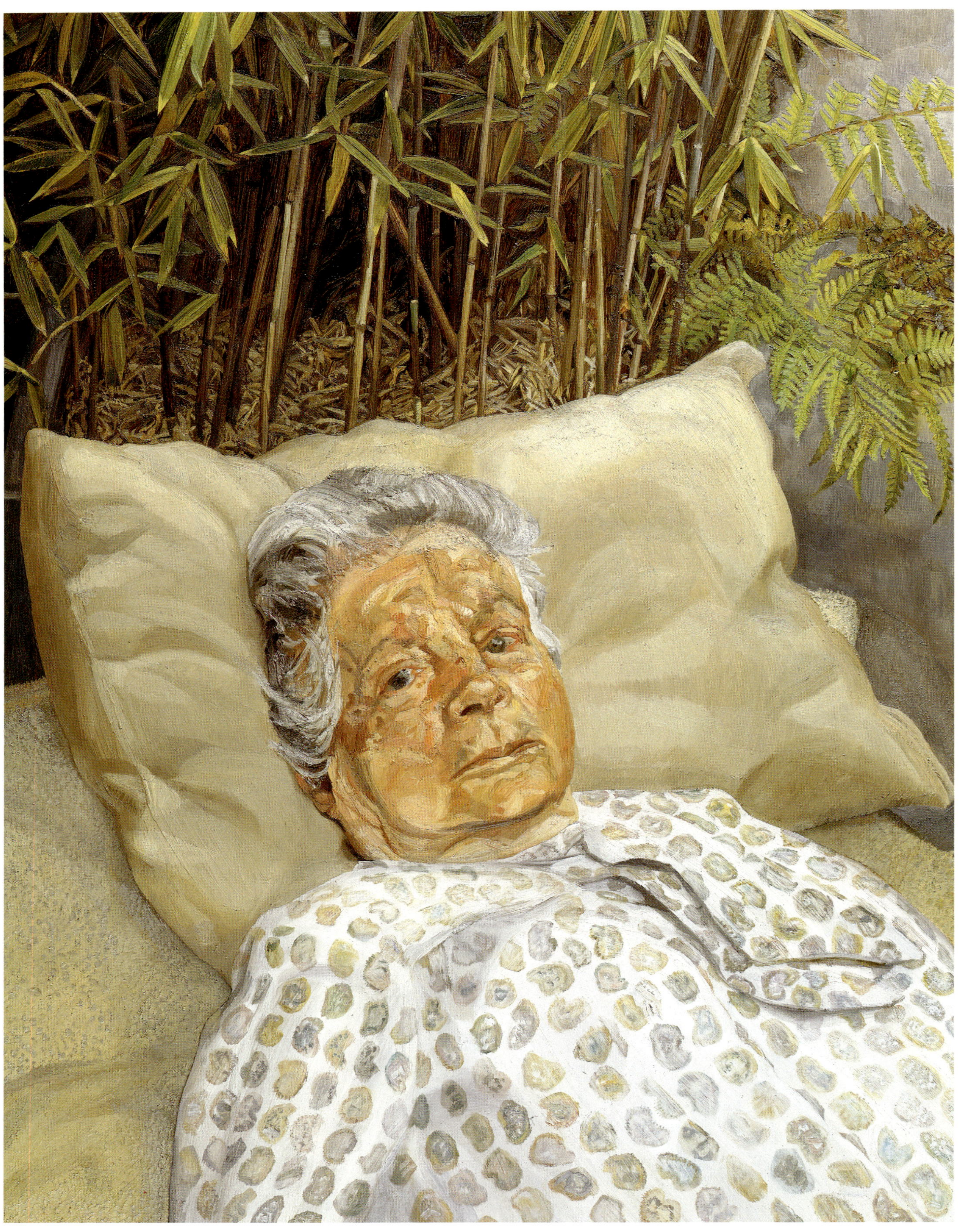

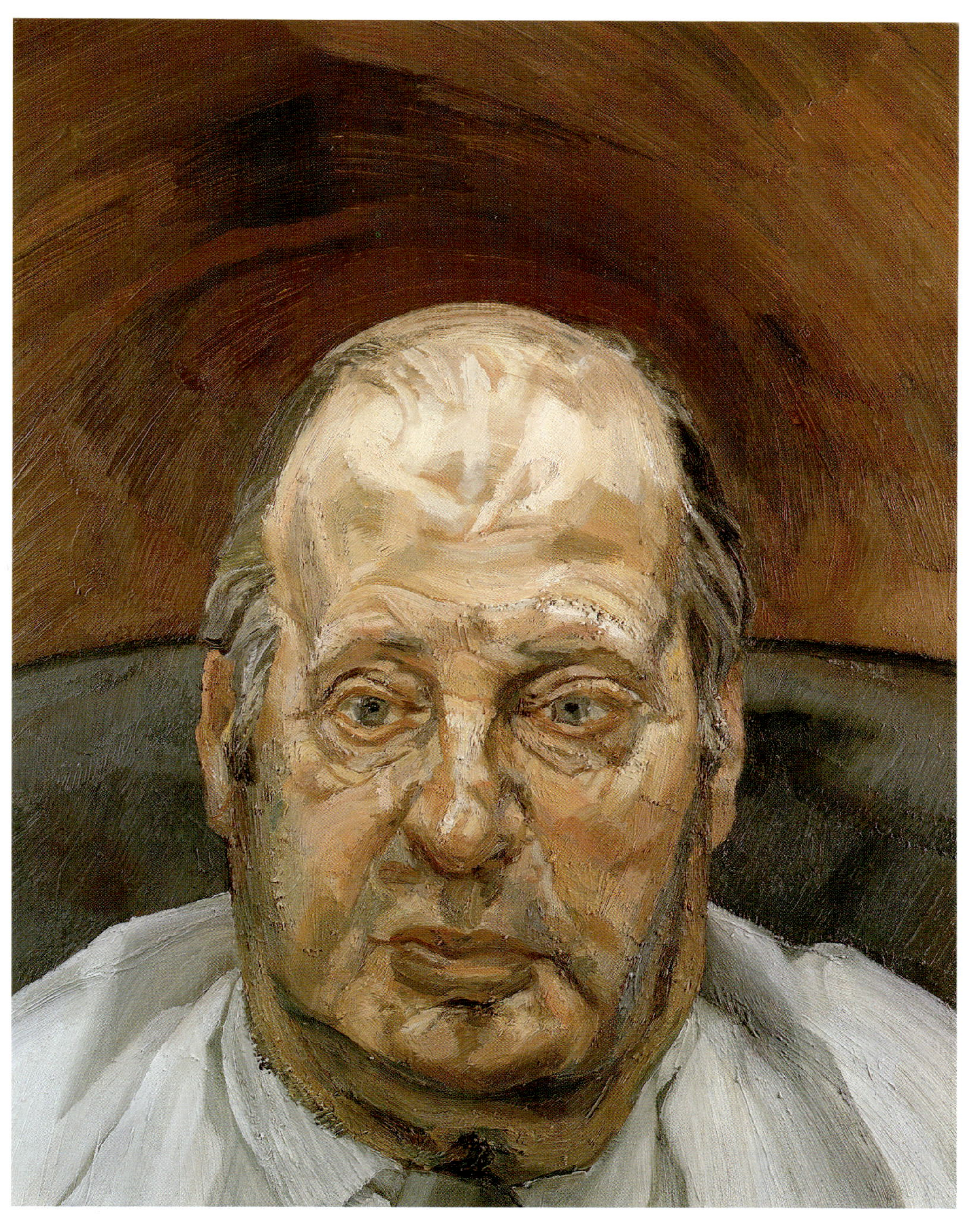

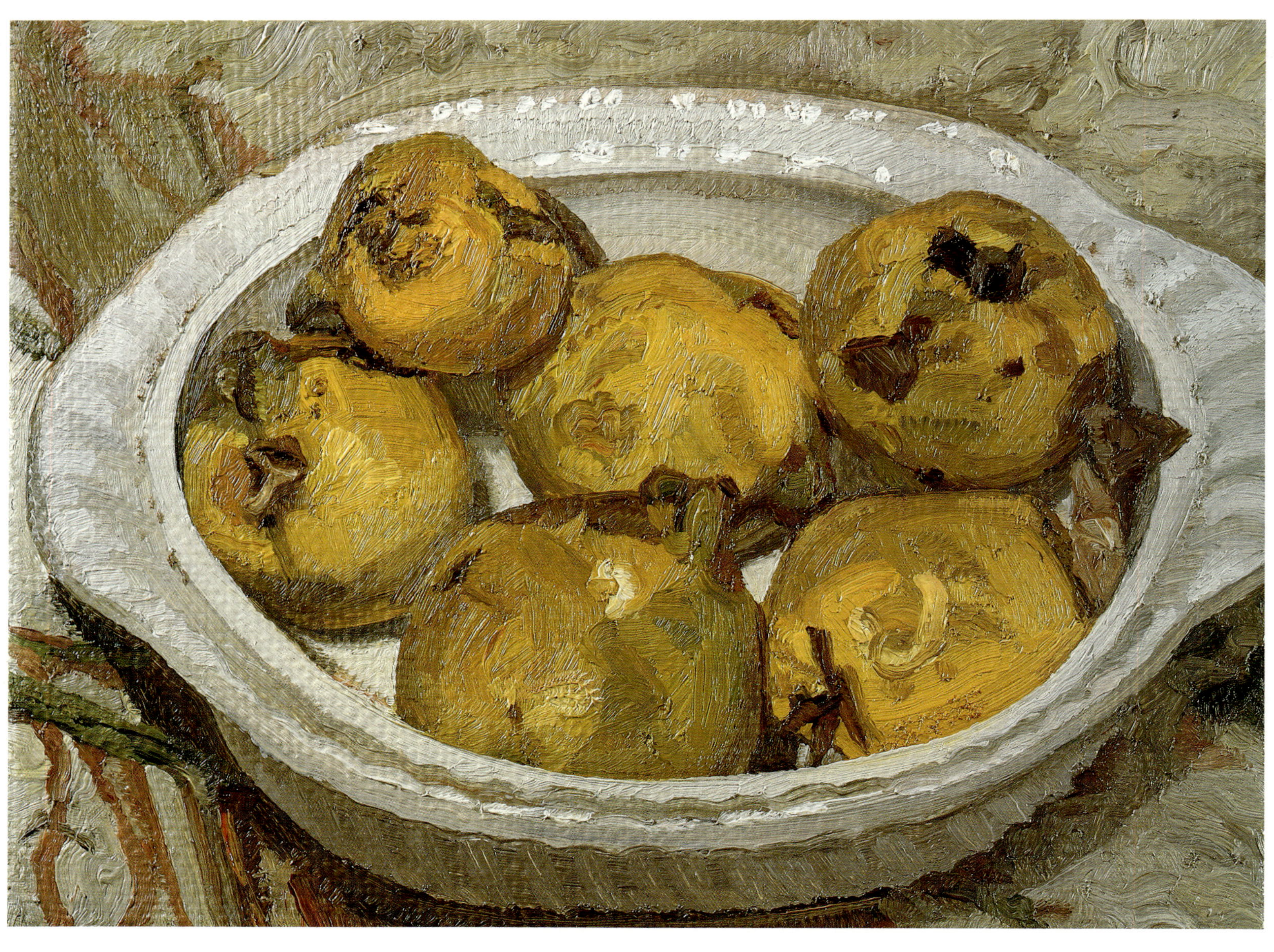

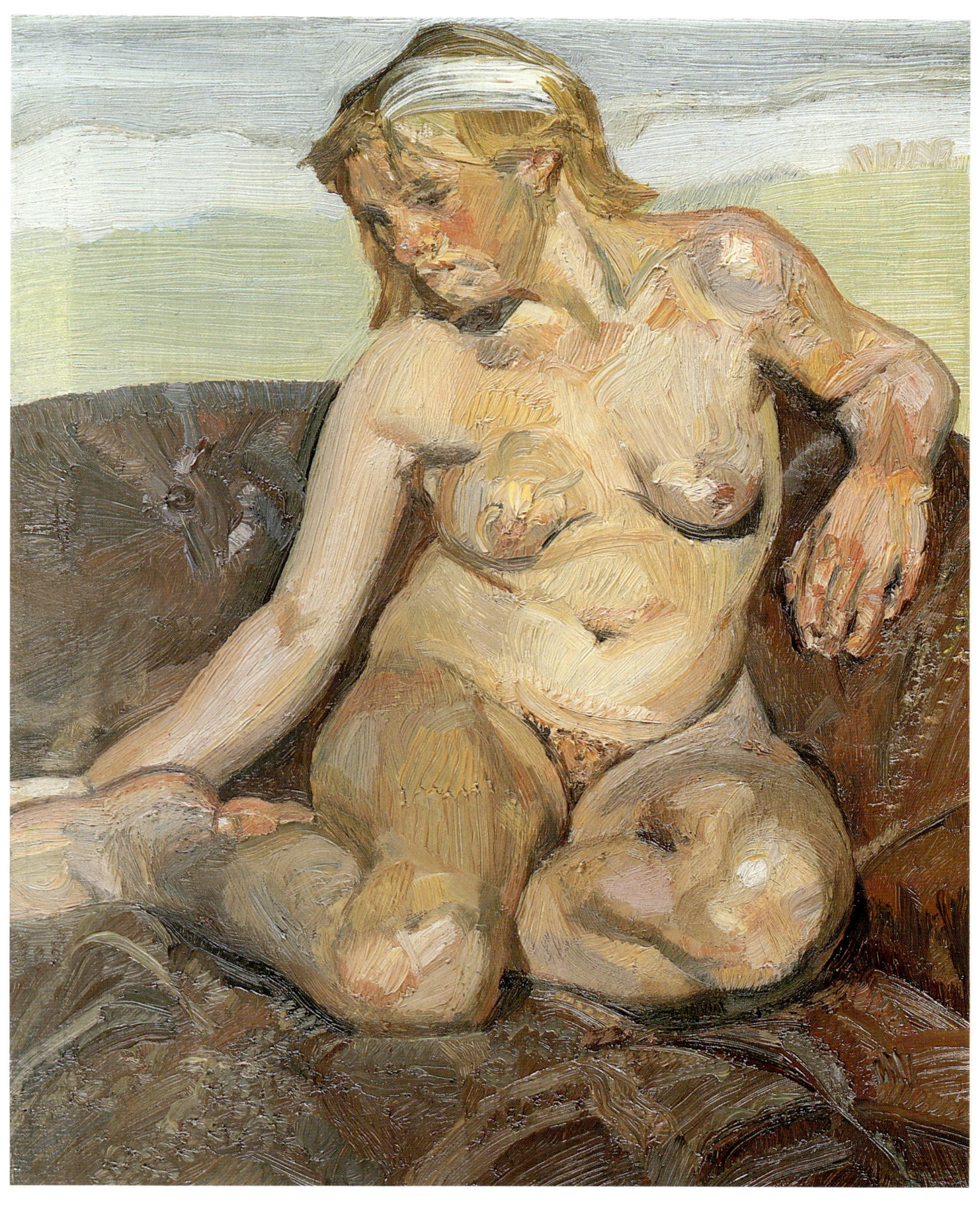

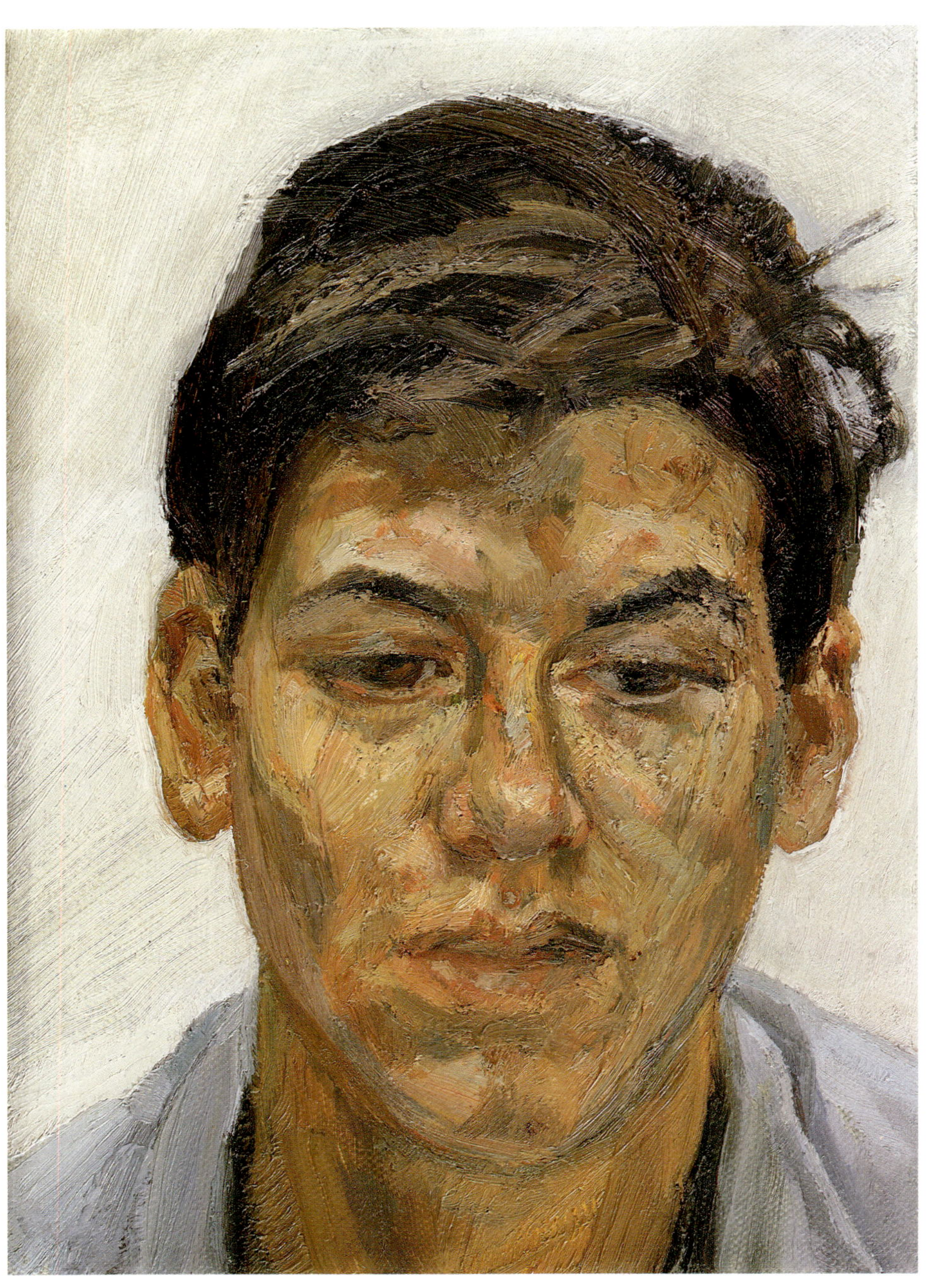

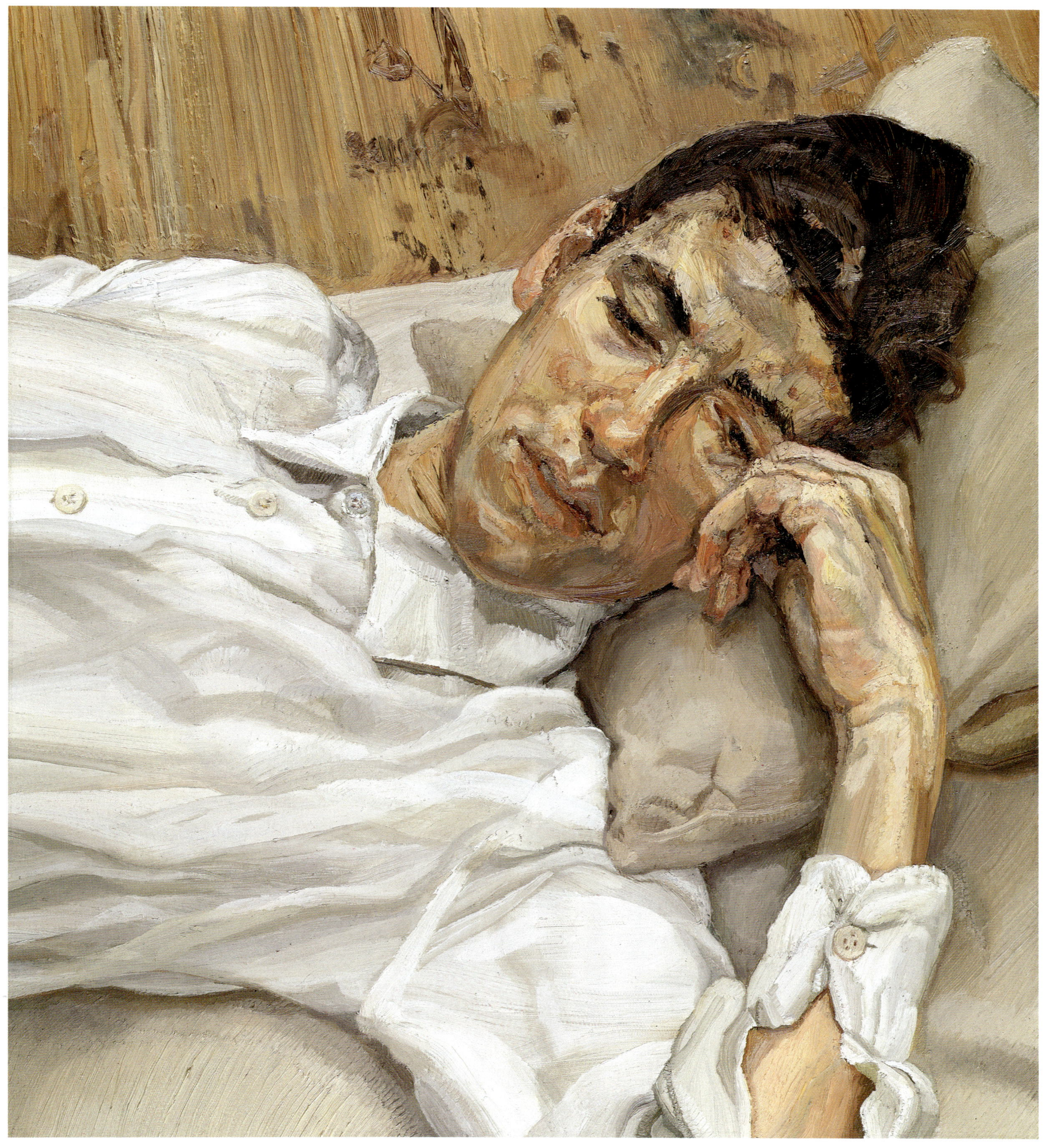

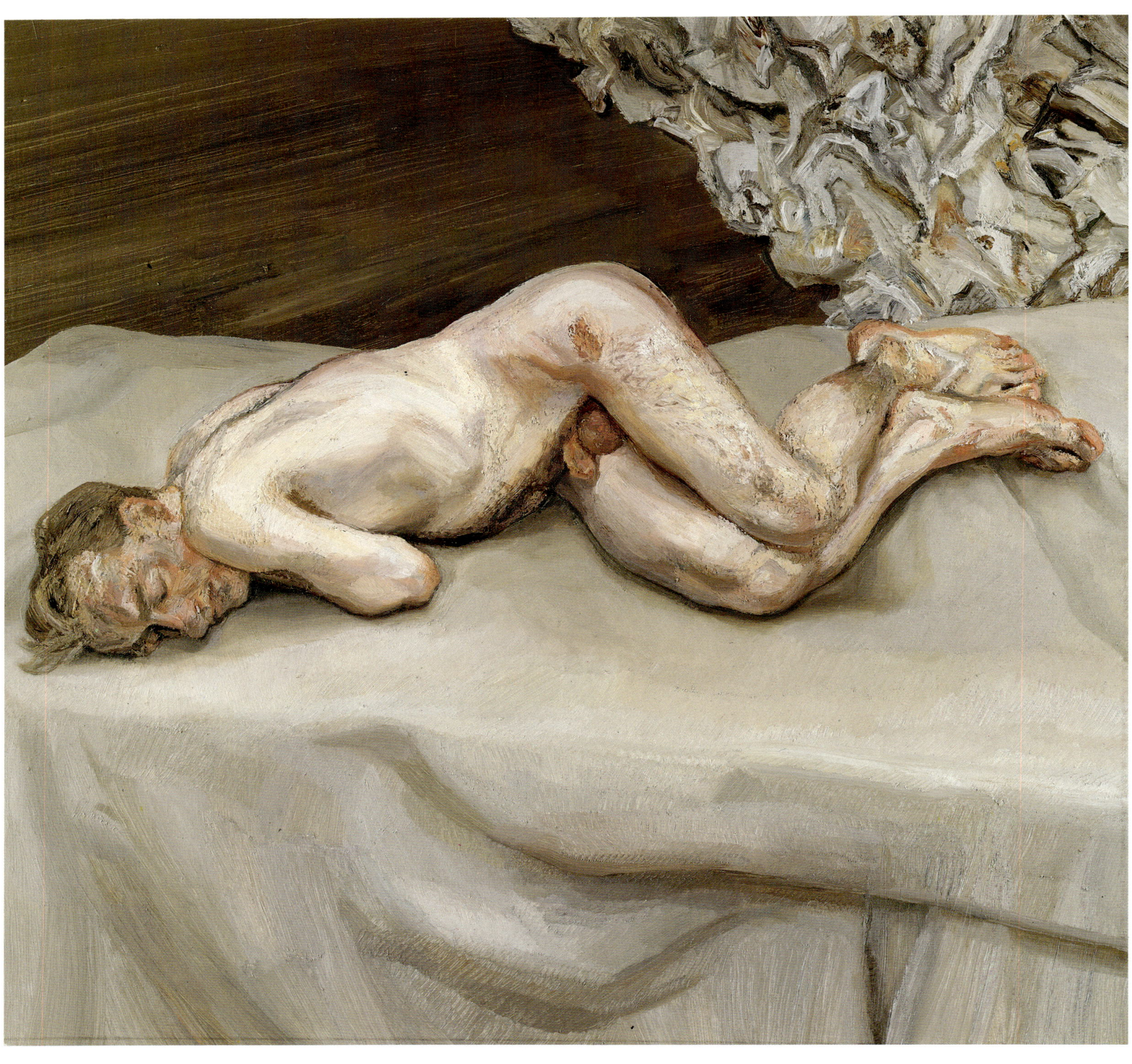

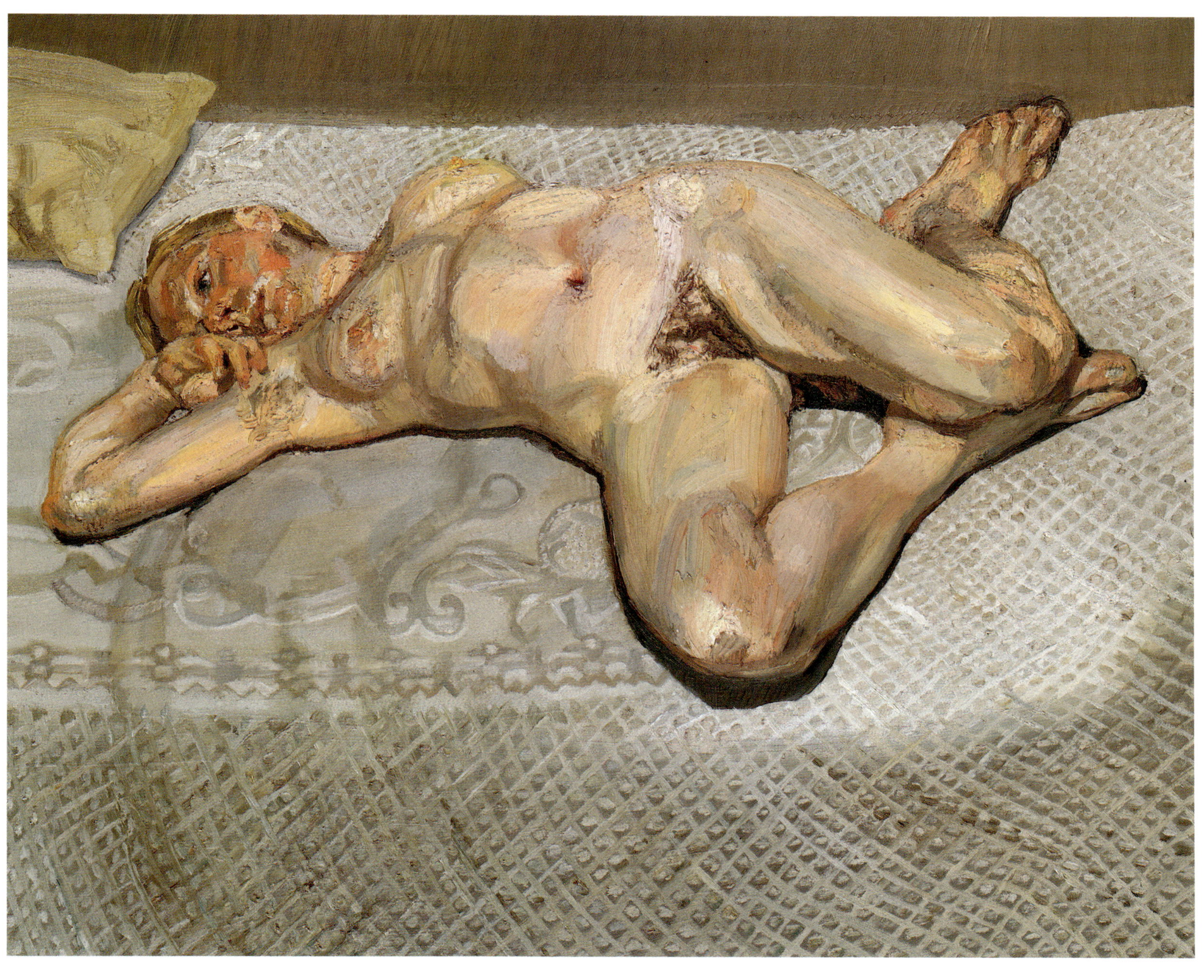

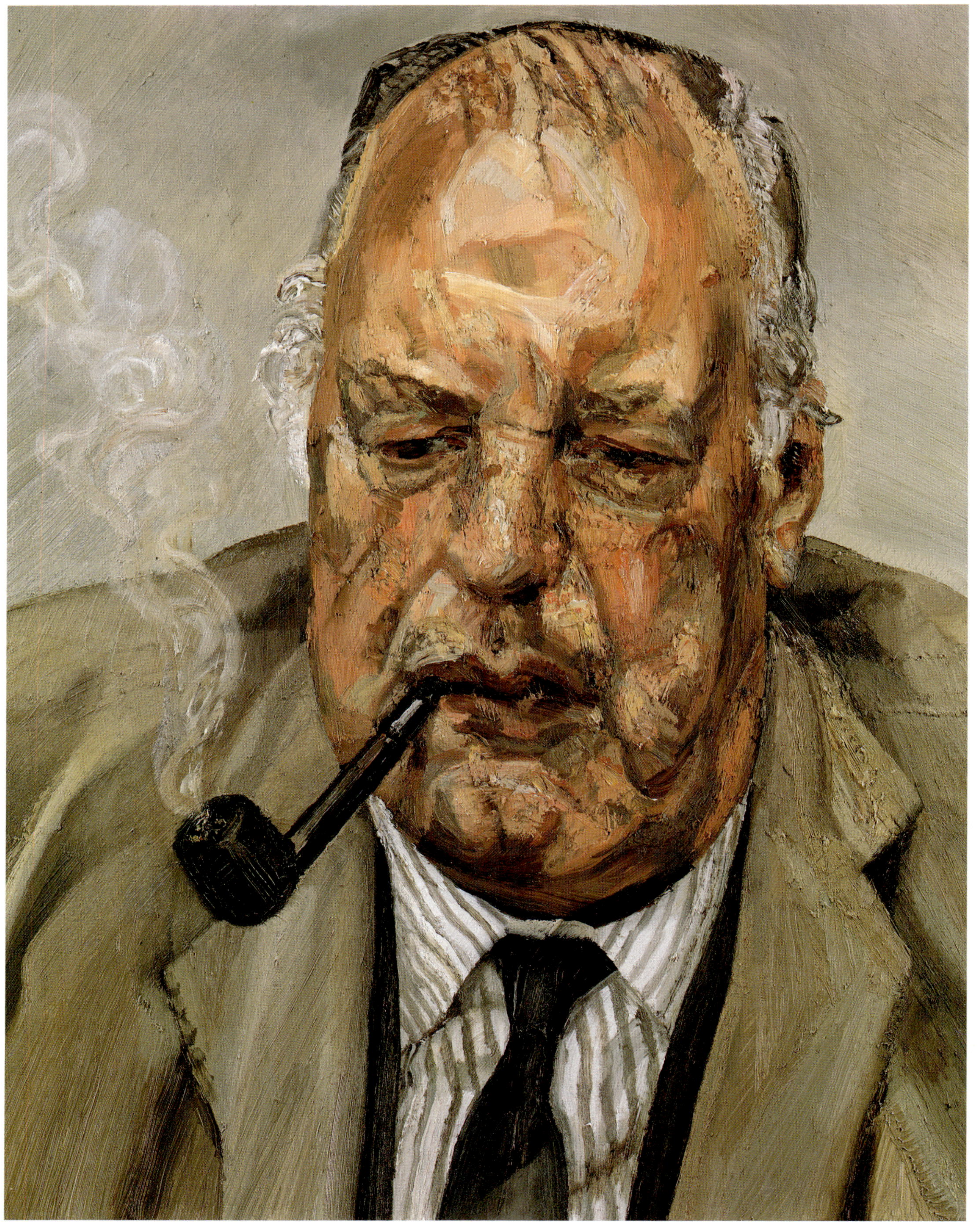

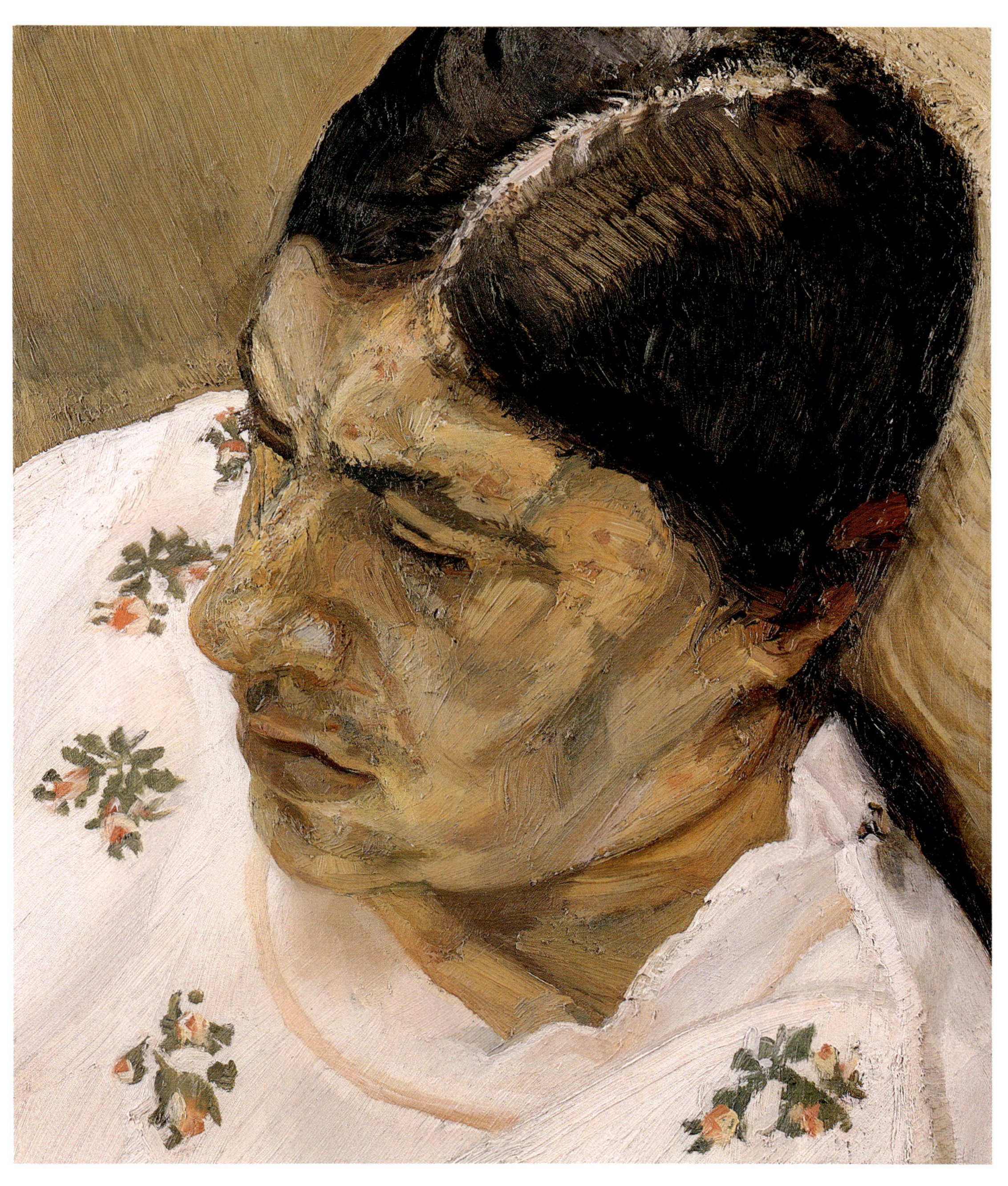

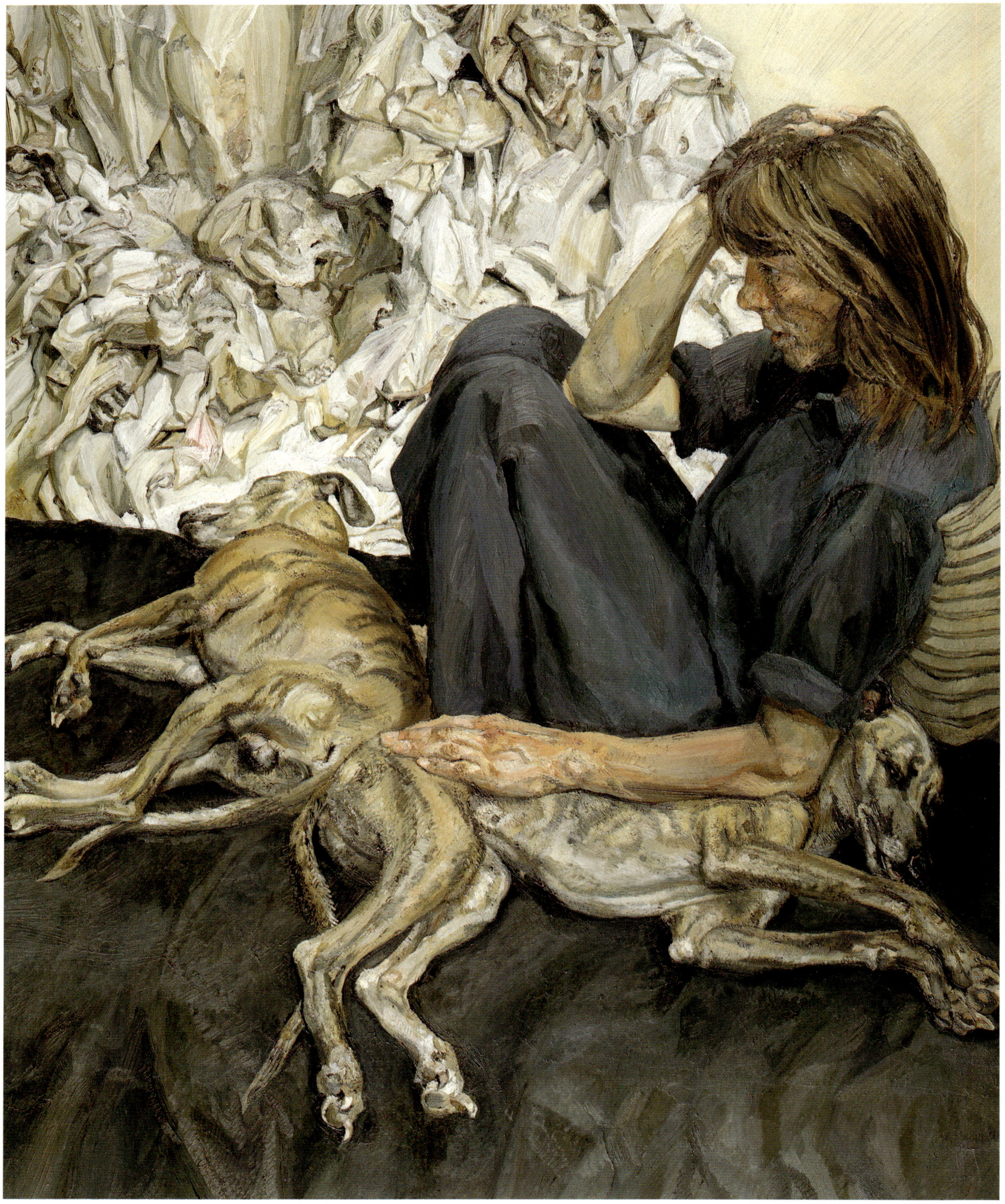

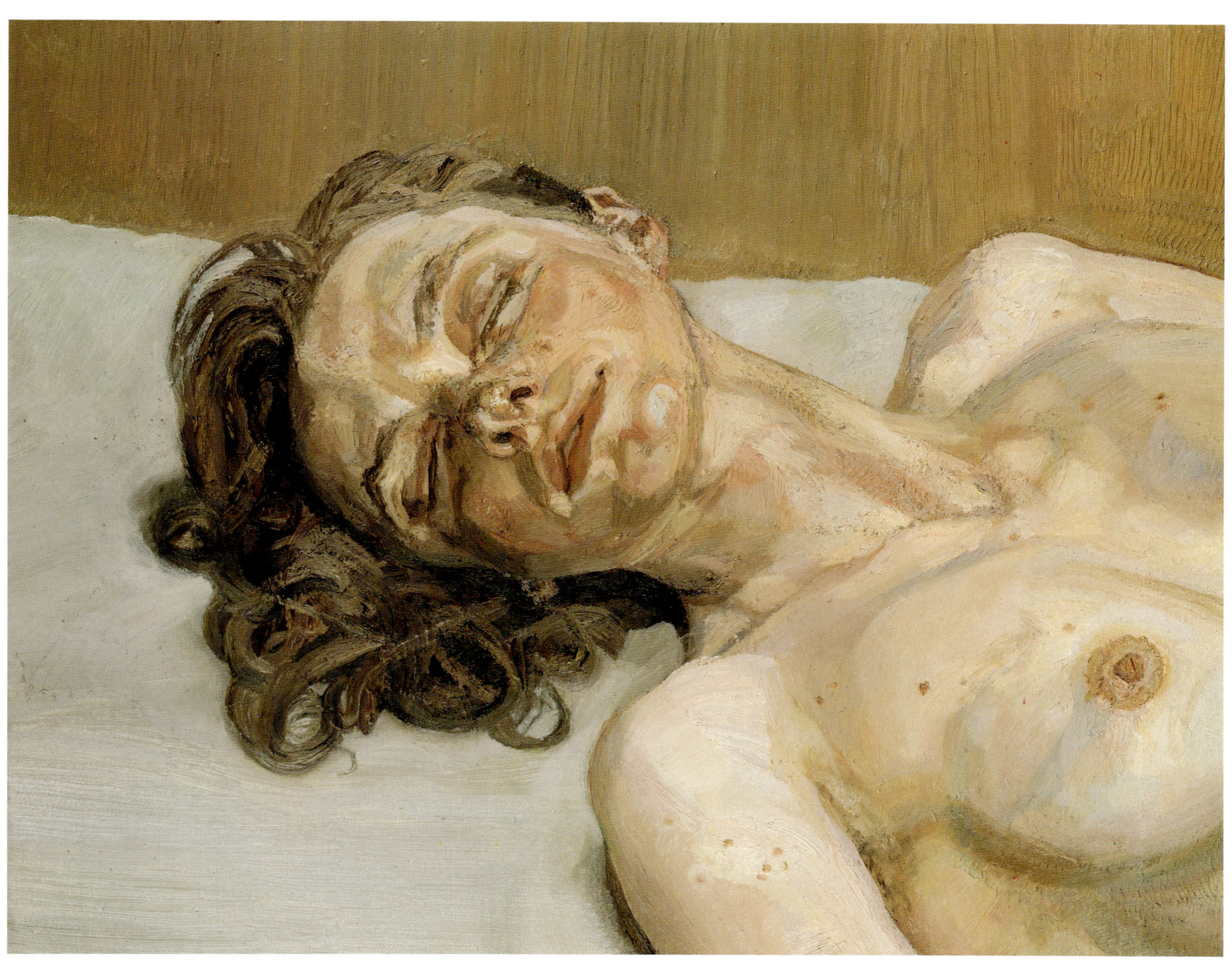

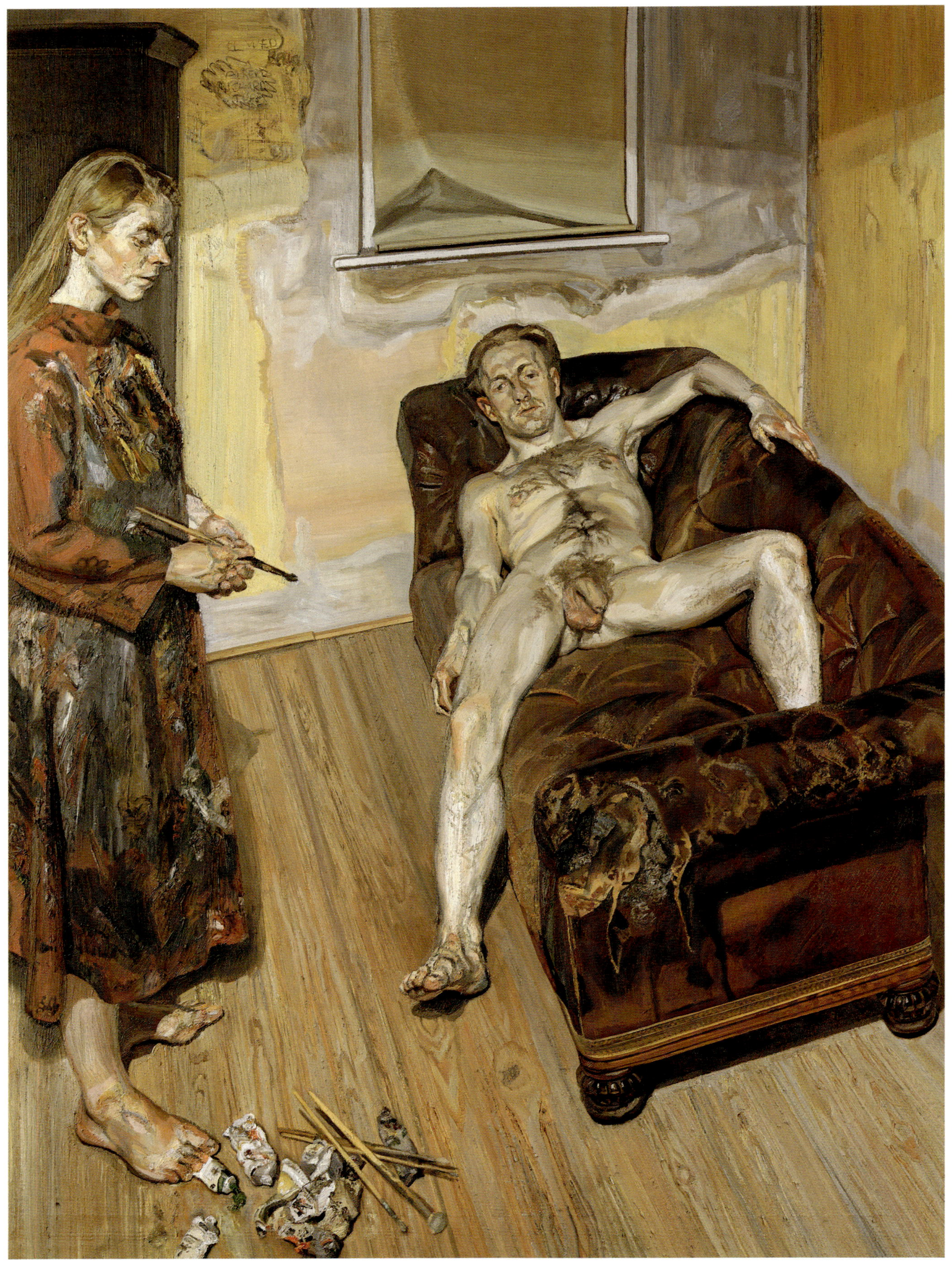

Lucian Freud

1922	Born December, in Berlin
1933	Came to Britain
1939	Naturalized British subject
1938/39	Studied at Central School of Arts and Crafts, London
1939/42	East Anglian School of Painting and Drawing, Dedham
1942/43	Part-time study at Goldsmiths' College, London
1946/47	Painted in Paris and Greece
1951	Arts Council Prize, Festival of Britain
1953/54	Visitor, Slade School of Fine Art, London
1983	Created a Companion of Honour
	Lives in London

List of Plates

1
Girl in a white dress, 1947
conté, crayon and pastel on buff paper
57 × 48 cm
Mrs Pamela Wynn

2
Girl in a dark jacket, 1947
oil on panel
47 × 38.1 cm
Private collection

3
Girl with a kitten, 1947
oil on canvas
39.5 × 29.5 cm
Private collection, courtesy James Kirkman Ltd., London

4
Girl with roses, 1947/48
oil on canvas
105.5 × 74.5 cm
The British Council

5
Girl with leaves, 1948
conté and pastel on grey paper
48 × 42 cm
Museum of Modern Art, New York

6
Sleeping nude, 1950
oil on canvas
76.2 × 101.6 cm
Private collection, Canada

7
Girl with a white dog, 1951/52
oil on canvas
76.2 × 101.6 cm
Trustees of the Tate Gallery

8
Head of a woman, 1950
oil on copper
19.5 × 14.5 cm
The Duke of Devonshire and the Trustees of the Chatsworth Settlement

9
Girl in a dark dress, 1951
oil on canvas
40.6 × 30.5 cm
Private collection, courtesy James Kirkman Ltd., London

10
Interior in Paddington, 1951
oil on canvas
152.4 × 114.3 cm
The Trustees of the National Museums and Galleries on Merseyside, Walker Art Gallery, Liverpool

11
Francis Bacon, 1952
oil on copper
17.8 x 12.8 cm
Trustees of the Tate Gallery

12
John Minton, 1952
oil on canvas
40 × 25.4 cm
Collection Royal College of Art, London

13
Girl in bed, 1952
oil on canvas
45.7 × 30.5 cm
Private collection

14
Girl reading, 1952
oil on copper
20.3 × 15.2 cm
Private collection

15
Boy's head, 1952
oil on canvas
21.6 × 15.9 cm
Private collection

16
A woman painter, 1954
oil on canvas
40.6 × 35.5 cm
Private collection

17
Hotel bedroom, 1954
oil on canvas
91.5 × 61 cm
The Beaverbrook Foundation, Beaverbrook Art Gallery, Fredericton, New Brunswick, Canada

18
A young painter, 1957/58
oil on canvas
40.8 × 39.4 cm
The Directors of Baring Brothers & Co. Ltd.

19
Man in a mackintosh, 1957/58
oil on canvas
61 × 61 cm
Private collection

20
Woman smiling, 1958/59
oil on canvas
71 × 55.8 cm
Private collection

21
Pregnant girl, 1960/61
oil on canvas
91.5 × 71 cm
Jacqueline and Gilbert de Botton, Switzerland

22
Head on a green sofa, 1960/61
oil on canvas
91.5 × 91.5 cm
By courtesy of the Lambton Trustees

23
Figure with bare arms, 1961/62
oil on canvas
91.5 × 91.5 cm
By courtesy of the Lambton Trustees

24
Baby on a green sofa, 1961
oil on canvas
55.8 × 62.2 cm
The Duchess of Devonshire

25
Sleeping head, 1962
oil on canvas
66 × 50.8 cm
Private collection

26
Red haired man on a chair, 1962/63
oil on canvas
91.5 × 91.5 cm
Erich Sommer

27
Man's head (self portrait), 1963
oil on canvas
53.3 × 50.8 cm
Whitworth Art Gallery, University of Manchester

28
John Deakin, 1963/64
oil on canvas
30.2 × 24.8 cm
Private collection

29
Naked child laughing, 1963
oil on canvas
34 × 28 cm
James Kirkman Ltd., London

30
Cyclamen, 1964
oil on canvas
45.7 × 49.2 cm
Private collection

31
A man and his daughter, 1963/64
oil on canvas
61 × 61 cm
Private collection

32
Michael Andrews and June, 1965/66
oil on canvas
60 × 70 cm
Private collection

33
Reflection with two children (self portrait), 1965
oil on canvas
91.5 × 91.5 cm
Thyssen-Bornemisza Collection, Lugano, Switzerland

34
Interior with hand mirror (self portrait), 1967
oil on canvas
25.5 × 17.8 cm
Private collection

35
Naked girl, 1966
oil on canvas
61 × 61 cm
Lent by Mr Steve Martin

36
Girl in a fur coat, 1967
oil on canvas
61 × 51 cm
The Fukuoka Sogo Bank Ltd.

37
Naked girl asleep, I, 1967
oil on canvas
61 × 61 cm
Private collection

38
Naked girl asleep, II, 1968
oil on canvas
55.8 × 55.8 cm
Private collection

39
Interior with plant, reflection listening (self portrait), 1967/68
oil on canvas
121.8 × 121.8 cm
Private collection

40
Buttercups, 1968
oil on canvas
53.3 × 50.8 cm
Private collection

41
Large interior, Paddington, 1968/69
oil on canvas
183 × 122 cm
Thyssen-Bornemisza Collection, Lugano, Switzerland

42
A filly, 1970
oil on canvas
19 × 26.6 cm
Anthony d'Offay Gallery, London

43
Paddington interior, Harry Diamond, 1970
oil on canvas
71 × 71 cm
University of Liverpool Art Gallery

44
Wasteground with houses, Paddington, 1970/72
oil on canvas
167.5 × 101.5 cm
Private collection

45
Factory in north London, 1972
oil on canvas
71 × 71 cm
Private collection

46
The painter's mother, II, 1972
oil on canvas
17.8 × 14 cm
Private collection

47
The painter's mother, III, 1972
oil on canvas
32.4 × 23.5 cm
Private collection

48
Large interior W.9, 1973
oil on canvas
91.5 × 91.5 cm
The Duke of Devonshire and the Trustees of the Chatsworth Settlement

49
Annie and Alice, 1975
oil on canvas
22.5 × 27 cm
Private collection, courtesy James Kirkman Ltd., London

50
Small naked portrait, 1973/74
oil on canvas
22 × 27 cm
Visitors of the Ashmolean Museum, Oxford

51
Last portrait, 1974/75
oil on canvas
61 × 61 cm
Thyssen-Bornemisza Collection, Lugano, Switzerland

52
Head of the big man, 1975
oil on canvas
40.9 × 27 cm
Private collection

53
Frank Auerbach, 1975/76
oil on canvas
40 × 26.5 cm
Private collection

54
The painter's mother resting, II, 1976/77
oil on canvas
26 × 40.6 cm
Private collection

55
The painter's mother resting, III, 1977
oil on canvas
59.1 × 69.2 cm
Private collection

56
The big man, 1976/77
oil on canvas
91.4 × 91.4 cm
Private collection

57
Two plants, 1977/80
oil on canvas
152.4 × 121.9 cm
Trustees of the Tate Gallery

58
Naked man with rat, 1977/78
oil on canvas
91.5 × 91.5 cm
Collection Art Gallery of Western Australia

59
Naked man with his friend, 1978/80
oil on canvas
90.2 × 105.5 cm
Private collection, courtesy James Kirkman Ltd., London

60
Night portrait, 1977/78
oil on canvas
71.1 × 71.1 cm
Private collection

61
Rose, 1978/79
oil on canvas
91.5 × 78.5 cm
Sukejiro Itani, Tokyo, Japan

62
Esther, 1980
oil on canvas
48.9 × 38.3 cm
Private collection, courtesy James Kirkman Ltd., London

63
Naked portrait with reflection, 1980
oil on canvas
90.3 × 90.3 cm
Private collection

64
Naked girl with egg, 1980/81
oil on canvas
75 × 60.5 cm
The British Council

65
Naked portrait, 1980/81
oil on canvas
90 × 75 cm
Private collection

66
Seated figure, 1980/82
oil on canvas
35 × 22.3 cm
Private collection

67
Bella, 1981
oil on canvas
35.5 × 30.5 cm
Collection of Roy and Cecily Langdale Davis

68
Large interior W.11 (after Watteau), 1981/83
oil on canvas
186 × 198 cm
Private collection, courtesy James Kirkman Ltd., London

69
Reflection (self portrait), 1981/82
oil on canvas
30.5 × 25.4 cm
Private collection

70
Man in a sports shirt, 1982/83
oil on canvas
50.9 × 40.7 cm
Private collection

71
The painter's mother, 1982/84
oil on canvas
105.4 × 127.6 cm
Private collection, courtesy James Kirkman Ltd., London

72
Blond girl, night portrait, 1980/85
oil on canvas
71 × 71 cm
Private collection

73
Girl with fair hair, 1983/84
oil on canvas
51 × 41 cm
James Kirkman Ltd., London

74
Girl in striped nightdress, 1983/85
oil on canvas
30.5 × 25.6 cm
Private collection

75
Fred, 1985
oil on canvas
17.9 × 12.1 cm
Private collection

76
Man in a chair, 1983/85
oil on canvas
120.7 × 100.4 cm
Thyssen-Bornemisza Collection, Lugano, Switzerland

77
Two Irishmen in W.11, 1984/85
oil on canvas
172.7 × 141.6 cm
Private collection

78
Naked woman on a sofa, 1984/85
oil on canvas
51 × 60.5 cm
Private collection, USA

79
Night portrait, 1985/86
oil on canvas
92.8 × 73.2 cm
Hirshhorn Museum and Sculpture Garden, Smithsonian Institution, Washington, D.C.

80
Double portrait, 1985/86
oil on canvas
78.8 × 88.9 cm
Private collection

81
Two Japanese wrestlers by a sink, 1983/87
oil on canvas
50.9 × 78.8 cm
Courtesy of the Art Institute of Chicago

82
Reflection (self portrait), 1985
oil on canvas
56.2 × 51.2 cm
Private collection

83
Bella, 1982/83
oil on canvas
61 × 55.9 cm
Private collection

84
Esther, 1982/83
oil on canvas
35.5 × 31 cm
Private collection

85
Ib, 1983/84
oil on canvas
30.5 × 35.6 cm
Private collection

86
Naked girl, 1985/86
oil on canvas
81 × 71 cm
Private collection

87
The painter's mother, 1984
oil on canvas
87.6 × 70 cm
Private collection

88
The painter's brother Stephen, 1985/86
oil on canvas
51.2 × 41 cm
The National Museum of Wales, Cardiff

89
Quinces in a fluted bowl, 1984
oil on canvas
16.5 × 21.6 cm
Thyssen-Bornemisza Collection, Lugano, Switzerland

90
Girl holding her foot, 1985/86
oil on canvas
18.2 × 15 cm
Lefevre Gallery, London

91
Bella, 1986
oil on canvas
22.3 × 16 cm
Private collection

92
Bella, 1986/87
oil on canvas
55.9 × 50.8 cm
Private collection

93
Naked man on a bed, 1987
oil on canvas
56.5 × 61 cm
James Kirkman Ltd., London

94
Blond girl on a bed, 1987
oil on canvas
41 × 51 cm
James Kirkman Ltd., London

95
Man smoking, 1986/87
oil on canvas
51 × 41 cm
Private collection

96
Annabel, portrait III, 1987
oil on canvas
35.6 × 30.7 cm
Private collection

97
Triple portrait, 1986/87
oil on canvas
120 × 100 cm
Private collection

98
Girl with closed eyes, 1986/87
oil on canvas
45.9 × 58.7 cm
Private collection

99
Painter and model, 1986/87
oil on canvas
159.6 × 120.7 cm
Private collection

Selected Exhibitions

1944 Lefevre Gallery, London (with Felix Kelly and Julian Trevelyan)
1946 Lefevre Gallery, London (with Ben Nicholson, Graham Sutherland, Francis Bacon, Robert Colquhoun, John Craxton, Robert MacBryde and Julian Trevelyan)
1947 The London Gallery (with John Craxton)
1948 The London Gallery (with James Glesson, Robert Kippel, John Pemberton, Cawthra Mulock
Galerie René Drouin, Paris
1950 Hanover Gallery, London (with Roger Vieillard)
1952 Hanover Gallery, London (with Martin Froy)
Vancouver Art Gallery
1954 British Pavilion XXVIII Venice Biennale (with Ben Nicholson and Francis Bacon)
1958 Marlborough Fine Art, London
1963 Marlborough Fine Art, London
1968 Marlborough Fine Art, London
1972 Anthony d'Offay, London
1974 Retrospective exhibition, Hayward Gallery (Arts Council of Great Britain) and tour
'Pages from a sketchbook of 1941', Anthony d'Offay, London
1978 Anthony d'Offay, London
1979 Davis & Long Co, New York
Nishimura Gallery, Tokyo
1982 Anthony d'Offay, London
1983 Thomas Agnew & Sons, London
Bernard Jacobson, New York

Selected Group Exhibitions

1942 New Year Exhibition, Leicester Galleries, London
'Imaginative Art since the War', Leicester Galleries
1948 'Forty Years of Modern Art', Institute of Contemporary Art, London
1950 'London–Paris', Institute of Contemporary Art
1951 'Sixty Paintings for '51', Arts Council, London
'British Painting 1925/50', Arts Council
1952 'Recent Trends in Realist Painting', Institute of Contemporary Art
1953 'Portraits by Contemporary British Artists', Marlborough Fine Art, London
1955 'Daily Express Young Artists' Exhibition', New Burlington Galleries, London
1962 'British Self Portraits from Sickert to the Present Day', Arts Council
1963 'British Painting in the Sixties', Tate Gallery, London
1966 'British Painting since 1945', Tate Gallery
1967 'English Paintings 1951–1967', Norwich Castle Museum
'Recent British Painting from the Peter Stuyvesant Collection', Tate Gallery
1976 'The Human Clay', Arts Council of Great Britain, Hayward Gallery
'Real Life: Peter Moores Liverpool Project 4', Walker Art Gallery, Liverpool
1977 'British Painting 1952–1977', Royal Academy of Arts, London
1979 'Treasures from Chatsworth: The Devonshire Inheritance', Royal Academy of Arts
'The British Art Show', Arts Council of Great Britain touring exhibition
1981 'Eight Figurative Artists', Yale Center for British Art, New Haven
'A New Spirit in Painting', Royal Academy
1984 'The Hard Won Image', Tate Gallery
'As of Now', Peter Moores Liverpool Project 7, Walker Art Gallery
1984/85 'The Proper Study', The British Council: Lalit Akademi, Delhi; Jehangir Nicholson Museum of Modern Art, Bombay
1985 'The British Show', Art Gallery of New South Wales, Sydney, in association with The British Council
'A Singular Vision', Royal Albert Museum, Exeter, and tour
1986 'Forty Years of Modern Art,' Tate Gallery
1987 'British Art in the 20th Century', Royal Academy of Arts
1987/88 'A School of London: Six Figurative Painters', Kunstnernes Hus, Oslo; Museum of Modern Art, Louisiana; Museo d'Arte Moderna, Ca'Pesaro, Venice; Kunstmuseum, Düsseldorf

Bibliography

Selected Catalogue Essays and Monographs

John Russell, *Lucian Freud*, catalogue introduction to exhibition at the Hayward Gallery, Arts Council of Great Britain, 1974
John Rothenstein, *Modern English Painters*, Macdonald, London, 1974
Lawrence Gowing, *Lucian Freud*, Thames and Hudson, London, 1982 (paperback 1984)

Selected Articles

Lucian Freud, 'Some Thoughts on Painting', *Encounter*, July 1954
Bernard Denvir, 'Masterpieces Explained', *The Artist*, June 1955
David Sylvester, 'Portrait of the Artist', *Art News and Review*, 17 June 1955
John Russell, 'Lucian Freud – Clairvoyeur', *Art in America*, vol. 59, January 1971
John Russell, 'Sights of London', *The Sunday Times*, 15 October 1972
William Feaver, 'New Realists', *London Magazine*, vol. 12, pt. 6, February/March 1973
Paul Overy, 'Lucian Freud's Visual Autobiography', *The Times*, 29 January 1974
Robert Melville, 'Brief Spell', *New Statesman*, 1 February 1974
William Feaver, 'Lucian Freud – The Analytical Eye', *Sunday Times Magazine*, 3 February 1974
Michael Shepherd, 'Faces of Freud', *The Sunday Telegraph*, 3 February 1974
Marina Vaizey, 'Lucian Freud', *The Financial Times*, 14 February 1974
Lynda Morris, 'Freud's Images', *The Listener*, 2 March 1978
John McEwen, 'No More Sugar-Coating', *The Spectator*, 16 October 1982
Marina Vaizey, 'When the Subject Matters', *The Sunday Times*, 17 October 1982
William Packer, 'The Best Painter in this Country', *The Financial Times*, 19 October 1982
Jeffrey Bernard, 'A Star for Me', *The Times*, 23 October 1982
Christopher Neve, 'Night Pictures: A Scrutiny', *Country Life*, October 1982
Timothy Hyman, review, *Artscribe*, no. 38, December 1982
E. B. Henning, 'New Paintings by Four Artists from Britain', *Bulletin of the Cleveland Art Museum*, vol. 69, pt. 10, December 1982
Michael Peppiatt, 'Lucian Freud', *Art International*, vol. XXVI, pt. 1, January 1983
Jonathan Keates, 'Lucian Freud', *Harpers and Queen*, October 1983
Marina Vaizey, 'The Rebirth of Painting', *Life*, September 1986
William Feaver, 'A Reasonable Definition of Love', *Architectural Digest*, July 1987

Photographic credits

AC Cooper Ltd., London
Prudence Cuming Associates, London
Tom Scott, Edinburgh
Tate Gallery, London
Rodney Todd-White, London
University of Liverpool
Walker Art Gallery, Liverpool
Whitworth Art Gallery, Manchester